Classical NEG Raising

Linguistic Inquiry Monographs
Samuel Jay Keyser, general editor

A complete list of books published in the Linguistic Inquiry Monographs series appears at the back of this book.

Classical NEG Raising
An Essay on the Syntax of Negation

Chris Collins and Paul M. Postal

The MIT Press
Cambridge, Massachusetts
London, England

MIT Press books may be purchased at special quantity discounts for business or sales promotional use. For information, please email special_sales@mitpress.mit.edu.

This book was set in Times Roman by Toppan Best-Set Premedia Limited. Printed and bound in the United States of America.

Library of Congress Cataloging-in-Publication Data is available.

ISBN: 978-0-262-02731-1 (hardcover); 978-0-262-52586-2 (pbk.)

10   9   8   7   6   5   4   3   2   1

Contents

Series Foreword

We are pleased to present the sixty-seventh volume in the series *Linguistic Inquiry Monographs*. These monographs present new and original research beyond the scope of the article. We hope they will benefit our field by bringing to it perspectives that will stimulate further research and insight.

Originally published in limited edition, the *Linguistic Inquiry Monographs* are now more widely available. This change is due to the great interest engendered by the series and by the needs of a growing readership. The editors thank the readers for their support and welcome suggestions about future directions for the series.

Samuel Jay Keyser
for the Editorial Board

Foreword
Classical NEG Raising: The First 900 Years

Laurence R. Horn, Yale University

The monograph by Chris Collins and Paul Postal (C&P) that you are about to read went to press on the Golden Anniversary of the first syntactic analysis for the "Transposition of NOT (EVER)" within a fragment of generative grammar: "Under certain conditions (e.g. after verbs like WANT or THINK which are themselves not negated), a NOT in the embedded sentence may be moved in front of the main verb . . . " (Fillmore 1963:220). In motivating both his rule and the syntactic cycle itself, illustrated by the "repeated applications" of this movement rule involved in his proposed derivation of (1a) from the structure directly underlying (1b), Charles Fillmore did not cite any explicit evidence for a syntactic analysis. He relied instead on the (purported) paraphrase relation between (1b) and one reading of the putatively ambiguous (1a) (Fillmore 1963:220n12):

(1) a. I don't believe that he wants me to think that he did it.
    b. I believe that he wants me to think that he didn't do it.

The paraphrase relation posited here rests on somewhat shaky ground; Dwight Bolinger was widely credited for pointing out (in a 1967 letter to George Lakoff) that the force of negative commitment is weaker in (the relevant reading of) (1a) than it is in (1b). In this, Bolinger was recapitulating the remark of the grammarian Poutsma (1928:105), who had noted four decades earlier that "the shifting of *not* often has the effect of toning down the negativing of a sentence." Poutsma's dynamic metaphor is striking: even 30 years before transformational rules, it was natural to conceive of the placement of *not* in movement terms.

After some years of neglect, Fillmore's syntactic approach to what had come to be called *negative transportation* or *NEG raising (NR)*, following the introduction of the NEG element in Klima 1964 (see Horn 1971 on the early terminological shifts), began to be supported with direct evidence. The most compelling argument was advanced by Robin Lakoff (1969b). Citing an earlier personal communication from Masaru Kajita, Lakoff pointed out that strict or strong polarity items (e.g., *until midnight, in weeks*) normally requiring a tautoclausal negative licenser are nevertheless well-formed in the scope of NR predicates with higher negation, and furthermore (for some speakers) license positive opposite-polarity tags formed on the embedded clause:

(2) a. I didn't think John would leave until tomorrow.
    b. *I didn't say John would leave until tomorrow.
    c. I don't suppose the Yankees will win the pennant, will they?
    d. *I don't suppose the Yankees will win the pennant, {won't they?/do I?}

These contrasts provide support for a grammatical rule of NR that accounts for the negative polarity item (NPI) licensing and tag formation before the NEG is raised into the main clause.

The functional transparency of NR predicates (and only NR predicates) that overrides the locality restriction on strict NPIs turns out to be more complex than it first appeared. While Fillmore's constraint that all predicates intervening between negative licenser and strict NPI must be NEG raisers is a necessary condition for grammaticality in sentences like (1a) and (2a), it is not sufficient, as seen in the licensing asymmetry between (3a) and (3b) from Horn 1971:120–121, an asymmetry for which Gajewski (2007) offers a new explanation:

(3) a. I don't believe John wanted Harry to die until Saturday.
    b. *I don't want John to believe Harry died until Saturday.

The polarity argument for NR, further chronicled in Horn 1978, is discussed insightfully and in great detail by C&P; see also Israel 2011 for general considerations on the character and distribution of strong polarity items.

Over the years, empirical and theoretical considerations have gradually led linguists away from Fillmore and Lakoff (and the Horn of 1971) and down the trail blazed by Jackendoff (1971:291): "The synonymy between *John thinks that Bill didn't go* and one reading of *John doesn't think that Bill went* is inferential in character and has nothing to do with the syntactic component—it may even have nothing to do with the semantic component." (This analytic trend is reviewed in Horn 1978 and Horn 1989 [2001:chap. 5].) The result has been a de facto rejection of the syntactic approach to NR, a rejection that C&P, on new grounds, urge us to reject.

In essence, the pragmatic view of the NEG-raising effect mirrors the assumptions in standard grammars of English, which tend to subsume NR (if it's noticed at all) under a more general tendency for formal contradictory negation (paraphrasable as 'It is not that case that p') to be strengthened to a contrary, as when *She's unhappy* or even *She's not happy* is understood as making a stronger negative claim than a mere denial that she is happy. These can be viewed as expressing lexicalized and virtual (or on-line) contrariety, respectively. But what of NR?

Following Horn 1989 [2001:chap. 5], Pullum and Huddleston (2002:sec. 9.5) note that negative clauses often "are taken to be making a stronger claim than they actually entail"; NR is cited (without being named) merely as "a further special case of this tendency to move to a more specific interpretation of a negative clause: the case where a clause containing a clausal complement has negation in the matrix clause interpreted as applying to the subordinate clause." In this respect, Pullum and Huddleston partially echo Jespersen (1917:53), who presents the use of *I don't think he has come* to "really mean" *I think he has not come* as both an instance of specialization of negative meaning and an illustration of "the strong tendency in many languages to attract to the main verb a negative which should logically belong to the dependent nexus." But note that unlike Jespersen, Pullum and Huddleston make no allusion to "attraction" or movement of the negative element.

For Jespersen, the tendency in question is part of a more general conspiracy in natural language to signal negation as early as possible. The effects of this *NEG-first* principle (Horn 1989 [2001:293], after Jespersen 1917:5) range from diachronic shifts in the expression of sentential negation (see van der Auwera 2011) to the emergence of ambiguities arising in contexts like [NEG S_1 because S_2] (Jespersen 1917:48), as in *He didn't marry her(,) because he really cares for her*, where the "illogical" scope reading—on which his affection was the non-cause of the wedding rather than the cause of the non-wedding—can be rendered more or less accessible by the intonation contour.

How does the weaker contradictory, *I don't believe that p* understood as $\neg(I\ believe\ that\ p)$, manage to strengthen to the contrary *I believe that $\neg p$*? The classic recipe is given by Bartsch (1973) in a paper that wears its conclusion on its sleeve: " 'Negative transportation' gibt es nicht." Like Jackendoff and other NR skeptics, Bartsch (1973:3) rejects any ambiguity for (4) but argues that, mirroring the semantic entailment from (4a) to (4b), there arises in certain contexts a pragmatic implication from (4b) to (4a):

(4) Peter glaubt nicht, dass Hans kommt.
      Peter believes NEG that Hans comes
      'Peter doesn't believe that Hans is coming.'
      a. Peter glaubt,   dass Hans nicht kommt.
          Peter believes that Hans NEG comes
          'Peter believes that Hans is not coming.'

    b. Es ist nicht so, dass Peter glaubt,   dass Hans kommt.
       it is NEG so that Peter believes that Hans comes
       'It is not the case that Peter believes that Hans is coming.'

This implication derives from the assumption that the subject *a* can be assumed to have given some thought to the truth of *p* and to have come to some conclusion about it, rather than that *a* hasn't thought about *p* or is neutral about whether *p* or $\neg p$. Propositional attitudes (*think, believe, want*) express the subject's cognitive or psychological stance toward the complement, inducing a disjunctive *pragmatische Voraussetzung* (pragmatic presupposition) of the form "[*a* believes that *p*] or [*a* believes that $\neg p$]." Thus, "NR" is not a rule of grammar or semantic interpretation but a (mere) *pragmatische Implikation;* (4a,b) are semantically distinct but can express the same information relative to a given *Sprechsituation*. Bartsch's inference schema can be given as follows:

(5) a. F (a, p) $\vee$ F (a, $\neg$p)   the pragmatically presupposed disjunction
    b. "$\underline{\neg\text{F (a, p)}}$"   the proposition actually asserted (hence the
                                    quotation marks)
    c. F (a, $\neg$p)   the proposition conveyed

The key is the assumed disjunction in (5a): if you can assume I either want to go or want to stay (= not-go) and I say (out of diffidence, politeness, cowardice, etc.) *I don't want to go*, you can infer that I want to stay: from the assumed disjunction *p or q* and the expression of *not-p*, infer q. This is the logical schema variously known as *disjunctive syllogism, modus tollendo ponens, reasoning by exclusion,* or (if you're a Stoic) *the fifth indemonstrable syllogism.* More recently, Klooster (2003:4) adduces a *"black and white" effect* to account for NR: "In a discourse where judgements and intentions are relevant, but reserving or deferring them are not, verbs of the considered type are easily interpreted as dichotomous."

    The problem is that this proposed solution to NR cannot handle variation within and across languages as to just which NR candidates can substitute for *F* in (5). When is the disjunction in (5a) actually assumed? Not just any predicate of the knowledge and belief class will do. In fact, membership in the class of propositional attitudes is neither necessary (given NEG raisers like *should, ought to, be likely,* or *be advisable*) nor sufficient (given non–NEG raisers like *know, realize,* or *be sure*) for "dichotomous" behavior. And then there is the problem of variation within and across languages. While German *hoffen* NEG-raises, English *hope* (usually) does not; Latin *sperare* 'hope' NEG-raised but French *espérer* doesn't (while *souhaiter* 'wish, hope' does). Parenthetical *guess* is a NEG-raising propositional attitude in Southern U.S. English but not in other U.S. or U.K. varieties. And so on: see Horn and Bayer 1984 for elaboration and a proposed fix.

But Bartsch's schema for pragmatic strengthening via disjunctive syllogism, while empirically flawed as a model of NR (a problem addressed in recent neo-Bartschian accounts by Gajewski (2011) and Romoli (2012)), in fact functions as a useful template for other cases in which formal contradictories are massaged into acting contraries via assumed disjunctions. Fodor (1970:158–168) describes the *all-or-none* effect resulting in the tendency for an apparent sentential negation with a (mass or definite) plural or generic bare plural to scope under the (explicit or implicit) quantification in subject and object terms. Thus, unlike (6a), (6b) "leaves no room for disagreements about different women," while the scopal possibility for negation with a universal in (6a) is unavailable with the plural definite in (6b); once again, the set in question behaves as a uniform entity with respect to negation. Example (7) illustrates similar facts.

(6) a.   All women enjoy/do not enjoy washing dishes; Do all women enjoy washing dishes?
    b.   Women enjoy/do not enjoy washing dishes; Do women enjoy washing dishes?

(7) a.   I didn't see all the boys, but I did see some of them.
    b.   #I didn't see the boys, but I did see some of them.

Mass terms exhibit similar behavior, as seen in (8):

(8) a.   I eat meat.
    b.   I don't eat meat.

In other words, meat in general is such that I {eat/don't eat} it. In each case, a formal contradictory is typically strengthened to a virtual contrary by a tacit (mis?)application of the law of excluded middle as in Bartsch's (5a). (See Löbner 1985 and von Fintel 1997 for discussion of similar cases, Geurts 2009 for a Bartschian approach to the "embedded implicature" phenomenon, Gajewski 2011 on NR and the excluded middle, and C&P's chapter 1 for more on this approach and its limitations.)

The view of NR as a special case of strengthening to a contrary considerably antedates Bartsch and even Jespersen. Time-traveling back to touch on a couple of high points in the history of NR, we meet up with the neo-Hegelian idealist philosopher Bernard Bosanquet and his dictum that "[t]he essence of negation is to invest the contrary with the character of the contradictory" (Bosanquet 1888:306). Two illustrations of this principle are the fact that "[f]rom 'he is not good' we may be able to infer something more than that 'it is not true that he is good'" (1888:310) and, relevant to our purposes, what Bosanquet termed "the habitual use of phrases such as *I do not believe it*, which refer grammatically to a fact of my intellectual state but actually serve as negations of something ascribed to reality . . . Compare our common phrase 'I don't think that'—which is really equivalent to 'I think that ____ not'" (1888:337). Anticipating Jespersen and Pullum and Huddleston, Bosanquet seeks here to reduce NR to an instance of the figure of litotes, the figure of speech in which "we say less and mean more" (*"minus dicimus et plus significamus,"* in the words of the fourth-century rhetoricians Servius and Donatus; see Hoffmann 1987, Horn 1991).

But this cannot suffice for NR, as recognized by Bosanquet's contemporary, the great Romanist Adolf Tobler (1882), in his eponymous paper on *Il ne faut pas que tu meures*. The standard (or only) meaning of this sentence in modern French is 'You mustn't die', amounting to a *logisch ungerechtfertigte Stellung* ('logically unwarranted position') of negation, since the higher-clause negation would be expected to yield the wide scope reading 'It is not necessary that you die'. Tobler cites a variety of German and French verbs reflecting this same pattern, including German *wollen* 'want' and *sollen* 'should, ought to' and their (older and modern) French counterparts *vouloir* and *devoir*, and contrasts the resultant (NR) readings as in (9) with standard instances of ironic negation like those in (10):

(9) a. Il ne faut   pas qu' elle entre.
         it PRT be.necessary NEG that she enter.SBJV
         'She must not enter.'

   b. Je ne veux jamais que son   nom soit   prononcé   devant
       I   PRT want (n)ever that his/her name be.SBJV pronounced before
       moi.
       me
       'I want her name never to be pronounced in front of me.'
       [Lit. 'I don't ever want her name to be pronounced in front of me.']

   c. Un peintre ne doit   penser que   le pinceau à la main.
       a   painter PRT should think COMP   the brush   at the hand
       [*ne . . . que* = 'only']
       'A painter should think only with brush in hand.'

(10) a. the holy saints by whom God was not hated (= was loved)
    b. He will do you little good. (= all the harm he can)
    c. We weren't in the best possible situation. (= we were in the worst
        situation)
    d. He didn't show that he had forgotten their kindness. (= he showed
        he hadn't forgotten)

As Tobler points out, the conscious sense of irony or litotes pervading the interpretation of the examples in (10) is absent from the interpretation of their more conventionalized counterparts in (9).

Tobler's own analysis of the true NR examples in (9), drawing on the sense that they involve a kind of fusion of the two clauses with the negation affecting the semantics in both, anticipates later observations:

> [T]he idea that in *I don't think he's coming* we have a negative element that belongs truly to the subordinate verb and that can be transferred, like a syntactic ping-pong ball, to another position without altering its logical connections, I think is not quite true. . . . It does not merely hop from one [clause] to another but belongs semantically to both. (Bolinger 1968:23–24)

> [W]e are used to thinking of a negative as occurring only on one specific S for each act of negation; but perhaps in the 'negative transportation' sentences . . . there is a requirement that each clause be under the umbrella of a negation. (Cattell 1973:636)

Sadly, despite the vividness of ping-pong balls and umbrellas as metaphors for negation, such fusion analyses have proved remarkably resistant to formalization.

A further problem for purely pragmatic analyses, as we have seen, is the existence of lexical idiosyncrasy. While there may be semantic generalizations about which predicates potentially license NR (as I have suggested in the mid-scalar hypothesis of Horn 1975, 1978), not all members of the suitable classes are NEG raisers in a given language. As Lauri Carlson (1983:120–121) characterizes the descriptive dilemma, on the one hand there is a "general tendency of any expression of doubt or indecision to suggest disbelief or disinclination," but on the other hand we must acknowledge that "the lexical selectivity of the negative transportation phenomenon does suggest that whatever process creates it has become a conventional rule in the clear cases." Thus, the negations in *I don't want that* and *I don't want to go* may both represent contraries in contradictory clothing, as do the lexicalized contraries resulting from prefixal negation (*uncommon, unhappy, infamous, impious*), but these construction types differ crucially from each other in the degree to which pragmatic strengthening has become conventionalized, a matter that casts doubt on purely meaning-based approaches without serving as decisive evidence for a syntactic theory of NR.

On this matter, I am on record as endorsing the Scottish verdict of "not proven." Following Prince (1976), I concluded my 1978 monograph on the topic by noting that, in light of the arguments I had reviewed over the previous 87 pages, "NR would thus constitute an example of a pragmatic process which has become grammaticized or syntacticized." My final and equally tentative and unsatisfying answer to the question I had posed—"Is NR a syntactic, semantic, or pragmatic phenomenon?"—was "YES, guilty as charged, on all counts, pending appeal to a higher court or the washing ashore of decisive new evidence" (Horn 1978:216). Whether the evidence set forth in the pages that follow this foreword is as decisive as it is new must be left to the mind of the beholder and the verdict of posterity.

One final historical note: Unlike most syntactic rules, NR has its own patron saint. St. Anselm observes in his argument against Paulus, a Roman jurist six centuries his predecessor, that *"non . . . omnis qui facit quod non debet peccat, si proprie consideretur"* ('not everyone who does what he *non debet* ('not-should') sins, if the matter is considered strictly [i.e., with the contradictory reading of negation as suggested by the surface structure]'). The problem, he sees, is the standard use of the string *non debere peccare* to convey the narrow scope contrary *debere non peccare*, rather than the literal wide scope contradictory (= 'it is not a duty to sin'). A man who does what is not his duty does not necessarily sin thereby, but (because of the interference of the NR reading) it is hard to stipulate for example (11a)—the proposition that a man need not marry—without seeming to commit oneself to the stronger (11b), an injunction to celibacy (Henry 1967:193ff.; cf. Williams 1964, Hopkins 1972, Horn 1978:200):

(11) a. non debet ducere uxorem
        Lit. 'NEG [he should take a wife]'
     b. debet non ducere uxorem
        Lit. 'he should NEG [take a wife]'

For Henry (1967:193), Anselm's take on modal/negative scope interaction is "complicated by the quirks of Latin usage" and his recognition that " *'non debet'*, the logical sense of which is 'It isn't that he ought', is normally used not to mean exactly what it says, but rather in the sense more correctly expressed by *'debet non'* ('he ought *not*')." Henry's assessment parallels that of logicians and epistemologists seeking to debug English of a similar flaw, from Quine's dismissal (1960:145–146) of the "familiar quirk of English whereby '*x* does not believe that *p*' is equated to '*x* believes that not *p*' rather than to 'it is not the case that *x* believes that *p*'" as an "idiosyncratic complication" to Hintikka's complaint (1962:13) that "the phrase 'a does not believe that p'[~B_ap in his notation] has a peculiarity . . . in that it is often used as if it were equivalent to 'a believes that ~p' [B_a~p]" and Deutscher's acknowledgment (1965:55) that *I do not believe that p* can be unfortunately ambiguous between *disbelief* and *not belief.* Grammarians too, find NR readings more to be censured than explained; for Vizitelly (1910), *I don't believe I'll go* and *I don't think it will rain* are "solecisms now in almost universal use. Say, rather, 'I believe I will not go'; 'I think it will not rain.'"

In fact, as demonstrated by the work of the last 50 years culminating in the present monograph, Quine's "quirk"—the lower-clause understanding of higher-clause negation over a semantically coherent but somewhat variable range of predicates and operators—is far more than an unfortunate foible or error in English (or Latin) usage.

In addition to commemorating the fiftieth anniversary of the establishment of a syntactic rule of NR within generative grammar (Fillmore 1963), the publication of *Classical NEG Raising* also marks precisely (more or less) the nine-hundredth anniversary of the discovery of NR in Western civilization, given that the Lambeth fragments, containing St. Anselm's disquisition on the (non-) obligations of marriage, were compiled "shortly after Anselm's death in 1109" (Uckelman 2009:41)—quite possibly, one might suppose, in 1114, give or take a few months. In unraveling the role played by NR in the confusion over the interpretation of *non debere* and thus dispelling the fallacy of Paulus's argument for celibacy, St. Anselm made the world safe for posterity (or, more exactly, for legitimate posterity), and a fortiori for those of us populating the earth 900 years later to continue the debate on the pros and cons of syntactic analyses of NEG raising.

Acknowledgments

In the German academic system, candidates for an advanced postdoctoral degree are required to submit a *Habilitationsschrift*. The book to follow can be thought of as a kind of *RE*-habilitationsschrift—not, of course, for the authors, who have advanced well beyond any such requirement, but for the syntactic rule of NEG raising, an old love of mine that I still have a warm feeling for, despite the occasional bumpy patches in our relationship over the last four decades. I am grateful to Chris Collins and Paul Postal, not only for inviting me to contribute this foreword and for their helpful comments on an earlier draft but also for the intellectually challenging and rewarding give-and-takes, via electronic and face-to-face exchanges over the last couple of years, on the grammar and pragmatics of NR, polarity licensing, negation, contrariety, and inversion. I commend them in particular for keeping the flame of NR scholarship alive in this study by which you are about to be engaged, enlightened, provoked, and thoroughly impressed—and without which there would be nothing for this foreword to precede.

Preface

The central claim of this monograph is that examples like (1a) instantiate a kind of syntactic raising that we call *Classical NEG Raising*. Involved is the raising of a negation (NEG) from the embedded clause to the matrix clause on the interpretation where (1a) is equivalent to (1b):

(1) a. I don't think this course is interesting.
    b. I think this course is not interesting.

We develop three main arguments in support of this claim. First, we show that Classical NEG Raising obeys island constraints. Since island constraints are associated with syntactic raising, and not associated with nonsyntactic relations, the fact that Classical NEG Raising is subject to island constraints strongly argues that it is a syntactic phenomenon.

Second, we show that a syntactic raising analysis predicts both the grammaticality and particular properties of what we call *Horn clauses*, named for Larry Horn, who discovered them (see Horn 1975:283). His example is given in (2):

(2) I don't think that ever before have the media played such a major role in a kidnapping.

In (2), the negative polarity item (NPI) *ever before* triggers Negative Inversion, the English construction involving a left-extracted XP and associated subject-auxiliary inversion. On all accounts that analyze nominal NPIs as indefinites, the complex of facts in (2) is unexpected, since indefinites do not otherwise trigger Negative Inversion.

Third, we show that the properties of parenthetical structures like those italicized in (3) provide a strong argument for the syntactic character of Classical NEG Raising:

(3) a. Sandra is not, *I don't believe*, having her yearly get-together.
    b. None of those steps will, *we don't deny*, be sufficient to solve the problem.

The main argument that has been presented in the literature *against* a syntactic raising analysis is called here the *composed quantifier argument*. This argument is based on the fact that sentences like (4) display various characteristics of Classical NEG Raising, yet manifest no *overt* NEG that could plausibly be taken to have raised from the embedded clause:

(4) No linguist imagined that Carla had told a living soul about her father.

We provide a detailed analysis of sentences like (4) and argue that they represent a variety of Classical NEG Raising in which the raised NEG is deleted. In support of this view, we show that the type of Classical NEG Raising involved in (4) is, like that in (1a), subject to island constraints, and gives rise to Horn clauses. Moreover, we show that parenthetical clauses corresponding to (4) pattern like the parenthetical clauses in (3), strongly supporting the existence of Classical NEG Raising in (4).

Acknowledgments

The first author taught the material presented in this work in a seminar at New York University during the spring semester of 2013. We would like to thank the following participants in that seminar for their judgments, ideas about negation, and feedback on our material: Judy Bernstein, Frances Blanchette, Dylan Bumford, Paola Cépeda, Stephanie Harves, Inna Livitz, Neil Myler, Jason Ostrove, Linmin Zhang, and Vera Zu.

The material on Horn clauses was presented by the first author at SUNY Stony Brook in March 2013. We thank the audience there for their helpful comments.

The experience of writing this monograph has been vastly different from that of writing Collins and Postal 2012. While the background literature on imposters and pronominal agreement was nonexistent to rudimentary, the background literature on negative polarity items and Classical NEG Raising is vast and sophisticated. For this reason, we are indebted to those who have helped us along the way. We have benefited from discussions with and comments by Christina Behme, Vincent Homer, Larry Horn, Pierre Larrivée, Jacopo Romoli, Yohei Oseki, Andrew Radford, Haj Ross, Manfred Sailer, Pieter Seuren, and three anonymous MIT Press reviewers.

We would like to express our appreciation to Anne Mark, whose copyediting has significantly improved the manuscript. We also thank Eve Tauss for preparing the index.

Background

1 Introduction

1.1 Domain of Inquiry

On one reading, English examples like (1a) seem to be paraphrases of corresponding examples like (1b):

(1) a. Karen expected that the moon would not turn purple.
    b. Karen did not expect that the moon would turn purple.

In addition to the interpretation of (1b) that is a paraphrase of (1a), (1b) has another interpretation where Karen had no expectations at all, perhaps because she had not thought about the matter, or because she had thought about the matter but was undecided.

This a priori unexpected semantic similarity between structures with negation in the complement clause and those with negation in the main clause, found in many other languages as well, has been the subject of a great deal of work; see Horn 1971, 1975, 1978, 1989 [2001] for extensive references to earlier periods dating back as far as St. Anselm in the eleventh century. Beginning with Fillmore 1963, within the generative grammar tradition there developed in the 1960s and 1970s considerable agreement that the roughly equivalent reading of pairs like (1a,b) was a function of a *syntactic* phenomenon of negation (henceforth: NEG) raising, from the complement into the main clause. That is, the shared reading was taken to be associated with cases like (1b) because the main clause NEG originates in the complement clause and is raised into the main clause. This conclusion involved the assumption that the preraising structure determined the meaning. The original syntactic conception is nicely represented in the following passage:

(2) (Horn 1971:120)
    "It is convincingly argued that the ungrammaticality of the sentences which result from substituting verbs such as *demand* or *claim* for *want* and *believe* —

(3) a. *Chauncey doesn't demand to die until he has touched fair
         Hermione's lips again.
     b. *I don't claim you have remembered to button your fly in
         years.
    reveals that NEG-raising is a minor rule applying to some predicates of
    opinion and expectation . . . , of intention . . . and of perceptual
    approximation . . ."

The posited raising involved a transformational movement rule, and we will informally assume such an approach in this monograph. But NEG raising, as argued for in this work, could equally be given a nontransformational syntactic account.[1]

We refer to the phenomenon illustrated in (1) as *Classical NEG Raising* (hereafter: *Classical NR*). The modifier is motivated by the fact that, following Postal 2005, we posit a wide variety of NEG raisings distinct from that taken to be present in (1b). This more general appeal to NEG raising is discussed in some detail in chapter 3.

While a syntactic approach to Classical NR was popular at the earlier period, not long after Fillmore's (1963) article, acceptance of such an approach began to erode; see Jackendoff 1971, Pollack 1974. Increasingly, a syntactic view of Classical NR was challenged by pragmatic and semantic approaches.[2] And even earlier adherents of a syntactic conception, such as Horn (1971:120, 127; 1972:228), came to reject it in favor of nonsyntactic views; see Horn 1978, 1989 [2001], Horn and Bayer 1984. Our goal in this monograph is to argue that this rejection was mistaken.

A key matter is the well-known fact that Classical NR only exists with a particular highly restricted subclass of higher-clause predicates. Horn (1975, 1978, 1989 [2001:322–330]) argued extensively that this class has a universal semantic characterization, while stressing that it is nonetheless subject to parochial lexical restrictions excluding elements that otherwise fall under the universal characterization. We simply refer to a predicate that permits Classical NR as a *Classical NR predicate* (hereafter: *CNRP*). Cited members of this class in English include the predicates in (3), although some exhibit a certain amount of speaker variation:

(3) advisable, advise, appear, believe, choose, expect, feel, feel (like),
     figure, find, guess (dialectal), imagine, intend, likely, look (like), mean,
     plan, reckon (dialectal), recommend, seem, sound (like), suggest,
     suppose, supposed, tend, think, turn out, used to (temporal form),
     want, wish

For concreteness, we will assume a syntactic version of Classical NR that has the form in (4):

(4) *Classical NR*

If NEG_1 raises from one clause B into the next clause above B, call it clause A, then the predicate of clause A is a CNRP.

A remark about the logic of formulation (4). It is designed to fit into our broader view that there is a general phenomenon of NEG raising (explicated in chapter 3 in particular). Under this view, NEGs arise in a variety of positions and in many cases raise from them to higher ones. In such terms, Classical NR is just a special case of this general NEG-raising phenomenon, where, in particular, a NEG raises across a clause boundary.

Of course, (4) is schematic and leaves various important properties unmentioned. Some of these are specified in what follows. In particular, (4) says nothing about the origin positions of raised NEGs nor about where they end up. It will be convenient to refer to the *minimal* clause where a putatively raised NEG actually sits as its *host*, and to the clause where it putatively originates, as its *origin*. Thus, in a syntactic view of Classical NR, a NEG raises from its origin to its host.

In Classical NR cases, NEG raises to a position right-adjacent to the finite auxiliary (Aux). It might seem that this fact should be built into our formulation of Classical NR, that is, into (4). But in present terms, NEGs that raise in ways different from Classical NR also end up directly after finite Aux positions. Thus, we view this typical locus for NEGs as a general English requirement on the position of raised NEGs rather than as something specific to Classical NR.

While intuitions about Classical NR readings are often subtle, the difficulties seem to arise in determining whether CNRP clauses with main clause NEGs have the reading equivalent to that where the NEG is only in the complement. But if one chooses a non-CNRP, the lack of such a reading is palpable. Consider:

(5) a. Karen figured that the moon would not disappear.
    b. Karen did not figure that the moon would disappear.
    c. Karen figured out that the moon would not disappear.
    d. Karen did not figure out that the moon would disappear.

In the examples with *figure out*, which, unlike *figure*, is not a CNRP, there is no hint of a Classical NR reading. So, whereas (5b) has a reading equivalent to (5a), (5d) clearly has no reading equivalent to (5c).

We have found that the relevant readings can be clarified by what we call the *agree* test. If the statements in (5b,d) are followed by *Do you agree?*, different interpretations result depending on the case. When (5b) is followed by *Do you agree?*, the most natural interpretation is that the speaker is asking the hearer whether he or she agrees with Karen that the moon will not disappear. This is shown in (6a). When *Do you agree?* follows (5d), the most natural interpretation is that the speaker is asking the hearer whether he or she agrees with the speaker's claim that Karen did not figure out that the moon would disappear.

(6) a. Do you agree? (following (5b))
     Yes, I agree that the moon will not disappear.
   b. Do you agree? (following (5d))
     Yes, I agree that Karen did not figure out that the moon would disappear.

A recurrent type of argument for a syntactic conception of Classical NR stands on the claim that there are various *negative polarity items (NPIs)* that require *local* licensers.[3] Sometimes these are called *strict* NPIs, a terminology we will follow.[4] However, although we will continue to use this now standard NPI terminology based on the stem *license*, in order to link this work with the huge literature on NPIs, a warning is in order. This terminology does not mesh well with our basic theoretical assumptions about NPIs. In what follows (especially in chapter 8), we return to the notions *licenser* and *local licenser*, and indicate how standard appeal to such ideas resolves in the current framework into appeal to various combinations of NEG raising and NEG deletion.

For present purposes, we can be rather vague about how *local* needs to be understood. Minimally, lack of separation by a clause boundary is required (the licenser and the NPI must be clausemates). The issue of locality is discussed in greater detail in chapter 8. Many NPIs (most notably *any* forms) do not manifest any locality requirement; see (7b). The English NPI most widely cited as requiring a local licenser is *until*, as in (7a) (on the meaning of *until*, see Karttunen 1974):

(7) a. Calvin did not believe/*claim that Mona would move in until June.
   b. Calvin did not believe/claim that Mona stole any of the money.

(In (7a), we only consider the reading where *until June* modifies the embedded clause. On the reading where it modifies the matrix clause, the sentence is irrelevantly acceptable.) Contrasts like that in (7a) are typical of the difference between CNRPs like *believe* and non-CNRPs like *claim*. In syntactic terms, such contrasts arise from the fact that the local NEG needed by the strict NPI can raise out of the complement clause and end up in the main clause with *believe* but not with *claim*.[5]

We will appeal to a variety of other strict NPIs throughout.[6] First, we take the idiomatic meaning of the phrase *stop at anything*, identical to that of the related *stop at nothing*, to define a strict NPI.[7] The fact that *stop at anything* is a strict NPI is shown by its unacceptability with *state* (a non-CNRP) in (8b):

(8) a. Ted will *(not) stop at anything to get promoted.
    b. I didn't believe/*state that Ted would stop at anything to get promoted.

The fact that negation is necessary in (8a) shows that *anything* as part of the idiom *stop at anything* is an NPI. The fact that the negation in (8b) cannot license *anything* in the embedded clause with non-CNRP *state* indicates that *anything* in that idiom is a strict NPI.

Second, we assume that the idiomatic expression *breathe a word* defines a strict NPI:

(9) a. Carolyn will *(not) breathe a word about it.
    b. Stanley doesn't anticipate/*predict that Carolyn will breathe a word about it.

Third, we take the expression *living soul* to represent a further strict NPI:

(10) a. Sandra *told/didn't tell a living soul about her sister.
    b. Shelly didn't figure/*figure out that Sandra told a living soul about her sister.

Fourth, phrases of the form *help Xself* on the meaning 'restrain oneself' are strict NPIs, as illustrated in (11):

(11) a. Ted *can/can't help himself.
    b. I didn't think that Ted could help himself.
    c. *I didn't agree that Ted could help himself.

Fifth, we find the expression *lift a finger* to form a strict NPI, as seen in (12):

(12) a. Karen would *(not) lift a finger to help Sidney.
    b. Karen did not think/*declare that Ted would lift a finger to help Sidney.

Sixth, minimizers of the class {*dick, diddly (squat), jack (shit), shit, squat,* . . .} are also assumed to be strict NPIs. Henceforth, we refer to this class as *JACK*. The relevant contrasts for the strict usages of these forms are illustrated in (13):

(13) a. Ted would *(not) understand jack(shit)$_A$/squat$_A$ about Turkish politics.
     b. Karen did not expect/*claim that Ted would understand jack(shit)$_A$/ squat$_A$ about Turkish politics.[8]

Seventh and last, adverbials of the class *in days/weeks/months/years* also form strict NPIs:

(14) a. Teresa has *(not) been seen in days/years.
     b. I don't think/*agree that Teresa has been seen in days/years.

In what follows, we freely cite sentences with one or another of the strict NPIs in (6)–(14) to make various points without further explicitly indicating their strict NPI status.[9]

In the literature advocating a syntactic view of Classical NR, contrasts between CNRPs and non-CNRPs like those in (6)–(14) have regularly been taken to support a syntactic raising view of the phenomenon. The logic is initially apparently straightforward. If strict NPIs require local licensers, then only a syntactic conception of Classical NR limited to CNRPs provides local licensers in the good cases and guarantees their absence in the bad ones. But chapter 9 discusses potential complications to this logic involving quantifier scope.

Strict NPIs have also been used to motivate the claim that Classical NR can function "successive-cyclically." In many cases, a particular NEG has been claimed to reach its host via several successive raisings, each into a clause containing a CNRP, hence a clause capable of independently acting as a host. Consider:

(15) a. I think/agree that he wants to not get here until 6:00.
     b. I think/agree that he doesn't want to get here until 6:00.
     c. I don't think/*agree that he wants to get here until 6:00.

(16) a. I imagine/concede that he believes that she cannot help lying.
     b. I imagine/concede that he doesn't believe that she can help lying.
     c. I don't imagine/*concede that he believes that she can help lying.

Here, the (a) examples show NEGs in their origin clauses, and the (b) examples show them having raised one clause up, while the (c) examples with the CNRPs *think/examine* show them raising to a host two clauses up from their origin. The (c) examples with the non-CNRPs *agree/concede* are ungrammatical, because in each case a NEG had to raise out of the complement of a non-CNRP.

However, we do not find these arguments for "successive cyclicity" particularly convincing. The reasons for our skepticism lie in the fact that examinations of data like (15) and (16) never discuss the scope of the NPIs in such examples. See chapter 9 for more on the scope of strict NPIs. But we are unable to pursue the issue of successive cyclicity in this monograph.

Over time, purely semantic or pragmatic approaches appear to have become increasingly favored, and our impression is that such views are dominant today.[10] Horn 1989 [2001:308–330] represents an extensive argument for a pragmatic approach. See Tovena 2001, Pullum and Huddleston 2002:838–843, Larrivée 2004:103–105, Gajewski 2005, 2007, 2011, Sailer 2006, Bošković and Gajewski 2008, Homer 2010, and Romoli 2012, 2013a, 2013b for more recent presentations of nonsyntactic views.

To clarify the issues dividing syntactic and nonsyntactic views of Classical NR, we will briefly characterize a particular nonsyntactic approach, due to Bartsch (1973) (see also Horn 1978, 1989 [2001], Horn and Bayer 1984, Gajewski 2007). This is not an arbitrary choice since Bartsch's account is arguably the essential source for all modern nonsyntactic conceptions of Classical NR.

Consider a pair like (17a,b), differing essentially only in whether or not the negation appears in the main or complement clause:

(17) a. I don't think it will rain today.
    b. I think it will not rain today.

Given Classical NR, (17a) is syntactically ambiguous. Either *not* is raised or it originates in the matrix clause without raising. Bartsch's conception, however, recognizes no syntactic ambiguity in cases like (17a). Rather, Bartsch assumed that (17a) will have only a single meaning determined by main clause negation but also that on a particular pragmatic assumption, the statement in (17a) can entail that in (17b). The pragmatic assumption is that the speaker either thinks it will rain today or thinks it will not rain today, and so definitely has some opinion one way or the other. In other words, it is not true that the speaker has not thought about whether or not it will rain (and hence has no opinion). Nor is it true that the speaker is undecided about whether or not it will rain. This state of affairs is characterized by the *excluded middle property*, which we will notate $F(x, p) \vee F(x, \sim p)$. Here, F stands for a particular CNRP and x for its subject.

Given the excluded middle property, the inference to (18c) from premises (18a,b) is justified:

(18) a. $F(x, p) \vee F(x, \sim p)$ (the excluded middle property)
b. $\sim F(x, p)$ (from statement (17a), taken to involve main clause negation)
c. $F(x, \sim p)$ (logical consequence via disjunctive syllogism of (18a,b))

So, assuming the excluded middle property, given an assertion of (17a), the apparent complement scope of the main clause NEG is simply a deductive logical consequence, seemingly rendering any syntactic raising unmotivated and redundant.

However, on the basis of earlier observations by George Lakoff (1970b) and others, Horn (1975:281–282, 1978:179, 183–187, 1989 [2001:321]) and Horn and Bayer (1984:399–401) stress that such an analysis cannot easily account for the seemingly idiosyncratic lexical differences within a language and between languages. For example, while cognates of *hope* allow the Classical NR type of reading in other languages, this verb is not a CNRP in English.[11]

Therefore, Horn and Bayer (1984:407) show how to render the excluded middle property *lexically specific*. They claim that there is an implicature that applies "to a proper subset of linguistic expressions appearing in the relevant frame" (see also Romoli 2012, 2013a, 2013b for a different implicature-based approach). Gajewski (2007:297n7) also adopts a lexical approach, where only certain lexical items introduce an excluded middle presupposition. We need not make any assumption about whether the excluded middle property should be taken to be an implicature or a presupposition in nonsyntactic approaches. More precisely, in criticizing nonsyntactic approaches, we assume only that the excluded middle property is lexically specified.

We do not claim that the lexical specificity of Classical NR argues in favor of a syntactic approach. Rather, both syntactic and semantic approaches must somehow specify the class of CNRPs. In a syntactic approach, the lexical specificity of Classical NR is analogous to the lexical specificity of subject-to-subject raising (see (19)) and of double object constructions (see (20)):

(19) a. It is likely that Bruce is intelligent.
b. Bruce is likely to be intelligent.
c. It is probable that Bruce is intelligent.
d. *Bruce is probable to be intelligent.

(20) a. I gave money to Bruce.
b. I gave Bruce money.
c. I donated money to the church.
d. *I donated the church money.

1.2   Organization

This monograph is divided into two parts. In part I, we present the general conception of negation we adopt. This conception is necessary to appreciate the full force of the arguments for a syntactic approach to Classical NR in part II. Part I is roughly based on the framework of ideas in Postal 2005, although many modifications, refinements, and improvements are introduced. Part II represents completely new work.

The ideas in part I drawn from Postal 2005 include the following:

(21) a. that NEGs are not limited to modifying clausal constituents;
      b. that there is NEG raising;
      c. that there is NEG deletion;
      d. that every NPI originates modified by at least one NEG; and
      e. that there is a fundamental distinction between two types of NPIs, those originating with one NEG (unary-NEG NPIs) and those originating with two NEGs (binary-NEG NPIs).

Here, these assumptions are clarified, modified in certain ways, formalized in certain cases, and embedded in a more precise and more justified system of conditions. Moreover, the present monograph goes considerably beyond (21) and, in addition to the arguments given for Classical NR in part II, develops a range of distinct ideas not subsumed by (21). The ideas developed in part I that extend (21) include these:

(22) a. integration of scope considerations into the analysis of NPIs (chapters 2, 5, and 9);
      b. expansion of the body of tests differentiating unary- and binary-NEG NPIs (chapter 4);
      c. development of a precise view of the syntax and semantics of the subtype of polyadic quantification relevant to NPIs (chapter 6);
      d. development of a series of case studies illustrating the utility of NEG deletion (chapter 7); and
      e. construction of arguments showing that appeal to antiadditivity is not sufficient to account for the distribution of strict NPIs (chapter 10).

In part II, we develop a number of arguments favoring a syntactic approach to Classical NR. In chapters 11 and 12, we show that Classical NR is sensitive to syntactic islands, a fact entirely unexpected under any nonsyntactic view, specifically under an approach like that exemplified in (18). In chapters 13–15, we cite certain contexts (dubbed *Horn clauses*) that demand the syntactic presence of a negative constituent. But such a negative constituent exists in Horn clauses only under the assumption that classical NR is syntactic. In chapter 16, we argue that a widely accepted and *apparently* devastating argument against a syntactic view of Classical NR (dubbed there the *composed quantifier argument*) is faulty and in no way conclusive, given our general framework for understanding negation. In chapter 17, we argue that parenthetical expressions provide a powerful argument for the syntactic nature of Classical NR. In chapters 18 and 19, we present additional arguments for a syntactic approach (and against a semantic/pragmatic approach). In chapter 20, we present our conclusions.

2 The Syntactic Representation of Scope

The representation of quantifier scope is critical at multiple points in this monograph. We thus spell out here, in partially informal terms, our general assumptions in this area. Crucially, we take the representation of scope to be syntactic to exactly the same extent as the representation of phrase structure, word order, categories, and so on.

We take the scope of quantifiers to be represented syntactically by the presence of DPs in clausal scope positions. For convenience, we follow May (1985, 1989) and assume that a scope position is a position adjoined to a clause $[_S DP_i S]$. In these cases, the embedded S contains a DP bound by $DP_i = [_{DP} D_i NP_i]$ (in the scope position). S in effect provides the syntactic representation of an open sentence defining the argument of the semantic value of the quantificational DP_i, where NP_i denotes the restriction of the quantifier represented by D_i. In other words, a quantificational DP will always have at least two distinct occurrences, one in a scope position and one in a nonscope position (an "argument" position in some approaches). There can of course be several DPs in scope positions of a single clause, yielding structures like $[_S DP_1 [_S DP_2 [_S DP_3 S]]]$.

The key feature of representations of the type just outlined is that relative semantic scope is represented by relative height in syntactic structures. Since the relations between multiple DPs in scope positions are hierarchically represented, the fact that some quantifier DPs in a clause scope over others falls out from the representation. We naturally assume that there are principles relating syntactic scope to the corresponding semantics (see Heim and Kratzer 1998:chap. 7 for one such specification). In general, we need not concern ourselves with the details of such principles but we do spell them out in detail for polyadic quantifier cases in chapter 6.

From the point of view of this monograph, it is mostly irrelevant whether the relation between a quantifier DP in scope position and the bound DP position in the associated S is due to quantifier lowering as in G. Lakoff

1971:238–243, McCawley 1971:228–230, 1973:150, 294–295, and Seuren 1974a:106, 118–120, 1974b:192–195, 1996:301, 318–319, 1998:522–524; quantifier raising as in May 1985, 1989, and much later work (e.g., Heim and Kratzer 1998); multiattachment of the quantificational phrases in their argument and scope positions with scope positions picked out by a designated edge label, as would be natural in the Metagraph framework of Johnson and Postal 1980 and Postal 2010; or raising to the specifier of a dedicated functional projection (ScopeP), in the spirit of Rizzi 1997. The reason we need not focus on the (of course real and not unimportant) differences among these views is that in all the approaches cited, a key shared notion is that the height of a quantificational expression in a graph/tree indicates scope. For example, in Principles and Parameters work, the c-command domain of a quantificational expression is identified as its scope. That is, a structurally higher quantificational expression by definition scopes over a lower one.

Given this background, in this monograph we represent (1a) as in (1b). Where necessary, we will provide a somewhat more elaborate representation.

(1) a. Myron saw no student.

    b. $[_S$ <[no student]$_1$> $[_S$ Myron saw DP$_1$]]

In this structure, DP$_1$ has two occurrences. One occurrence is in scope position and the other is in direct object position (on the definition of *occurrence*, see Collins and Stabler 2012). The notation <X$_i$> coindexed with a distinct X$_i$ is utilized throughout to represent distinct occurrences of the same constituent X, where the one in "< >" is unpronounced.

As noted above, we take no position on whether structures like (1b) are formed by quantifier raising, formed by quantifier lowering, or simply nonmovement multiattachment structures. In particular, unlike May (1985, 1989), we do not assume that structures like (1b) are formed by covert movement, although such an approach would be consistent with our results.

In the framework of Postal 2010, each member of the set of coindexed DPs would represent a single phrase, each X occurrence marking a separate arc sharing as head the single phrase represented by X.

As is evident in (1), the assumptions just made must go hand in hand with principles determining which of the multiple occurrences of a DP are deleted, that is, which are pronounced and which not. One clear generalization is that DP occurrences in scope positions are *never* pronounced. This fact might be the ground for skepticism concerning the syntactic reality of phrases in syntactic scope positions.

Significantly, then, clear evidence for the syntactic reality of syntactic scope positions directly related to negation was in fact provided by Klima (1964:285–286, 303–304), although he did not frame his observations in these terms. Klima observed first that an example like his (2a) was ambiguously equivalent to either (2b) or (2c):

(2) a. I will force you to marry no one.
    b. I won't force you to marry anyone.
    c. I will force you not to marry anyone.

Critically, Klima observed that the reading of (2a) equivalent to (2b) correlates with the fact that the main clause behaves as *syntactically* negative, according to tests for main clause syntactic negation, in particular, the possibility of *neither* tags. Compare:

(3) a. Carl did *(not) claim that penguins were mammals and neither did I.
    b. Carl claimed that penguins were not mammals (*and neither did I).

Such contrasts support the claim that only main clause syntactic negation permits a *neither* clause.[1]

Strikingly, then, despite the ambiguity of (2), the grammatical (4) is unambiguously interpretable only as (2b):

(4) I will force you to marry no one and neither will he.

Given the dependence of *neither* on main clause syntactic negation, the grammaticality of (4) and its exclusive interpretation with main clause scope for the quantifier DP *no one* argue directly for the syntactic representation of scope. That is, in this case the scope position of *no one* must be analyzed in such a way that the negation associated with *no one* is in the main clause.

In our terms, then, the two readings of (2a) equivalent to (2b,c) would be represented respectively as follows:

(5) a. <[[NEG SOME] one]>$_1$ [I will force you to marry DP$_1$]
    b. I will force you [<[[NEG SOME] one]>$_1$ [to marry DP$_1$]]

The support for the syntactic representation of quantifier scope derivable from *neither* expressions is not isolated. Other tests for (main clause) syntactic negation give results parallel to the *neither* test. This is true of both negative parentheticals (see chapter 17) and following negative clauses of the form [DP CNRP not] (see Ross 1973:157), as shown in (6c,d):

(6) a. Donna did not prove they discovered a new element, (I don't think).
    b. Donna proved they did not discover a new element, (*I don't think).

    c. Donna did not prove they discovered a new element. (No, I guess not.)

    d. Donna proved they did not discover a new element. (*No, I guess not.)

Compare, then:

(7) a. They will force you to marry no one, I don't think.
    b. They will force you to marry no one. No, I guess not.

In each case, the addition forces the reading of (2b). This follows from the claim that *no one* in such cases takes scope in the matrix clause.

Finally, the conclusions just drawn are supported as well by confirmation tag questions, known to require that the tag have a polarity opposite to that of the main clause:

(8) a. They did not force her to marry anyone, did/*didn't they?
    b. They forced her not to marry anyone, *did/didn't they?

As expected at this point, the analog of Klima's (2a) with a confirmation tag is disambiguated depending on the choice of polarity for the tag:

(9) a. They will force her to marry no one, will they?
    b. They will force her to marry no one, won't they?

That is, (9a) has unambiguous main clause scope for *no one*, and (9b), unambiguous complement clause scope.

The joint force of the different pieces of evidence from *neither* expressions, negative parentheticals, appended phrases like *I guess not*, and confirmation tags provides solid evidence for the syntactic reality of quantifier scope positions even though occurrences in these positions are never overt. We take these facts to provide independent support for the kind of syntactic representation of quantifiers we adopt.

3 NEG Raising

3.1 NPIs

This study of Classical NR should be understood against a background assumption about *negative polarity items* (NPIs), sketched in Postal 2005. This view makes the entirely nonstandard assumption that what are normally called NPIs are expressions underlyingly associated with a NEG, which has raised away from the NPI. Such a view contrasts radically with the range of consensus views about NPIs.

Consider a standard NPI example like *ever* in (1b):

(1) a. *Chloe ever tasted beer.
    b. Chloe did not ever taste beer.

On the standard view, because *ever* is an NPI, it can only occur in contexts where it relates in specific ways to a form standardly called its *licenser*. This licenser must have certain semantic characteristics (usually taken to be decreasingness; see Ladusaw 1979) and needs to be in an appropriate syntactic position vis-à-vis the NPI, for example, one c-commanding the NPI. In (1b), the licenser would be *not*, while (1a) would be ungrammatical because of the absence of a legitimate licenser.

With respect to (1b), we claim that the *not* found immediately following the Aux originates as part of the adverbial form. In effect, we posit a single original structure common to the *ever* of (1b) and the clearly negative *never* of (2):

(2) Chloe never tasted beer.

Artificially ignoring scope structures for the moment, a first schematic account of the structure underlying both (1b) and (2) would be (3a) or, a bit more explicitly, (3b):

(3) a. Chloe [NEG ever] tasted beer
    b. Chloe [[NEG SOME] ever] tasted beer

The relation between structures (3a,b) and (2) is relatively straightforward, involving the morphological specification that a [[NEG SOME] ever] constituent (out of which its NEG has not raised) takes the form *never*. NEG in this case is realized simply as *n-* and SOME is not pronounced.

But more is required to relate (3a,b) to (1b). In particular, the NEG must raise out of the adverbial form to a position immediately adjacent to the Aux. Such an analysis requires an overall syntactic framework in which separation of NEG from its original structural locus is both well-defined and permitted— that is, in effect, a syntactic framework that *countenances some notion of NEG raising*. The resulting analysis of (1b) is given in (4):

(4) Chloe did NEG_1 [[<NEG_1> SOME] ever] taste beer

In this structure, NEG has raised from a position adjacent to SOME, to a position right-adjacent to the Aux *did*. The higher occurrence of NEG_1 in (4) is realized as *not* or *n't*. The lower occurrence is covert. (We note in passing that the movement of NEG_1 in (4) violates Ross's (1967 [1986:127]) Left Branch Condition. We return to a detailed discussion of the locality constraints on NEG raising in chapters 11 and 12.) The NEG-raising analysis of (1b) accounts for the truth-conditional equivalence between (1b) and (2). Both sentences have the same underlying structure, and the movement of the NEG does not contribute to the semantic interpretation of (1b). That is, even though the NEG's superficial position immediately follows the Aux in (1b), its interpretation is a function of its preraising position (internal to the DP).

There are distinct ways of capturing the fact that the raising of the NEG in (1b) is semantically vacuous. In the Metagraph framework of Johnson and Postal 1980 and Postal 2010, this conclusion follows from the defining assumption that semantic interpretation ignores noninitial arcs. In Minimalist syntax, the natural treatment of the semantic vacuity of NEG raising would be in terms of reconstruction. We do not pursue these issues here.

This brief discussion illustrates that within a framework accepting the view taken in Postal 2005 about NPIs, the NEG raising required by a syntactic view of Classical NR (see chapter 1) should be viewed as a special instance of a much broader syntactic phenomenon of NEG raising. We view NEG raising in general as being possible from any position. Many, no doubt a majority, of the resulting structures are ill-formed. We assume these are blocked by various filtering conditions. One class of these will specify possible landing sites where NEGs can remain. In English, raised NEGs that are not ultimately deleted (see chapters 7 and 8 on NEG deletion) mostly end up as right sisters of the finite Aux.

3.2 *Some/Any*

A similar NEG-raising analysis can be given for pairs such as the following:

(5) a. I saw no widow.
    b. I didn't see any widow.

The underlying structure of both examples, again initially ignoring scope occurrences for simplicity, is the following:

(6) I saw [[NEG SOME] widow]

In (5a), NEG does not raise, and [[NEG SOME] widow] is spelled out as *no widow*. In this case, NEG is realized as *no*, and SOME is unpronounced. In (5b), NEG raises to a position right-adjacent to Aux. The higher occurrence of NEG is realized as *n't*, and the lower occurrence of NEG is not pronounced.

Furthermore, we assume that *any* in (5b) is a suppletive form of *some*, determined by the rule in (7) (where <NEG> means 'unpronounced occurrence of NEG'):[1]

(7) *The SOME→*any *mapping (first version)*
    a. SOME → *any*, in the context [<NEG> ___] (NEG unpronounced)
    b. SOME → null, in the context [NEG ___]   (NEG pronounced)
    c. SOME → *some*, otherwise

NEG itself has various realizations depending on context, including *no, n-, not, n't, non*. We have not represented the fact that in [[NEG SOME] ever], neither SOME nor *any* is ever pronounced, whether or not NEG raises away (see section 3.1). See section 3.5 for a parallel fact about *jackshit*$_A$ and similar forms.

3.3 Verbal Negation

Given the above account of NPIs, how should negation be analyzed when no NPIs are present (to serve, in our framework, as sources for NEGs), as in the following example?

(8) Melissa didn't leave.

The most uniform analysis possible for negation would claim that the post-Aux NEG is always raised from some other position. To maintain that view, we suggest that the NEG immediately following a finite Aux is always in a derived position (a noninitial position in the framework of Postal 2010).

Absent an NPI in (8) to serve as the origin of NEG, we are then led to claim that the NEG in such cases raises from the verb or possibly the verb phrase:

(9) Melissa did NEG$_1$ [$_{VP}$ <NEG$_1$> [$_{VP}$ leave]]

We do not have evidence to distinguish between NEG directly modifying V and NEG modifying VP (as in (9)). Henceforth, to leave the choice open, we simply say that NEG modifies V/VP.

In (9), the higher occurrence of NEG is spelled out as *n't*, and the lower occurrence is unpronounced. Negation of predicate adjectives would receive a parallel analysis (e.g., for *Melissa isn't happy*).

3.4 Support for the Negation Analysis of NPIs

The nonstandard assumption that NPIs are inherently associated with a NEG gains some support from the fact that many, though by no means all, NPIs actually occur as components of overt phrases formed with NEG:

(10) a. Lauren won't show up *until Thursday*.
 b. Not until Thursday will Lauren show up.

(11) a. Lauren hasn't worked *in weeks*.
 b. Not in weeks has Lauren worked.

(12) a. Lauren didn't contribute *a damn thing*.
 b. Not a damn thing did Lauren contribute.

(13) a. Lauren didn't call *even one* student.
 b. Not even one student did Lauren call.

Uncontroversially, the italicized phrase in each data set in (10)–(13) is an NPI. Moreover, the following three relevant properties hold:

(14) a. The NPI in the (b) example occurs as a constituent of a phrase with a superficially visible instance of syntactic negation.
 b. Truth-functionally, the (b) example is equivalent to the corresponding (a) example.
 c. The (a) example is syntactically naturally relatable to the (b) example by positing that the original NEG of the (a) example has raised out, whereas that of the (b) example has not.

Some NPIs, such as *yet*, do not allow constructions such as the (b) examples in (10)–(13) (**Not yet have I seen him*). In our framework, the NEG of [NEG yet] would be forced to move away from the NPI, as in the case of *jackshit$_A$* in section 3.5.

3.5 The JACK Class Minimizers

In present terms, some types of NPI DPs *require* raising of the NEG present in the DP. One such type consists of the NPI versions of the slang forms *dick, diddly, diddly squat, jack, jackshit, shit, squat,* the class abbreviated as JACK in chapter 1. We take members of JACK to be nouns, occurring in their NPI usages with a determiner of the form [NEG SOME], as in (15):

(15) [_DP_ [_D_ NEG SOME] JACK]

Such a representation helps to account for the synonymy of *I didn't see jackshit_A* and *I didn't see anything*, both of which incorporate the structure [[NEG SOME] NOUN].

Example (16b) is unacceptable because the NEG associated with a member of the noun class JACK has failed to raise out of the associated D:

(16) a.   Karen doesn't know jackshit_A about relativity.
     b.   *Karen knows no jackshit_A about relativity.
     c.   *Karen doesn't know any jackshit_A.

A further constraint, needed to block (16c), must guarantee that SOME→*any* is always deleted when the associated NP has a member of JACK as its head noun. Thus, the rule spelling out SOME needs to be revised as follows:

(17) *The SOME→any Mapping (second and final version)*
     a.   SOME → *any*, in the context [<NEG> ___] (NEG unpronounced)
     b.   SOME → null, in the context [NEG ___]   (NEG pronounced)
     c.   SOME → *some*, otherwise
     d.   *any* → null, in the context [___ [_NP_ JACK]]

Let us consider how these rules work with minimizers. For instance, consider (18a), whose structure is given in (18b):

(18) a.   John did not drink a drop.
     b.   John drink [NEG a drop]

What is the relationship between the indefinite article *a* in (18) and the *some* that NEG usually modifies? We suggest two possibilities, but do not take up a serious discussion of this issue. The first possibility is that the indefinite article is a reduced form of *some*. Then one could simply say that NEG modifies *a* in (18) just as NEG modifies *some* in other examples. Another possibility is that examples like *a drop* are really analyzed as [SOME a drop], where the indefinite article is not an existential quantifier at all. Then the NEG in (18b) would be modifying the null SOME in such a structure.

3.6 *Many*

Classical NR aside, descriptive appeal to NEG raising is by no means original
in the framework of Postal 2005 or this monograph, nor is it limited to cases
taken to involve NPIs. For instance, consider triples like (19a–c):

(19) a. Veronica did not read many books.
  b. Not many books did Veronica read.
  c. Many books, Veronica did not read.

Lasnik (1972:32) noted that cases like (19a) are scope ambiguous. On one
reading, (19a) is synonymous with (19b), and on the other it is synonymous
with (19c).

Lasnik (1972) proposed an analysis of such cases where on the reading of
(19a) synonymous with (19b), the NEG originates in the object, raises out of
it, and ends up in the post-Aux position. That is, Lasnik had even then made
proposals partially in line with our current assumptions and, notably, radically
at odds with those of Klima (1964), whose assumptions greatly influenced
much early generative work on negation in English. For Klima, the NEG in
both readings of (19a) had to be a sentential negation.

So, as long ago as 1972, acceptance of Lasnik's assumption already determined the following fact:

(20) Some English instances of NEG have a surface position distinct from
      (and higher than) their position of origin.

In other words, Lasnik had already recognized the existence of NEG
raising. However, such ideas have, to say the least, hardly been prominent
since then.

Partial representations of the readings in (19b,c) are given in (21b,c) (ignoring scope occurrences to be discussed in chapter 5):

(21) a. Veronica did not read many books.
  b. Veronica did NEG_1 read [<NEG_1> many books]
  c. Veronica did NEG_1 [$_{\text{VP}}$ <NEG_1> read [many books]]

Structure (21b), where NEG raises away from the object DP, yields the reading
of (19a) synonymous with (19b). Structure (21c), where the scope-bearing DP
contains no NEG and the post-Aux NEG originates on the V/VP, ultimately
yields the reading of (19a) synonymous with (19c). In chapter 5, we argue that
NEG raising in cases like (21b) must be restricted to raising from the scope
occurrence of the DP dominating the raised NEG. In this, our position deviates
from Lasnik's view, which did not recognize DPs in scope positions.

Support for an analysis like (21b) that invokes NEG raising comes from the
fact that the [NEG many] constituent posited there clearly occurs independently in Negative Inversion cases like (19b) and in subjects—specifically, in
either passives or middles:

(22) a.   Not many people believe in witches.
      b.   Not many books were read by Veronica.
      c.   Not many books edit as easily as that one.

However, the [NEG many] constituent unmodified by NEG raising does not,
for many speakers including ourselves, occur in object positions themselves,
although, in our view, the structure of (23a) provides the input to the NEG
raising seen in (19a) on one reading:

(23) a.   *Veronica read not many books.
      b.   *Veronica read to not many children.
      c.   *Veronica's study of not many manuscripts was unpublished.

These ungrammatical cases reveal the existence of a condition, call it the *Not-
Initial Constraint*, which blocks a range of DPs beginning with *not* from a
variety of positions including verbal and prepositional object positions. Determining exactly which *not*-initial phrases are subject to the restrictions and
precisely formulating this constraint are complicated matters, and we will not
attempt them here. It appears from (19b) and (22) that the relevant type of
NEG phrase is required to be preverbal in a clause, regardless of how that
status is achieved.

3.7 The Semantics of Negation

The view of NPIs and negation sketched so far demands a particular view of
the semantics of negation. We reject the traditional "sentential" conception of
negation whereby it is limited to operating on the interpretation of clausal
constituents. Rather, we assume NEGs can modify verbs (or perhaps verb
phrases), adjectives (or perhaps adjective phrases), DPs, Ds, and NPs, as well
as clauses.

The idea that NEG can modify smaller constituents than clauses is no doubt
controversial, and an opposing view that negation originates exclusively in a
high position modifying clauses has been defended:

(24) (McCawley 1998:582)
      "If no such analysis proves viable, it might be necessary, for example,
      to allow the scopes of some negations to be something other than a S,

though it is hard to see how something could be a negation without having a S as its scope."

This amounts to the assumption that semantically, all negation is propositional. But that claim, which McCawley did not defend, is arguably baseless. Often, the view that negation is essentially clausal/propositional is restricted somewhat to allow something called "constituent negation," almost always treated as marginal and secondary. But our view is almost the opposite: the number of instances of actual clausal negation is quite restricted. Our view, which is contrary to the emphasis on clausal/propositional negation, is consistent with the positions taken in the following works (see also Landman 1991:288):

(25) a. (Keenan and Faltz 1985:6)
"Thus we can directly interpret conjunctions, disjunctions, and negations in most categories by taking them to be the appropriate meet, join, and complement functions of the interpretations of the expressions conjoined, disjoined, or negated. The sense in which we have only one *and*, *or*, and *not* is explicated on the grounds that they are always interpreted as the meet, join, and complement functions in whatever set we are looking at."
   b. (Ladusaw 1996b:322)
"If negation is based upon an opposition of elements within a certain domain, we can recognize what is logically the same negative opposition in different semantic and pragmatic domains."
   c. (Haspelmath 1997:203n6)
"The Fregean view of negation as a sentence operator contributes little to our understanding of the form of negation in natural languages."

In such terms, there is no semantic barrier whatever to taking negation to originate in diverse constituents, including DPs, Ds, and so on. The idea of restricting all negation to the propositional level was also rejected by Horn (1989 [2001]); see especially his chapter 7.

Our fundamental assumption about the semantics of the syntactic element NEG is as follows:

(26) For an interpreted syntactic constituent K = [NEG [X]], the semantic value in model M of K is, as in Keenan and Faltz 1985, the complement of the semantic value of X in M.

In a view where negation is treated as sentential, the semantic value of NEG is applied exclusively to the semantic value of a clause C, yielding the value

False if C has the value True, and True if C has the value False. In our view, this account is subsumed under a more general conception not limited in particular to clausal categories and in which any constituent with predicative semantics can be negated.

This intuition can be semantically formalized as (27). We assume that the body of the lambda term (shown as [. . .] below) has type t. P_i is a variable of any type, and the P variables do not have to have the same type.

(27) NEG takes X with semantic value $\lambda P_1 \ldots \lambda P_n [\ldots]$
     And returns Y with semantic value $\lambda P_1 \ldots \lambda P_n \neg[\ldots]$

This rule is actually a schema for an infinite number of semantically different NEGs. There will be a distinct semantic value for NEG for each different semantic type, $\lambda P_1 \ldots \lambda P_n [\ldots]$. For propositional variables p (no predicate abstraction), the negation is simply $\neg p$. This approach is completely compositional.

The following remarks deal with the case of a negated quantifier. Other cases (negated V/VP) would be treated analogously, and further illustrative examples are given throughout the monograph.

First, we give the semantic values of the quantifier *some*, NP, and NEG:

(28) *Quantifier with semantic value of type <<e,t>, <<e,t>, t>>*
     $[\![some]\!] = \lambda P \lambda Q [\exists x (P(x) \& Q(x))]$

(29) *NP of semantic value of type <e,t>*
     $[\![boy]\!] = (\lambda x.\ x \text{ is a boy})$

(30) *NEG with semantic value of type <<<e,t>, <<e,t>, t>>, <<e,t>, <<e,t>, t>>>*
     $[\![NEG]\!] = \lambda X \lambda P \lambda Q \neg[X(P)(Q)]$

Given these semantic values, we calculate the semantic value of [no boy], which for us has the syntactic structure [[NEG SOME] boy]. First, we show how to calculate the semantic value of *some boy*:

(31) $[\![some\ boy]\!] = [\![some]\!]([\![boy]\!])$
     $= (\lambda P \lambda Q [\exists x (P(x) \& Q(x))]) (\lambda x.\ x \text{ is a boy})$
     $= \lambda Q [\exists x ((x \text{ is a boy}) \& Q(x))]$

Given the semantic value of *some boy*, the semantic value of *some boy runs* is the following:

(32) $[\![some\ boy\ runs]\!] = \exists x ((x \text{ is a boy}) \& (x \text{ runs}))$

In our framework, *no* is a NEG which modifies SOME:

(33) $[\![\text{NEG SOME}]\!] = [\![\text{NEG}]\!]([\![\text{SOME}]\!])$
$= (\lambda X \lambda P \lambda Q \ \neg[X(P)(Q)]) \ (\lambda P \lambda Q \ [\exists x \ (P(x) \ \& \ Q(x)])$
$= \lambda P \lambda Q \ \neg[\exists x \ (P(x) \ \& \ Q(x))]$

Combining this with an NP yields the following semantic value:

(34) $[\![\text{no boy}]\!] = [\![[[\text{NEG SOME}] \ \text{boy}]]\!]$
$= (\lambda P \lambda Q \ \neg[\exists x \ (P(x) \ \& \ Q(x))]) \ (\lambda x. \ x \text{ is a boy})$
$= \lambda Q \ \neg[\exists x \ ((x \text{ is a boy}) \ \& \ Q(x))]$

Finally, combining this with a clause, as in *no boy runs*, yields the following semantic value:

(35) $[\![\text{no boy runs}]\!] = \neg[\exists x \ ((x \text{ is a boy}) \ \& \ (x \text{ runs}))]$

3.8 A Preliminary Minimalist Account

In Minimalist syntax, the above analysis of NEG raising can be implemented in terms of movement to the specifier of a functional projection. We will call this phrase *NMP* (for NEG Merge Phrase). This is a phrase into whose specifier NEG is merged (either internally or externally, as we will show). We make the following assumption (see Haegeman 1995, 2000 on the NEG Criterion):

(36) a. NEG is in Spec,NMP at Spell-Out.
      b. Spec,NMP is occupied by NEG at some point in the derivation.

So all cases of NEG following a finite Aux would be analyzed as in (37), where NEG raises to Spec,NMP.

(37)

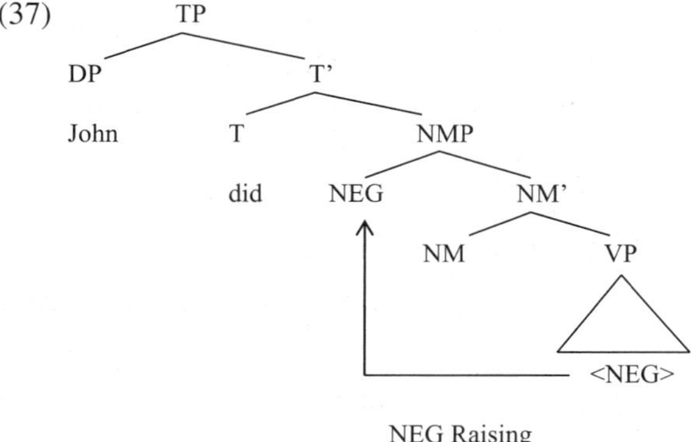

NEG Raising

As noted in (36b), we assume that any instances of NMP must have a filled specifier (an EPP feature). So if NMP is generated, then its specifier will have to be filled by either internal or external Merge before Spell-Out. At the present time, we do not know of languages in which NM is overt.

Recall that our analysis of nominal NPIs involves an underlying negative quantificational DP: [[NEG SOME] NP]. We assume that NEG modifies SOME, where NEG is the specifier of NMP and SOME is the complement of NMP. This yields the DP structure (38) for *no boy*:

(38)

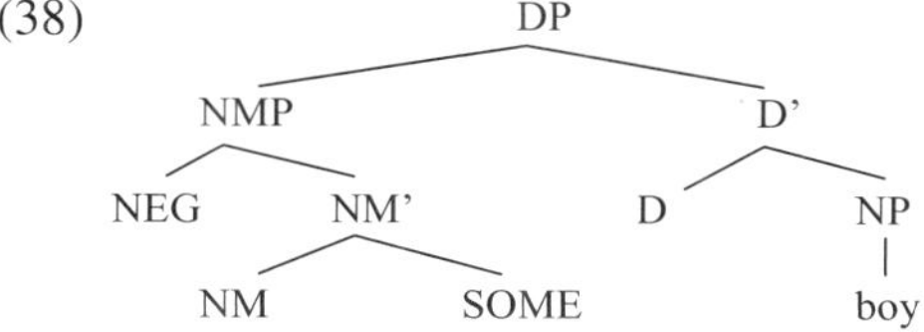

On these assumptions, SOME and [NEG SOME] are not actually determiners, but rather occupy Spec,DP; the actual determiner is a null head. Nevertheless, we will continue to refer to [NEG SOME] as a determiner in the lingua franca terminology of the present monograph.

Finally, consider the structure of Classical NR on these assumptions. We assume that Classical NR takes place successive-cyclically through the embedded Spec,CP position. So consider the following sentence:

(39) a. I don't think that John knows jackshit$_A$.
    b. I do NEG$_1$ think [$_{CP}$ <NEG$_1$> COMP [$_{IP}$ John knows [$_{DP}$ [<NEG$_1$> SOME] jackshit$_A$]]]

We assume that NEG$_1$ starts out in the DP [[NEG$_1$ SOME] jackshit$_A$]. It then raises to Spec,CP of the embedded clause. Finally, from Spec,CP, it raises into Spec,NMP of the matrix clause. Such an analysis predicts that if Spec,CP is filled, then Classical NR will be blocked. This prediction holds, as shown in chapters 11 and 12.

4 Reversals

4.1 Two Types of NPIs

In the preceding chapter, we outlined an analysis of certain NPIs in which NEG starts out as a sister of SOME and raises away (usually to a position immediately right-adjacent to Aux). Such a view of NPIs provides a straightforward account of the relations between pairs like (5a,b) of chapter 3, repeated here:

(1) a. I saw no widow.
    b. I didn't see any widow.

As discussed in chapter 3, providing the object DPs in such pairs with the same underlying structure accounts for their semantic equivalence, while analyzing (1b) in terms of NEG raising and the SOME→*any* mapping accounts for the differences in form. In the terms developed so far, (1b) has the structure in (2):

(2) I did NEG_5 see [[<NEG_5> SOME] widow]

    A basic problem is that the view of NPIs represented in (2) appears to leave cases like (3) without an obvious analysis:

(3) a. At most half of the class knows any physics.
    b. Everybody who steals any candy will get caught.
    c. If you steal any candy, you will be caught.

    The assumption that these cases are subject to the SOME→*any* mapping given in chapter 3 might seem to create a dilemma. Focus on (3b), under the assumption that the structure of *any candy* originates with NEG as a sister to SOME. The result would be (4):

(4) Everybody who steals [[NEG SOME] candy] will get caught

In this structure, NEG would somehow need to be forced to be unpronounced and SOME would be realized as *any* since the unpronounced occurrence of NEG creates the environment for the SOME→*any* mapping. However, such an analysis determines the wrong truth conditions, since (3b) does not mean 'Everybody who steals no candy (who doesn't steal any candy) will get caught'. Similar problems arise for (3a) and (3c).

Rather, all three examples are truth-conditionally equivalent to examples where the NPI determiner *any* that they contain is replaced by the indefinite *some*:

(5) a. At most half of the class knows some physics.
    b. Everybody who steals some candy will get caught.
    c. If you steal some candy, you will be caught.

Following the general assumptions made in Postal 2005, we propose to analyze these cases in terms of double NEG structures, dubbed *reversals*, a term motivated by the fact that a second NEG scoping over the first nullifies the semantic consequences of the first one, as formally shown in (7). On this analysis, the structures of the examples in (3) are respectively (6a–c):

(6) a. At most half of the class knows [[NEG$_2$ [NEG$_1$ SOME]] physics]
    b. Everybody who steals [[NEG$_2$ [NEG$_1$ SOME]] candy] will get caught
    c. If you steal [[NEG$_2$ [NEG$_1$ SOME]] candy], you will be caught

Given the semantics for negation proposed in section 3.7, the structures in (6a–c) will yield the same interpretations as those of (5a–c), respectively. In other words, [NEG [NEG SOME]] has exactly the same semantic value as SOME. This is shown formally in (7):

(7) a. $[\![\text{SOME}]\!]$ $= \lambda P \lambda Q\ [\exists x\ (P(x)\ \&\ Q(x))]$

    b. $[\![\text{NEG}]\!]$ $= \lambda X \lambda P \lambda Q\ \neg[X(P)(Q)]$

    c. $[\![\text{NEG SOME}]\!]$ $= [\![\text{NEG}]\!]([\![\text{SOME}]\!])$

                         $= (\lambda X \lambda P \lambda Q\ \neg[X(P)(Q)])\ (\lambda P \lambda Q\ [\exists x\ (P(x)\ \&\ Q(x))])$

                         $= \lambda P \lambda Q\ \neg[\exists x\ (P(x)\ \&\ Q(x))]$

    d. $[\![\text{NEG (NEG SOME)}]\!] = [\![\text{NEG}]\!]([\![\text{NEG}]\!]([\![\text{SOME}]\!]))$

                         $= (\lambda X \lambda P \lambda Q\ \neg[X(P)(Q)])\ (\lambda P \lambda Q\ \neg[\exists x\ (P(x)\ \&\ Q(x))])$

                         $= \lambda P \lambda Q\ \neg[\neg[\exists x\ (P(x)\ \&\ Q(x))]]$

                         $= \lambda P \lambda Q\ [\exists x\ (P(x)\ \&\ Q(x))]$

                         $= [\![\text{SOME}]\!]$

So we are arguing that there are at least two kinds of contrasting NEG structures depending on whether they involve single NEGs, as in (8a) (henceforth: *unary-NEG structures*), or two NEGs, as in (8b) (henceforth: *binary-NEG* or *reversal structures*). Critically, in the structures (8a,b) and in definition (9), X is not of the form [NEG Y].

(8) a. [$_\alpha$ NEG X]   (unary-NEG NPI)
    b. [$_\alpha$ NEG [NEG X]]   (binary-NEG NPI/reversal)

In a reversal structure, the outer NEG is called a *reversal NEG*. More precisely:

(9) *Definitions:* Reversal NEG *and* reversal structure
    NEG_2 is a *reversal NEG* and Z is a *reversal structure* if and only if
    there is a NEG_1 such that Z = [NEG_2 [NEG_1 X]].

The distinction between unary- and binary-NEG structures interacts with our view that all NPIs involve at least one instance of NEG to yield a parallel typology of NPIs based on whether they represent unary- or binary-NEG structures. The reason that both the patterns in (8) may yield *any* when X = SOME is a function of the SOME→*any* mapping (17) of chapter 3.

Having argued that reversal structures like those in (6) get the meaning right for the relevant NPIs, we must address the obvious syntactic issue that neither NEG posited in (6) is overt. Given our general framework for analyzing NPIs, both of the NEGs in each structure of (6) must then have been deleted. This points to a characteristic and no doubt controversial feature of most reversal structures: namely, there is no overt representation of either NEG. While this property evidently makes the notion of reversal structure quite abstract, it in no way precludes the existence of evidence for such structures. And in section 4.9, we provide such evidence.[1]

In a binary-NEG structure, there are two unpronounced NEGs. We attribute this to a phenomenon of NEG deletion, which we discuss in detail in chapters 7 and 8. NEG deletion involves a relation between individual NEGs and other phrases, their NEG deleters, which we call the *NDEL relation*. In our view, NEG deletion requires NEG deleters. In (6a–c), we take the relevant NEG deleters to be *at most half of the class*, *every*, and *if*, respectively (reversal NEGs are also NEG deleters; see chapter 8 for details). Each of these represents a nonincreasing function with respect to the relevant constituents. We refer to such NEG deleters as *general NEG deleters* as opposed to what we call *lexical NEG deleters*. The distinction is explained in chapters 7 and 8.

Reversals do not play a *direct* role in our syntactic treatment of Classical NR because the overt NEGs raised by Classical NR are never reversals. For example, in *I don't think Allan will get here until 6:00*, the raised NEG is not a reversal NEG. But the reversal concept is nonetheless critically relevant because understanding many of the facts involving NPIs and Classical NR involves disentangling different kinds of NPIs (many of which we analyze as reversal NPIs).

4.2   A Constraint on NEG Deletion in Reversals

An important issue whose discussion we postpone until chapter 8 is that allowing NEG deletion of the type seen with reversals seems to allow a range of wrong predictions. We have claimed that the sentences in (3) have the respective structures in (6), where both NEGs are deleted. Why then can the sentences in (3) not have the respective unary-NEG structures in (10), with only the single NEG deleted in each case?

(10) a. At most half of the class knows [<NEG> SOME physics]
      b. Everybody who steals [<NEG> SOME candy] will get caught
      c. If you steal [<NEG> SOME candy], you will be caught

On such analyses, an example like *At most half of the class knows any physics* would have the interpretation that at most half of the class knows no physics. Since the structures in (10) yield the wrong interpretations, they must be blocked.

A related issue is why an example like (11) cannot have an indefinite existential reading:

(11) We saw no student.

That is, why can (11) not have the interpretation determined by structure (12)?

(12) We saw [<NEG$_2$> [NEG$_1$ SOME]] student

Here, only one of the two NEGs is deleted. For the moment, we assume the following informal constraint based on Szabolcsi 2004:

(13) *The NEG Deletion Evenness Condition (first version)*
      If X is a general NEG deleter, X deletes an even number of NEGs.

We return to this condition in chapter 8, explicating a much more adequate version and embedding it in a framework of general assumptions about NEG deletion.

In the sections that follow, we offer various types of evidence distinguishing unary-NEG NPIs from reversal ones.

4.3 Alternation with Non-NPI Indefinites

A general test distinguishing reversal NPIs from unary-NEG NPIs is provided by the semantic equivalence found when reversal DP NPIs are replaced by corresponding non-NPI DPs whose D is the indefinite element *some*, as already illustrated in (5). What needs to be shown is that unary-NEG NPIs do not share this property. Consider:

(14) a. I do not see any zebra.
     b. I do not see some zebra.

(15) a. Nobody saw any zebra.
     b. Nobody saw some zebra.

Here, replacement of what we take to be unary-NEG NPIs by *some* forms does not preserve the semantics of the NPI. In (14b) and (15b) the existential quantifier associated with *some* must scope over negation, while in (14a) and (15a) the scopes are reversed (see Szabolcsi 2004 for discussion of such scope facts). We find that this test is a good initial heuristic for determining the character of an NPI with respect to the unary- versus binary-NEG dimension.[2]

4.4 Discourse Anaphora

Reversal NPIs as opposed to unary-NEG NPIs support a kind of discourse anaphora that one finds with indefinites:

(16) a. If you steal any candy, you should hide it.
     b. If you meet any students, say hello to them for me.
     c. If they know any physics, they learned it in high school.

In all cases, the NPI can be the antecedent of a pronoun, just as a non-NPI indefinite can:

(17) a. If you steal some candy, you should hide it.
     b. If you meet some students, say hello to them for me.
     c. If they know some physics, they learned it in high school.

As a condition distinguishing unary- from binary-NEG NPI structures, we propose the following condition relating NPIs to discourse anaphora:

(18) If an NPI DP is the antecedent of a discourse (non-c-commanded) anaphor, then it is a reversal NPI.

The following minimal pair illustrates that unary-NEG NPIs cannot serve as discourse antecedents:

(19) a. If you steal any candy$_1$, give it$_1$ to me.   (reversal antecedent)
     b. If you steal [[NEG [NEG SOME]] candy]$_1$, give it$_1$ to me

(20) a. *If you don't steal any candy$_1$, give it$_1$ to me.
                                                    (unary NEG DP antecedent)
     b. If you steal [[NEG SOME] candy]$_1$, give it$_1$ to me

Condition (18) plausibly also underlies the following appositive modification contrast:

(21) a. If they know any physics$_1$, which$_1$ they probably learned in high
         school, they can take Physics 102.
     b. *If they don't know any physics$_1$, which$_1$ they probably learned in
         high school, they can't take Physics 102.

To the extent that (21a) is acceptable, *any physics* is serving as the anteced-ent of the appositive relative *which*. No such appositive modification is possible for unary-NEG NPIs.

4.5 Negative Inversion

As we will discuss in much more detail in chapters 13, 14, and 15, unary-NEG NPIs can license Negative Inversion in what we call *Horn clauses*. A Horn clause is a clause embedded under a negated CNRP, where an NPI in the fronted phrase triggers Negative Inversion in the embedded clause:

(22) I don't think that at any point will he steal that money.

Reversal NPIs never license Negative Inversion in such cases:

(23) a. *At most half of the class thinks that at any point will he steal that
         money.
     b. *Everybody who thinks that at any point will he steal that
         money. . .
     c. *If you think that at any point will he steal that money, you are
         crazy.

Arguably, the ungrammaticality of (23a–c) is related to the fact that indefinites do not trigger Negative Inversion:

(24) a. *At most half of the class thinks that at some point will he steal
         that money.

b. *Everybody who thinks that at some point will he steal that money. . .

c. *If you think that at some point will he steal that money, you are crazy.

That is, as elaborated in chapter 14, the general conditions on Negative Inversion block cases like (24a–c) and also block those like (23a–c), while permitting cases like (22). Thus, the contrast between (22) and (23a–c) strongly supports the distinction between unary and reversal structure NPIs.

4.6 VP Ellipsis

The two types of English NPIs that we distinguished earlier, nonstrict and strict, arguably behave differently under VP ellipsis. This difference between nonstrict and strict NPIs can be understood in terms of the binary-NEG/unary-NEG distinction (see section 9.4). Constituents containing nonstrict NPIs can easily be elided, as shown in (25a–c). That situation contrasts with the VP deletion facts found with strict NPIs, which for some speakers are degraded, as shown in (26a–d):

(25) a. A: Not everybody knows any physics.   B: I do.
      b. A: No more than three people know any physics.   B: I do.
      c. A: Few students have ever been to Paris.   B: I have.

(26) a. A: Nobody here knows shit about Turkish.   B: *I do.
      b. A: Nobody has seen Sally in ages.   B: *I have.
      c. A: Nobody got there until 6:00.   B: *I did.
      d. A: Nobody here is all that smart.   B: *I am.

A very informal account of these facts can be given as follows, assuming a view of VP ellipsis that requires the satisfaction of both semantic and syntactic identity conditions. We cannot consider these conditions in any detail here, as this is a subject with a huge literature and one about which many fundamental issues remain unresolved.

Consider first Speaker B's response in (25a), which would have the structure in (27):

(27) I do <know some physics>

In the overall example, the reversal *any physics*, which we analyze as [[NEG$_2$ [NEG$_1$ SOME]] physics], counts as identical to *some physics* in the deleted VP in the second clause of (25a). Assuming a semantic account of the needed identity for VP ellipsis, the acceptability of cases like (25a) is understandable since *some physics* and [[NEG$_2$ [NEG$_1$ SOME]] physics] have identical semantic values (and identical SYNNEG values, a syntactic property; see chapter 14). But the strict NPIs in (26a–d) are not semantically equivalent to indefinites. So under the same assumption about semantic identity for VP ellipsis, no deletion should be possible.[3]

4.7 Intensives

A further argument for distinguishing two classes of NPIs is based on the possibility of DP continuations with phrases such as *not even* DP, *not any, not a single one, not a drop, not a bit*. For lack of better terminology, we will call such phrases *intensives*. They are systematically possible with unary-NEG NPIs:

(28) a. I did not read any report, not even yours/not a single one.
    b. Nobody saw any students, not even Jane.
    c. Nobody drank any beer, not a drop/not a bit.

But they are ruled out with reversal NPIs:

(29) a. *At most half of the class knows any physics, not even Newton's laws.
    b. *Everybody who steals any candy, not a bit, will get caught.
    c. *If you drink any sodas, not a single one, you will be sorry.

We claim that this contrast follows from the contrast between structures of the two types of NPIs, given the following informal condition:

(30) *The Intensive Condition*
If an intensive is associated with X, then X is an antiadditive DP formed with a unary NEG.

Evidence for condition (30) is provided by facts like these:

(31) a. Nobody/Not one doctor (not even Sandra) claimed that.
    b. Not everyone/Not every doctor (*not even Sandra) claimed that.
    c. Zero doctors/Less than one doctor (*not even Sandra) claimed that.
    d. Some doctors/All doctors (*not even Sandra) claimed that.

In (31a), each of the DPs with which the intensive is associated is formed with a NEG and is antiadditive. In (31b), the subject is decreasing but not antiadditive. In (31c), the modified DPs are antiadditive but not formed with NEG. Finally, in (31d), the modified DPs are neither formed with NEG nor antiadditive.

Given condition (30), the contrast between (28) and (29) is accounted for, because only the unary-NEG subset of NPIs represent antiadditive DPs.

To maintain the utility of condition (30), it is important to dispose of an alternative hypothesis that would deny its relevance to distinguishing unary-NEG from binary-NEG structures. The alternative would be the following:

(32) Intensives can only occur in the scope of an antiadditive operator, and moreover, one formed with a NEG.

On this hypothesis, the grammatical status of an intensive is not dependent on the structure of the DP that it associates with. To refute this, one needs to find a reversal NPI in the scope of an antiadditive operator formed with NEG where the reversal can nonetheless not be associated with an intensive.

Forms (33a,b) arguably illustrate such a case. The NPIs in both (33a) and (33b) appear in the scope of an antiadditive operator (the negated verb [NEG find]), but intensives are nonetheless impossible. It is important that these examples be read with only weak stress on the *any* forms. Contrastive stress raises a general high-scope confound issue discussed at length in chapter 9.

(33) a.   I didn't find a doctor who gave any poisoned medicine to those patients.
           (*any* means 'some')
      b.   *I didn't find a doctor who gave any poisoned medicine, not a drop, to those patients.
      c.   That doctor didn't give any poisoned medicine, not a drop, to those patients.

Example (33c) shows that the mere presence of the intensive between the direct object and the PP *to those patients* in (33b) is not the basis for its ungrammaticality. What is, we claim, is condition (30), which blocks (33b) on the assumption that a weakly stressed *any* inside a relative clause R can have its licenser external to R only under a reversal analysis. The alternative condition (32) offers no basis for the fact in (33b) (see also section 12.10 for further relevant discussion).

The same argument can be made on the basis of (34):

(34) They didn't consider the possibility that he gave any poisoned medicine (, *not a drop,) to those patients.

Here, [NEG consider the possibility that S] forms an antiadditive context containing *any poisoned medicine* (again read with weak stress on *any*), but the presence of the intensive still yields ungrammaticality. This follows if the context only allows reversal NEG structures. That claim is independently supported by the fact that this context refuses NPIs like *in years*—that is, refuses strict NPIs, which we suggested earlier do not permit reversal structures. If this is correct, they should be barred in the context of (34), which they are:

(35) *They didn't consider the possibility that he had visited his mother in years.

We claim that a case like (35) is ungrammatical because (i) strict NPIs, which are always unary-NEG NPIs, cannot appear in the relevant environment given that (ii) *in years* can only represent a unary-NEG NPI structure. The classification of *in years* as a unary-NEG NPI is supported in (36):

(36) a. At most half of the students have seen their mothers anytime recently/*in years.
   b. Every person who has visited a nursing home at any time/*in years should do so again.
   c. If he had attended a church at any time/*in years, he wouldn't have said that.

These examples show that forms that sanction reversal NPIs like *any* systematically fail to permit *in years*.

So we have now shown with respect to the environment in (34) that it permits reversal NPIs but not strict NPIs. That means it does not permit what are in our terms unary-NEG NPIs. And that, given condition (30), entails the impossibility of an intensive, which is what (34) illustrated. But the hypothetical alternative condition (32) allows the ungrammatical intensive case in (34).

The cases in (33) and (34) together then argue strongly that condition (32) on intensives is too weak. Specifically, the feature that differentiates condition (32) from condition (30)—that is, nonreference to the unary-NEG structure of the DP with which intensives are associated—is what renders (32) too weak.

4.8 NPI Types That Do Not Permit Reversal Structures

While we have argued that some NPIs can represent either unary- or binary-NEG structures, some NPIs do not allow reversal structures. We already suggested this for the *in years* type. We will further support this claim via the class called JACK in chapter 1. The evidence takes the form of systematic contrasts between members of JACK and *any* forms. Consider the following data:

(37) a. Jerome doesn't know anything/jackshit$_A$ about Turkish.
b. At most half of the class knows anything/*jackshit$_A$ about Turkish.

(38) a. Dorothy didn't say anything /jackshit$_A$ about California.
b. Less than three people said anything/*jackshit$_A$ about California.

(39) a. If he doesn't write anything/jackshit$_A$ about that, it is a sign he is ill.
b. If he writes anything/*jackshit$_A$ about that, it is a sign he is ill.

(40) a. Because he didn't steal any cocaine/jackshit$_A$, he was not arrested.
b. Not because he stole any cocaine/*jackshit$_A$ was he arrested.

(41) a. Why he didn't steal any cocaine/jackshit$_A$ has not been determined.
b. Whether he stole any cocaine/*jackshit$_A$ has not been determined.

(42) a. Nobody said anything/*jackshit$_A$ to the detainee.
b. Nobody who said anything/*jackshit$_A$ to the detainee was released.

The contrasts in (37)–(42) reveal the following pattern. The distribution of *jackshit$_A$* parallels that of *any* forms only insofar as the latter are analyzed as unary-NEG structures. This means that members of JACK contrast with *any* forms in environments where the latter are semantically equivalent to *some* forms (and hence analyzed as binary-NEG structures).

The evidence in (37)–(42) is supported by the fact that adding intensives to the *any* forms that alternate grammatically with JACK forms yields well-formed outputs, but adding them to the other class of *any* forms yields ill-formed outputs. We illustrate only with (41), leaving it to the reader to check the others:

(43) a. Why he didn't steal any cocaine (, not any/not even Ted's,) has not been determined.
b. Whether he stole any cocaine (*, not any/*not even Ted's,) has not been determined.

We conclude that English grammar includes a principle informally representable as follows:

(44) *The JACK Determiner Restriction Condition*
If DP$_x$ = [D$_1$ [$_{NP}$ N]], where N is a member of JACK, then
a. D$_1$ = [zero] or
b. D$_1$ = [NEG SOME].

The reason for case (44a) here is that Postal (2004b:chap. 5) argues at length that the non-NPI variants of the JACK class take the determiner *zero* (e.g., *He knows shit about physics*). Case (44b) limits the case where D_1 is associated with a member of JACK but does not dominate the determiner *zero* to the unary-NEG case. We observe that both alternatives in (44) define antiadditive Ds.

Members of the *in ages/days/months/weeks* . . . set and the JACK set are not the only NPI forms that preclude reversal NEG structures. Others include punctual *until, so good/hot/great, half bad, anything* in the phrase *stop at anything*, and so on. We leave documentation of this fact to the reader.

4.9 Do Reversal Structures Really Contain NEGs?

Traditional approaches to NPIs like *any* would of course not claim that what we take to be reversal NPIs contain any NEGs at all; see note 1. This is just a special case of the fact that no previous view of NPIs has taken them to systematically represent negative forms.

However, there is evidence that even reversal NPIs incorporate syntactic negation. This derives from the distribution of the DP modifiers *at all* and *what(so)ever*, which argues against traditional accounts that recognize no NEGs in NPIs.

Consider *at all* data such as (45a–h) (since the facts for *what(so)ever* are fully parallel, we omit discussing them for brevity's sake):

(45) a. I saw a/some linguist/several linguists/certain linguists (*at all).
    b. I saw the linguists/those linguists/both linguists (*at all).
    c. I saw two/three/four linguists (*at all).
    d. I saw each/every linguist (*at all).
    e. I saw all the linguists (*at all).
    f. I saw most linguists (*at all).
    g. At most three linguists (*at all) were there.
    h. Zero linguists (*at all) were there.

These examples contrast with (46a–b):

(46) a. I saw no linguist (at all).
    b. Not many linguists (at all) showed up.

These data suggest that something like (47) is a necessary condition on appending the *at all* modifier to a DP:

(47) *The* At all/What(so)ever *Condition*
    In a structure A = [[$_{\mathrm{DP}}$ X] at all/what(so)ever], the determiner D of X contains NEG.

The condition covers such complex cases as these:[4]

(48) a. Absolutely nobody at all would help me.
  b. Not a SINGLE person at all wants to go out?
    (www.meetup.com/patgirls/messages/boards/thread/33004692)

Cases like (49a,b) might be considered counterexamples to (47):

(49) a. Few diamonds at all were recovered.
  b. Little money at all was recovered.

While these judgments conflict with those given by Horn (1972:161), whose generalization claimed they were impossible, Google supplies many examples supporting the grammaticality of such cases, as illustrated in (50):

(50) a. And so far very few people at all are brought up by gay couples!
    (www.courage.org.uk/articles/article.asp?id=48)
  b. Oct 4, 2010 – porn stars actually make very little money at all.
    (www.formspring.me/kpooz/q/1259684268)
  c. Still, they certainly don't skimp you here, as all the favorites can be found and enjoyed for very little money at all.
    (www.gogobot.com/kapolei-korean-barbecue-kapolei-ko-olina
    -restaurant)

We hypothesize that these occurrences of *few* and *little* represent the forms [NEG many] and [NEG much], respectively. Then the analyses of (49a–b) would be (51a–b), respectively:

(51) a. [NEG many] diamonds at all were recovered
  b. [NEG much] money at all was recovered

Under this hypothesis, the relevant DPs in (49) are formed with NEG in conformity with condition (47).[5]

We can conclude that the *At all/What(so)ever* Condition determines that any DP modified by *at all* has a D containing a NEG. And we can consider the interaction of that condition with the Intensive Condition (30), which requires a unary-NEG analysis for an associated NPI:

(52) a. I didn't see any linguist(s) (at all), not even Gail/not a single one.
  b. At most seven philosophers know any linguists (at all), *not even Wayne/*not any.

Evidently, the modifier *at all* is possible on NPI *any* forms. Given what was argued about intensives, that in (52a) has to be a unary-NEG *any* form, whereas that in (52b) is arguably a reversal one. Both types of expression (*at all* and intensives) are possible in (52a) because it is a unary-NEG structure and hence represents an antiadditive negative DP, as condition (30) requires, and also represents a DP whose D contains NEG, as condition (47) requires. But only the *at all* modifier is possible on the NPI in (52b) because, in our terms, it represents a reversal NEG structure, which does not form an antiadditive (or even a decreasing) operator. We see no basis for these results in standard ideas about NPIs in which both NPIs in (52) are simply some form of existential indefinite, differing semantically or syntactically from *some* only in having to occur under the scope of a decreasing (or at least nonincreasing) form.

We stress that condition (47) is by no means a fully adequate account of the distribution of *at all*. For example, it is not clear that (47) blocks the following cases:

(53) a. Not every philosopher (*at all) believes that.
      b. Not all philosophers (*at all) believe that.
      c. No less than five philosophers (*at all) believe that.
      d. No more than five philosophers (*at all) believe that.
      e. Not even five philosophers (*at all) believe that.
      f. Nowhere near/Not nearly twenty linguists (*at all) believed that.
      g. Not only Barbara/the doctor (*at all) believes that.

Fortunately, the limitations of condition (47) are not relevant to the conclusion that the distribution of *at all/whatsoever* supports the claim that NPI *any* forms, of both the unary and the reversal type, represent NEG-containing structures.

4.10 Free Choice *Any*

In the previous section, we argued that modification by *at all* and *whatsoever* diagnoses the presence of a NEG. From this, plus the fact that reversals can be modified by *at all* and *whatsoever*, we concluded that reversals have the structure [[NEG$_2$ [NEG$_1$ SOME]] NOUN]. We now consider the consequences of this diagnostic for the analysis of free choice *any*. There is a voluminous and complicated literature on free choice *any*, and what we say here cannot begin to do justice to it. We stick narrowly to the consequences of our own system.

Free choice *any* is illustrated in (54). We call *any child* a *FCA phrase*.

(54) Any child can read this book.

Any child in (54) can be modified by *at all* and *whatsoever* just like an NPI:

(55) Any child at all/whatsoever can read this book.

Furthermore, just as some NPIs can be modified by exceptives, so can *any child* in (54). Since indefinites cannot be modified by exceptives (see (56c)), it is unlikely that FCA phrases are indefinites (in light of the distribution of exceptives, Dayal (1998:438, 449) also argues against analyzing FCA phrases as indefinites):

(56) a. Any child but John can read this book.
     b. No child but John can read this book.
     c. *Some child but John can read this book.

Given this evidence, we claim that FCA phrases are really negative quantifier DPs. A first approximation to an analysis of (54) might then be the following:

(57) [[NEG SOME] child] can read this book

Such a structure successfully predicts that *any child* can be modified by *at all/whatsoever* and *but*. However, it yields the wrong meaning, since it is equivalent to 'No children can read this book'.

A possible adjustment would analyze FCA phrases as reversals:

(58) [[NEG_2 [NEG_1 SOME]]] child can read this book

Such a structure would be equivalent semantically to 'Some child can read this book'. This analysis is also wrong, since under its semantic interpretation, (54) would be true if Kim, but no other child, could read the book. And clearly, that is not the interpretation of (54).

Therefore, we suggest that an extra clausal negation is needed in (54), as in (59), where we represent *any child* in its scope position:

(59) <[[<NEG_1> SOME] child]$_1$> [$_s$ <NEG_2> [$_s$ DP$_1$ can read this book]]

The interpretation of (59) is 'No child is such that it is not the case that he/she can read this book', in turn equivalent to 'Every child can read this book'. This is the approximate interpretation of (54).

The structure in (59) raises the question of how NEG_1 and NEG_2 are deleted. Since [[<NEG_1> SOME] child] defines a decreasing function, it represents a suitable NEG deleter in terms of the conditions on general NEG deleters developed in chapter 8; see the General NEG Deletion Condition there. But certain features of structures like (59) raise issues for other conditions, in particular, the claim in chapter 8 (see the NDEL C-Command Condition there) that a NEG deleter must c-command the NEG it deletes. While in its position of origin [[<NEG_1> SOME] child] c-commands NEG_2, it evidently does not c-command NEG_1, nor does NEG_1 c-command NEG_2 (and obviously, NEG_2

does not c-command NEG_1 either). The issue of how these two covert NEGs are deleted is thus problematic.

We see two distinct potential approaches to these issues. Under the first proposal, NEG_1 could raise to be a sister of its originally containing DP. Then [[<NEG_1> SOME] child] would c-command NEG_1, which would c-command NEG_2, and each covert NEG would have a c-commanding NEG deleter. However, this proposal violates the widely accepted constraint permitting only binary-branching structures, since raising NEG to be sister of DP would yield a ternary-branching structure.

Under the second proposal, NEG_1 would not raise but would be directly deleted in its origin position by [[<NEG_1> SOME] child]. This proposal would require a general view of NEG deletion in which a NEG deleter can either c-command or dominate a NEG it deletes.

Both of these possibilities involve a situation we will call *autocannibalistic NEG deletion*, illustrated in (59) by the idea that the DP [[<NEG_1> SOME] child] could delete its own component NEG_1. Each proposal has certain virtues, but each raises various problems. We will not be able to resolve the relevant issues in this monograph. However, doing so is clearly integral to justifying the kind of analysis of FCA structures proposed in (59). We note that the questions about NEG deletion raised by structure (59) arise again in a quite different domain in note 3 of chapter 15.

5 NEG Raising from Scope Positions

In the previous chapter, we argued that NEG raises away from a negative quantificational DP, giving rise to such structures as (1b):

(1) a. I didn't say anything.

    b. I did NEG_1 say [[<NEG_1> SOME] thing]

We proposed that the NEG raises from the NPI in object position and lands in a position right-adjacent to the finite Aux. In this chapter, we argue that the structure outlined in (1b) is considerably oversimplified. We modify the simpler view to take account of our assumption (i) that the NPI phrase occupies a scope position as well as the object position, and we propose (ii) that NEG raising takes place only from the scope position.

As for point (i), we claim first that [[NEG SOME] thing] must occupy a scope position. This is a common assumption in the syntax and semantics literature; see May 1989 and Heim and Kratzer 1998. Assuming as earlier that the scope position is left-adjoined to the clause, (1a) would be represented as follows:

(2) $[_S$ <[[<NEG_1> SOME] thing$]_3$> $[_S$ I did NEG_1 say DP_3]]

In this structure, DP_3 has both lower and higher occurrences. Only the lower one is pronounced, as the bracketing of the higher one indicates.

Given representation (2), one can ask whether NEG raising takes place from the higher or lower occurrence of [NEG_1 SOME thing]. NEG raising from the higher position of [[NEG_1 SOME] thing] would be impossible in cases like (2) if, as we assume, the following very general constraint on movement holds:

(3) *The C-Command Condition on Movement*

    If X moves from P_1 to P_2, then X's occurrence in P_2 c-commands X's occurrence in P_1.

In (2), the higher occurrence of [NEG$_1$ SOME thing] c-commands the moved NEG, and not vice versa, violating (3).

However, we argue in the remainder of this chapter that the following condition also holds:

(4) *The Raising from Scope Position Condition*
If XP$_x$ has a scope position occurrence O and NEG$_1$ raises out of XP$_x$, then NEG$_1$ raises from O.

Given structures like (2), conditions (3) and (4) appear to be inconsistent. To resolve this contradiction, we propose that structure (2) must be rejected. We assume instead that there are more scope positions than just the one indicated in (2) and that, in particular, another scope position exists immediately under the finite Aux:

(5) I did NEG$_1$ [$_{YP}$ <[<NEG$_1$> SOME thing]$_3$> [$_{YP}$ say DP$_3$]]

In (5), [NEG$_1$ SOME thing] occupies a scope position lower than the finite Aux. Just as in (2), we assume that this is an adjoined position. So in (5), [NEG$_1$ SOME thing] is left-adjoined to some YP. We do not take a precise stand on the syntactic identity of this YP. Under Minimalist assumptions, a plausible candidate would be vP (the maximal projection of "little v"), which is the complement of Infl. However, other possibilities are equally consistent with our account.

From this scope position adjoined to YP, NEG$_1$ can raise to its position immediately to the right of the finite Aux in accordance with the c-command condition in (3).

We now argue that the Raising from Scope Position Condition (4) is justified. The claim is that for a DP with a scope occurrence, the scope occurrence is the unique available launching point for NEG raising. The argument shows that if the NEGs of quantifier DPs raise out of nonscope positions, "overgeneration" will result in certain clear cases, whereas if such raising can only launch from scope positions, the overgeneration is avoided.

Consider (6a):

(6) a. Rodney claimed that Evelyn did not own any cheetah.
   b. Rodney claimed that Evelyn did NEG$_1$ [<[[<NEG$_1$> SOME]
      cheetah]$_5$> [own DP$_5$]]
   c. Rodney claimed that there was no cheetah such that Evelyn owned it.

Structure (6b) claims that the scope of the quantifier DP in (6a) is internal to the complement clause, which is the case. The main clause verbal denotation is not part of the material quantified over by [[NEG$_1$ SOME] cheetah] in (6a).

Now consider a structure with negation in the main clause:

(7) a. Rodney did not claim that Evelyn owned any cheetah.
   b. [Rodney did NEG$_1$ <[[NEG$_1$ SOME] cheetah]$_5$> claim that [Evelyn owned DP$_5$]]
   c. There is no cheetah such that Rodney claimed that Evelyn owned it.

In this case, (7b) claims that the quantifier DP takes high scope, which is correct (*any* should be stressed to favor this reading). This analysis also satisfies the C-Command Condition on Movement (3), given that the scope position of the quantifier DP is below *did*. We know that *any cheetah* in (7) is a unary-NEG structure, not a reversal, because it can be followed by intensives (e.g., *not a single one*, *not even a spotted one*) and, as argued in chapter 4, reversals can never be followed by intensives.

The key case is then (8a), with structure (8b) and interpretation (8c):

(8) a. Rodney claimed that Evelyn didn't own any cheetah.
   b. Rodney <[[<NEG$_1$> SOME] cheetah]$_5$> claimed that [Evelyn did NEG$_1$ own DP$_5$]
   c. There is no cheetah such that Rodney claimed that Evelyn owned it.

Structure (8b) claims that (8a) can have the high-scope reading given in (8c). But such an interpretation is in fact impossible. Example (7a) with its legitimate structure (7b) shows that the high scope of the *any* DP is not *in itself* illegitimate with main verb *claim*. Given that, some principles must prevent the NEG associated with the high-scope DP from ending up in the complement as in (8a). The C-Command Condition on Movement (3) guarantees that (8a) cannot result from the displacement of the NEG$_1$ in the higher scope position to a position in the complement. So far so good.

But since the DP in scope position is the same DP filling the object position of *owned*, the C-Command Condition on Movement (3) does not suffice to block a high-scope reading of (8a). It is also necessary to account for why NEG$_1$ cannot raise out of the object position occurrence internal to the complement, which would not violate the requirement that all displacement is to a c-commanding position.

However, raising NEG$_1$ out of the complement of *own* in (8b) is just what the Raising from Scope Position Condition (4) precludes. The latter blocks the ungrammatical reading of (8a), because it only allows NEG$_1$ to raise from its main clause (scope) position in (8b), not from its lower-clause object position. So there is no possibility that a NEG raised from a scope position in clause A can end up in a lower complement clause of A. In particular, then, NEG$_1$ in (8b) can rightly not appear in the complement clause of *claimed*.

6 Polyadic Quantification

6.1 Basics

Consider the following ordinary standard English sentence:

(1) No one ever showed me anything.

Common views of course take the *any* phrase here to be an NPI, licensed by the c-commanding *no one* phrase. And common views take a nonstandard English example like (2) (equivalent to (1)) to represent a distinct phenomenon, so-called *negative concord*:

(2) No one ever showed me nothing.
    (onlinelibrary.wiley.com/doi/10.1111/j.1548-1492.2012.01193.x/abstract)

See Labov 1972 for discussion of negative concord in one type of nonstandard English and Haegeman and Zanuttini 1996, Ladusaw 1996a, Déprez 1997, Giannakidou 2000, Zeijlstra 2008, and references in these works, for general discussions of negative concord.

However, we find it at best odd to treat related, synonymous sentences like (1) and (2) in closely related variants of the same language as representing entirely distinct grammatical phenomena. Significantly, in the framework adopted in this monograph, we are led to view both (1) and (2) as representations of the same underlying structures. That is, we regard cases like (1) as instances of negative concord, deformed by various NEG deletions.[1]

To elaborate, we focus on (3):

(3) No man loves any woman.

On our view, to account for the presence of *any* in the DP *any woman*, we would naturally postulate an underlying [NEG SOME], where NEG is deleted. The appearance of *any* as the morphological representative of SOME then should be a consequence of the SOME→*any* mapping of chapter 3.

The claim that an NPI phrase like *any woman* in (3) represents an underlying unary-NEG structure [NEG SOME], just as that in (4a) does, is supported by the common distribution of intensives seen in (4b,c):

(4) a. Xavier does not love any woman.
   b. No man loves any woman, not even Sylvia/not any/not a single one.
   c. Xavier does not love any woman, not even Sylvia/not any/not a single one.

In our terms, there are only two possibilities for the underlying structure of *any woman* in (3), given in (5) (we ignore scope position occurrences for the moment):

(5) a. No man loves [[NEG$_2$ SOME] woman]

   (unary-NEG structure)
   b. No man loves [[NEG$_2$ [NEG$_1$ SOME]] woman]

   (reversal structure)

We tentatively suggest that both structures are possible for (3). However, they give rise to subtly different (but logically equivalent) interpretations. First, consider structure (5a). Interpreting the two NEGs as independent yields the following equivalent interpretations, represented in predicate logic (supplemented with restricted quantification):

(6) a. $\neg\exists$x: x a man. $\neg\exists$y: y a woman. x loves y
   b. $\forall$x: x a man. $\exists$y: y a woman. x loves y

Clearly, these do not represent any correct interpretation of (3). We suggest that while (5a) is a possible structure, when (3) is so represented it is not interpreted as in (6). Rather, (3) represents polyadic quantification, with the two quantifier DPs yielding a single polyadic quantifier.

Polyadic quantification exists when n-tuples (n > 1) of DPs yield a single quantifier interpreted as quantifying over n-tuples of individuals. For discussions, see Keenan 1987, 1992, 1996, May 1989, Moltmann 1995, 1996, de Swart 1999, de Swart and Sag 2002, and Peters and Westerståhl 2006.

Under the polyadic interpretation of (3), the two quantifiers are not interpreted independently. Rather, the meaning is 'there is no man-woman pair <x, y> such that x loves y'. This can be represented as follows in logical notation:

(7) $\neg\exists$<x, y>: x a man, y a woman. x loves y

The idea that a sentence with multiple negative DPs can be given a polyadic interpretation has much support crosslinguistically. First, for the standard

English variety spoken by one of us, *No man loves no woman* may have the interpretation in (7) (see also May 1989). Second, as illustrated in (2), in various nonstandard English dialects, multiple negative forms are interpreted as containing a single logical negation (Labov 1972), the negative concord reading. Third, parallel negative concord examples are quite productive in other languages (see de Swart and Sag 2002 for an extensive discussion of French).

As for (5a) and (5b), we speculate that both structures are possible and that their slightly different interpretations can be diagnosed via appeal to stress patterns and certain continuations. The polyadic reading is clearest if the determiners *no* and *any* are both stressed. In that circumstance, it is natural to follow up with a use of *in particular* that points out a specific ordered pair for which the generalization expressed by the quantifier holds:

(8) a. NO man loves ANY woman.
    b. In particular, Myron does not love Mary.

The reversal reading is most natural if the negative D of the first DP alone (*no man*) is stressed. Under that condition, it is natural to follow up with a use of *in particular* that points out some specific individual (not an ordered pair of individuals) for whom the generalization expressed by the quantifier holds:

(9) a. NO man loves any woman.
    b. In particular, Myron doesn't.

We have not studied whether the so-called negative concord forms of nonstandard English reveal the same subtle ambiguity claimed here for standard English NPIs. In other words, we have not investigated whether or not negative quantifiers in negative concord dialects may have (in different contexts) both unary-NEG and binary-NEG (reversal) analyses.

In the remainder of this monograph, we focus on the polyadic interpretation of sentences like (3) and leave the possibility of a reversal structure (such as that in (5b)) to future work.

6.2 Determiner Sharing

We now make the nonstandard theoretical proposal that the syntactic basis of polyadic quantification structures such as (8a) involves syntactic determiner sharing between the different DPs whose NPs denote the sets quantified over, as partially represented in (10) for (8a) (wherever relevant, we use subscripted lowercase letters to indicate shared constituents—here, specifically Ds and their components):

(10) [NEG$_e$ SOME$_f$]$_a$ man loves [NEG$_e$ SOME$_f$]$_a$ woman

According to the present proposal, (10) contains two occurrences of a single determiner, [NEG SOME]. We observe that the assumption that multiple constituents, here the subject and object of *loves*, can share a subconstituent is a special case of structures permitted only under grammatical views in which tree structure is not fully maintained. Put differently, this is possible if the Single Mother Condition is not uniformly imposed. Allowing such structures is a characteristic of the framework developed in Johnson and Postal 1980 and Postal 2010.

We stress that the idea of multiple occurrences of the same phrase subsumed under the rubric *sharing* is different from the more common recognition of different occurrences of the same constituent due to movement or its analogs. The present usage of *sharing* corresponds in the framework of Johnson and Postal 1980 and Postal 2010 to *initial* arcs with the same head node (overlapping initial arcs), whereas multiple occurrences corresponding to those formed by movement involve at least one noninitial arc (a Type I successor in the framework of Postal 2010).

Structures like those with shared Ds are not, however, standard in Minimalist work. And in particular, because of its Definition 14, the framework of Collins and Stabler 2012 does not permit them. However, the idea of shared constituents could be executed in Minimalist terms if that definition were revised. One would assume that the determiner [NEG SOME] can be merged in at several places. First, Merge([NEG SOME], woman) would take place, and subsequently Merge([NEG SOME], man). So a single determiner would be used to form two different DPs.

We assume, following the discussion in chapter 2, that both DPs in (10) have scope position occurrences as well as nonscope position occurrences via one of the mechanisms (e.g., quantifier raising) referred to earlier. So a more detailed structure of (10) is the following:

(11) [$_C$ <[[NEG$_e$ SOME$_f$]$_a$ man]$_1$> [$_A$ <[[NEG$_e$ SOME$_f$]$_a$ woman]$_2$> [$_B$ DP$_1$ saw DP$_2$]]]

A relevant remark at this point concerns crosslinguistic variation. Richter and Sailer (2006), among others, observe that there are at least three attested possibilities for a language that allows multiple N-words (in our terms, [NEG SOME] Ds) in a single clause. In German, no polyadic readings are possible.

In French, both polyadic and nonpolyadic readings are found (de Swart and Sag 2002). And in Polish, only polyadic readings are possible.

For us, these three situations represent the following *syntactic* differences:

(12) a. Multiple [NEG SOME] DPs cannot share Ds.   (German)
    b. Multiple [NEG SOME] DPs can share Ds or not.   (French)
    c. Multiple [NEG SOME] DPs must share Ds.   (Polish)

We assume that English falls under (12b), but determining this is complicated by the fact that we classify English with French on the basis of our theory of NPIs.

Our assumption is that the shared-D structure of DPs in scope position is what provides the syntactic basis for the polyadic interpretations at issue here. Put differently, the reason that German combinations of [NEG SOME] Ds do *not* yield polyadic readings is that German syntax bars the type of determiner sharing specified above. In contrast, we would say that Polish requires such sharing for the DPs found in scope positions.

An issue arises with respect to cases like the following:

(13) a. No man drank a drop.
    b. No man read a word.
    c. No woman contributed a red cent.
    d. No woman said a single thing.

These examples also arguably have polyadic interpretations and, in particular, their objects cannot be interpreted as representing reversal structures since none of the contained minimizers permit reversal analyses. And yet it might seem that the determiners in the objects here do not represent [NEG SOME], but at best NEG plus the indefinite determiner, *a*.

As discussed in section 3.5, one approach to such cases would analyze them as underlying instances of [NEG SOME], where the SOME is realized as *a* under a restricted set of circumstances with some minimizer nouns and related forms. Alternatively, the minimizers might involve a null SOME in the structure [SOME a drop]. Under either analysis, the examples in (13) can be analyzed in terms of determiner sharing.

6.3 The Semantics of Determiner Sharing

Recall that in chapter 3, we gave the rule for the interpretation of [NEG SOME] as follows:

(14) a. ⟦SOME⟧ $= \lambda P \lambda Q\ [\exists x\ (P(x)\ \&\ Q(x))]$
    b. ⟦NEG⟧ $= \lambda X \lambda P \lambda Q\ \neg X(P)(Q)]$

c. $[\![\text{NEG SOME}]\!] = [\![\text{NEG}]\!] ([\![\text{SOME}]\!])$
$= (\lambda X \lambda P \lambda Q \,\neg[X(P)(Q)]) \,(\lambda P \lambda Q \,[\exists x \,(P(x) \,\&\, Q(x))])$
$= \lambda P \lambda Q \,\neg[\exists x \,(P(x) \,\&\, Q(x))]$

The following section maintains exactly these semantic values. The only change is that we allow the predicates to be true of n-tuples. We will use s as the variable for n-tuples of individuals, and the notation s_i to denote the ith coordinate of the n-tuple. Given this background, we propose the following semantic rule to interpret shared-D structures like (11). This rule is not restricted to negative quantifiers (adapted from May 1989:406):

(15) In a syntactic structure, $[DP_{i_1}[DP_{i_2} \ldots [DP_{i_n} \, S]]]$,
       where $DP_{i_1}, DP_{i_2}, \ldots, DP_{i_n}$ share determiner D and $DP_k = [D \, NP_k]$,
       $[\![[DP_{i_1}[DP_{i_2} \ldots [DP_{i_n} \, S]]]]\!] = [\![D]\!](P)(Q)$
       D = the shared determiner
       $P = \lambda s \,[[\![NP_{i_1}]\!](s_1) \wedge \ldots \wedge [\![NP_{i_n}]\!](s_n)]$
       $Q = \lambda s \,[[\![S]\!]^g]$, where g assigns $i_1, i_2, \ldots, i_n$ the values $s_1, s_2, \ldots, s_n$

A few notes on the above interpretation rule. First, we take the indices on the DPs to be part of the syntactic structure of the DP, hence visible to the rules of semantic interpretation. Second, strictly speaking this rule is noncompositional. The semantic value of $[DP_{i_1}[DP_{i_2} \ldots [DP_{i_n} \, S]]]$ is not calculated in terms of the semantic values of a DP_i and of S. Rather, the interpretation operates on a structure containing a whole sequence of DPs that share a determiner. Third, we assume that (15) applies to the maximal sequence of DPs in scope position sharing a determiner (so it cannot apply to any proper subset of the set of DPs sharing a determiner).

Fourth, we assume that common NPs are interpreted as predicates. For example:

(16) $[\![\text{dog}]\!] = \lambda x. \; x$ is a dog

Fifth, we assume that the interpretation of traces is given by this rule (from Heim and Kratzer 1998:116):

(17) $[\![t_i]\!]^g = g(i)$

Under the multiple-occurrence theory adopted here, there are no traces. Therefore, the rule is a bit more complicated, but has basically the same form:

(18) $[\![DP_i]\!] = g(i)$ if DP_i is bound by another occurrence

Sixth, there are no rules of semantic interpretation for quantifiers other than statement (15), which covers the trivial case of one DP in a scope position as well. In that case, the determiner-sharing condition is still met since the share relation is reflexive (a DP shares determiner D with itself). Condition (15) also unproblematically covers the case of multiple DPs in scope positions with no determiner sharing. In that case, (15) applies recursively to each [$_s$ DP S] combination.

Now consider (19):

(19) No boy loves no girl.

We want to show the calculation of its truth conditions on the polyadic interpretation. First, the structure interpreted by the semantic rules is given in (20):

(20) [$_s$ <[[NEG$_e$ SOME$_f$] boy]$_1$> [$_s$ <[[NEG$_e$ SOME$_f$] girl]$_2$> [$_s$ DP$_1$ loves DP$_2$]]]

In this example, the determiner [NEG$_e$ SOME$_f$] is shared between the two DPs in scope position. So the calculation of truth conditions goes as follows:

(21) ⟦<[[NEG$_e$ SOME$_f$] boy]$_1$> [$_s$ <[[NEG$_e$ SOME$_f$] girl]$_2$> [$_s$ DP$_1$ loves DP$_2$]]⟧ = 1
   if and only if
   ($\lambda P \lambda Q \ \neg[\exists s \ (P(s) \wedge Q(s))]$) ($\lambda s \ [⟦boy⟧(s_1) \wedge ⟦girl⟧(s_2)]$) ($\lambda s \ [⟦S⟧^g]$),
                                                          where g assigns 1, 2 the
                                                          values s_1, s_2
   if and only if
   $\neg[\exists s \ (⟦boy⟧(s_1) \wedge ⟦girl⟧(s_2) \wedge ⟦S⟧^g \ )]$,   where g assigns 1, 2 the
                                                          values s_1, s_2
   if and only if
   It is not true that there is an s = <x, y> such that x is a boy, y is a girl,
       and x loves y
   if and only if
   There is no <x, y> such that x is a boy, y is a girl, and x loves y.

6.4   The Realizations of Polyadic Quantifier Structures

We turn to the issue of how the sort of syntactic structures taken here to underlie the negative polyadic cases under discussion relate to the actual superficial morphology of such sentences, as well as to our ideas about the structure of NPIs, NEG deletion, and so on. We focus on the following example:

(22) No doctor treated any patient in any bar.

Internal to our assumptions, the important feature of such cases is the presence of *any* forms in two of the positions where our analysis posits a single shared underlying determiner of the form [NEG SOME]. NEG deletion is one of the basic elements of our approach to NPIs, the other being NEG raising. Moreover, ideally, the presence of the form *any* should be a function of the SOME→*any* mapping of chapter 3.

As noted in the previous sections, we start from the assumption that the NPIs in examples like (22) are of the form [[NEG SOME] N] underlyingly. So the representation of (22) is as follows:

(23) [[NEG_a $SOME_b$] doctor] treated [[NEG_a $SOME_b$] patient] in [[NEG_a $SOME_b$] bar]

The three orthographic strings [NEG_a $SOME_b$] represent distinct occurrences of a single determiner. We assume that in nonstandard dialects of English having negative concord, these multiple occurrences are realized as copies of the single D. In other words, while there is a single underlying D shared among the DPs in the syntactic structure that determines the polyadic quantification, that shared D is realized in different syntactic positions by independent copies. The notion of copy we use here can be described in terms of the notion of replacer arc of Postal 2010.

Crucially, we are making a distinction between copies and occurrences. One constituent XP can have several occurrences, but no copies at all. We are suggesting that in the case of determiner sharing, the distinct occurrences are replaced by distinct copies, and these distinct copies can be independently manipulated (e.g., by the SOME→*any* mapping).

The same notion of copy is arguably also found in the domain of anaphora. Consider, for instance, the following quotations:

(24) (Lee 2003:84, 85)

> "San Lucas Quiaviní Zapotec (SLQZ), an Otomanguean language spoken in southern Mexico, regularly allows apparent Principle B and C violations: Pronouns may locally bind identical pronouns, and R-expressions may bind identical R-expressions."

> "In this paper, I will propose that 'bound' pronouns and R-expressions in these languages are not in fact violations of Principles B and C. Rather, they are bound variables spelled out as copies of their antecedents."

The phenomena described by Lee show that the copy mechanism appealed to here for negative concord structures is independently motivated in the anaphora domain.

Return to the posited underlying structure (23). We are suggesting that this structure, with its single D, [NEG_a $SOME_b$], shared by DP_1 and DP_2, is converted into a partially distinct one in which the occurrence of D in each of the DPs is replaced by a distinct but morphologically identical D. This yields the following structure:

(25) [[NEG$_c$ SOME$_d$] doctor] treated [[NEG$_e$ SOME$_f$] patient] in [[NEG$_g$ SOME$_h$] bar]

In this structure, each NEG is a copy of the single underlying shared NEG, and each SOME is a copy of the single underlying shared SOME.

The general principle determining that all occurrences of D in such shared-D cases are replaced is this:

(26) *The Shared-Determiner Copy Condition*
In a set Q of DPs originating with a shared D$_a$, each occurrence of D$_a$ is replaced by a distinct copy of D$_a$.

In the negative concord cases (of nonstandard English), the resulting NEG copies are not deleted. But in standard English, such deletion of the NEG parts of copies of [NEG SOME] Ds is required, subject to the following constraint:

(27) *The Standard English Negative Concord Reduction Principle*
Let DP$_1$, DP$_2$, . . . , DP$_n$ be a maximal sequence of n > 1 DP occurrences in scope position (in a single clause) sharing a D = [NEG SOME], where DP$_1$ c-commands each of DP$_2$, . . . , DP$_n$. And for all i, $1 \leq i \leq n$, let D$_i$ be the copy of D in DP$_i$ and let NEG$_i$ be the NEG of D$_i$. For each occurrence of DP$_i$ (i ≠ 1), NEG$_i$ is deleted.

Principle (27) determines that a standard English polyadic quantifier DP structure undergoes a modification operating on the copies. This forces the NEG of each copy to be deleted. In chapter 8, we propose two slightly different reformulations of this principle and consider the possible integration of those variants into a more general view of NEG deletion.[2]

Principle (27) forces NEG deletion of all copies (except where n = 1) in polyadic quantification structures in standard English. Here we note two exceptions. The first case, discussed by May (1989:403–407), is (28a) with interpretation (28b) (acceptable for only one of us):

(28) a. No man loves no woman.
b. ¬∃<x, y>: x a man, y a woman. x loves y

Principle (27) does not admit this sentence with the polyadic interpretation since according to (27), one of the NEGs must be deleted (see discussion under (7)). Unfortunately, we have at present no account that rescues such examples.

Another problematic type of case is represented by (29a) with interpretation (29b):

(29) a. No man saw NO woman in NO bar.
     b. Every man saw some woman in some bar.
     c. No man saw NO woman in NO bar in NO town.

What is relevant about these examples is that the first negative quantificational DP takes the second under its scope, but the second and the third arguably form a single polyadic quantifier. In fact, more DPs can be added, without changing the interpretation of those in the simpler example, as shown in (29c). These facts are incompatible with principle (27), because (27) forces NEG deletion with polyadic quantification in standard English. We also cannot offer any solution to this problem here.

We observe that many nonstandard English negative concord/polyadic examples manifest a distinct NEG in addition to the ones of the negative quantifier DPs defining the polyadic structure, as in (30a,b):

(30) a. Don't no woman need no man playing with her emotions.
     (answers.yahoo.com/question/index?qid = 20111230094127AAw 3zC3)
    b. I'm not fighting no woman over NO man!
     (www.prisontalk.com/forums/archive/index.php/t-546259.html)

Clearly, the NEG found right-adjacent to Aux in such examples makes no contribution to the semantics of such cases. While an important issue, consideration of the origin of such NEGs is not directly relevant here. We might well take the NEG right-adjacent to Aux to be a NEG raised from the highest-scoping negative DP (e.g., *no woman* in (30a)), the raising leaving a copy in the position vacated, where *copy* is understood as in our earlier discussion. In any event, we suspect that standard English manifests a covert analog of the Aux-adjacent NEGs in examples like (30).

7   NEG Deletion: Case Studies

7.1   Goal

A key basis of our defense of syntactic approaches to Classical NR, especially that in chapter 16, depends on the concept of NEG deletion. This concept has also obviously played a key role in our analysis of reversals (chapter 4) and polyadic quantification (chapter 6). The basic idea of NEG deletion is that a deleted NEG has no direct morphological realization, and so is unpronounced.

The idea of NEG deletion is not original here but goes back at least to Klima's (1964) analysis of Classical NR in terms of "NEG absorption" (an account sharply different from our own). Another early analysis was by Fauconnier (1971:222), who proposed a rule of the form NEG NEG → ∅.

In this chapter, we consider several cases that give plausible initial support for the existence of NEG deletion. Then in chapter 8, we briefly sketch a general theoretical conception of NEG deletion adequate for describing the cases in this monograph.

7.2   French *Pas* Deletion

The standard French finite clause negation pattern is illustrated in (1):

(1) Le   ministre ne   viendra   pas.
      the   minister PRT   come.FUT   NEG
      'The minister will not come.'

In such cases, negation is represented by the postverbal form *pas*, accompanied by the marker *ne*, glossed as PRT. In colloquial forms of French, especially in more recent decades, *ne* is frequently absent. In cases where there is a negative quantifier, *ne* is also found in more formal usage, as in (2), but again often absent in colloquial usage:

(2) Personne ne   viendra.
     no.one   PRT come.FUT
     'No one will come.'

These data suggest that while historically derived from a true negative form, current French *ne* does not have that function.

Nonetheless, the latter conclusion is partially controversial, as has long been observed. Thus, Martinon (1927:538–548) provided a section titled "The Negation *Ne* Employed Alone" that considered a restricted variety of cases where one might argue that *ne* functions as a negation, and not as a semantically redundant marker as in (1) and (2). In addition, Martinon claimed that exactly four verbs could be conjugated with *ne* without *pas*: *pouvoir* 'can/be able', *cesser* 'cease', *oser* 'dare', and *savoir* 'know'. Martinon (1927:539–540) gave these examples in particular (see also Muller 1991:230):

(3) a. Il ne   cessait (pas) de crier.
        he PRT ceased (NEG) of shout
        'He didn't cease shouting.'
    b. Tu   ne sais (pas) ce que tu   veux.
        you.FAM PRT know (NEG) what   you.FAM want
        'You don't know what you want.'
    c. Cette circonstance ne   pouvait vous dispenser   de . . .
        that circumstance PRT could   you exempt/excuse/avoid from
        'That circumstance can't exempt you from . . .'

In addition to indicating the optionality of the phenomenon in all of these cases and others, Martinon noted many restrictions on the possibility of *ne* unaccompanied by *pas*, restrictions of apparently both a semantic and a syntactic order. We propose that such clauses involve NEG deletion, which brings about the covert status of *pas*.

Focus on cases like the following:

(4) a. La tête à   Hollande Mr Bontaz ne peut la piffrer comme moi
       the head of Hollande Mr. Bontaz PRT can it stand like me
       d'ailleurs.
       moreover
       'Hollande, Mr. Bontaz can't stand even seeing, just like me
       moreover.'
       (actu-people.staragora.com/maroc-chaine-france.html)

b. en clair   plus personne ne peut la   piffrer dans ma famille.
   to put it clearly more no.one   PRT can her stand in   my family
   'Frankly, no one in my family can stand her anymore.'
   (lonelyness.journalintime.com/2010/04/22-ce-mercredi-ma-dit)

In our terms, (4a) involves deletion of the NEG associated with *peut* 'can', which would otherwise show up as *pas*. It is the deleted form that actually provides the negative force seen in the translation. The particle *ne* is present but has no semantic function, just as it has none in (4b), where the form *personne* provides the negative force.

Statement (5) represents the informal rule for NEG deletion in these cases:

(5) A NEG in the context Verb_x ___ is deleted by Verb_x only if $\text{Verb}_x =$ *pouvoir, cesser, oser,* or *savoir*.

We refer to this case of *pas* deletion as an instance of *lexical* NEG deletion since in each instance of this type of deletion, there is a specific lexical item that triggers the deletion and is grammatically marked to have that function. In chapter 8, we locate this rule in a more general theoretical framework.

Suppose one rejects the view that NEG (*pas*) is deleted in the pattern illustrated in (4a). Then one must adopt an alternative hypothesis and inevitably assign the negative force in (4a) to *ne*. But that implies that there are two distinct *ne*, one that has negative force (in (4a)) and one that lacks it (as in (1) and (2)). We take this conclusion to be theoretically undesirable.[1]

7.3 A German Case

Sailer (2006:383–384) discusses two forms he refers to as "specialized negators":

(6) einen Dreck
     a   dirt

(7) einen feuchten Kehrricht
     a   wet   dirt

These occur in sentences with a highly restricted set of verbs, to yield clauses that express negation, even though they manifest no overt form that regularly expresses negation. The following example illustrates this point (from Sailer 2006:383):

(8) Das interessiert mich einen Dreck/einen feuchten Kehrricht.
     this interests   me   a   dirt a   wet   dirt
     'I am not at all interested in this.'

Hereafter, for simplicity, we illustrate only with *einen Dreck*.

Sailer (2006:383) characterizes the relevant verb class in part as in (9):

(9) "The NP-negatives in [(6) and (7)] can only be used to negate a highly restricted set of verbs, such as those of intellectual concern . . ."

Beyond *interessieren*, other verbs in the class include *angehen* 'concern', *kümmern* 'mind, pay heed, care, worry', *scheren* 'concern', *verstehen* 'understand':[2]

(10) a. Du verstehst   einen Dreck.
          you understand a   dirt
          'You don't understand a thing.'
      b. Er denkt dass Du einen Dreck verstehst.
          he thinks that you a   dirt   understand
          'He thinks you don't understand a thing.'

Sailer (2006) concludes from these data that forms like *einen Dreck* are *themselves* expressions of negation. But in the overall context of the existence of the class of minimizers, this view is quite suspect. That follows because forms with meanings like that of *einen Dreck* fall into the class that yields minimizers crosslinguistically. These are forms whose standard meanings denote things of small size, little value, or minimal importance. Horn (1989 [2001]) characterizes them as follows:

(11) (Horn 1989 [2001:400])
      "When these items occur in positive contexts (if they do), they denote a minimal quantity; when they occur in negative contexts, the negation denotes the absence of a minimal quantity and hence the presence of no quantity at all."

The grammatical presence of a minimizer is often tied to a limited and perhaps semantically delimited class of forms. The conclusion that expressions like *einen Dreck* fall into the class of minimizers is a conclusion accepted by Manfred Sailer (personal communication).

Given that *einen Dreck* is a minimizer, one expects a priori that there would be distinct forms as in examples like (8) where an overt NEG is present. That is, one would expect that forms with a minimizer like *einen Dreck* would behave like other minimizers such as that in (12a,b):

(12) a. Ich mag sie kein bisschen.
          I   like her no   bit
          'I don't like her one bit.'

   b. Ich mag sie nicht ein bisschen.
      I   like her not a bit
      'I don't like her one bit.'

Here, the minimizer *ein bisschen* occurs in two variant structures, each with an overt NEG. In (12a), the NEG forms a complex D *kein*, parallel to English *no*, while in (12b), the NEG occurs as a clausal *nicht*. In present terms, the NEG in (12b) owes its position to having raised out of the same structure that underlies (12a).

The same pattern is seen with the minimizer in the following example:

(13) a. Er hat kein Wort gesagt.
      he has no   word said
      'He didn't say a word.' = 'He didn't say anything.'
   b. Er hat nicht ein Wort gesagt.
      he has not a   word said
      'He didn't say a word.' = 'He didn't say anything.'

Such paradigms are not unique to minimizer structures but merely represent a special case of a general German alternation possible between *kein* forms and *nicht ein* forms, as seen in the following example:

(14) a. Karen sah keinen Drachen.
      Karen saw no   dragon
      'Karen saw no dragon.'
   b. Karen sah nicht einen Drachen.
      Karen saw not a   dragon
      'Karen didn't see any dragon.'

Given this background, if minimizer forms like *einen Dreck* behaved like regular German minimizers, one would expect them to occur in paradigms like (12) and (13). And, in fact, as already documented by Richter and Sailer (2006:311, (8)), parallels to sentences like (8) are possible with *keinen* in place of *einen*:[3]

(15) a. Das geht   dich einen Dreck an.
      this concerns you a   dirt   PRT
      'This is none of your business.'
   b. Das geht   dich keinen Dreck an.
      this concerns you no   dirt   PRT
      'This is none of your business.'

Thus, under the proposal that forms like *einen Dreck* are "specialized negators," these expressions must be dually analyzed both as instances of negation, for sentences like (8) and (15a), and as minimizers that occur with negation, for sentences like (15b). This is hardly a desirable result.

The obvious proposal in present terms is that with the restricted class of verbs cited earlier, the NEG associated with the minimizer *einen Dreck* deletes. Given this proposal, there is no motivation for a dual analysis of *einen Dreck* as both minimizer and "specialized negator."

Our proposal that cases like (8) and (10) involve NEG deletion remains partially vague since, inter alia, we have not specified the context of the deletion.

One expects then that alongside cases like (15b) one would find those like (16) in which the NEG originally associated with *einen Dreck* has raised and appears as *nicht*:

(16) ?? Das geht   dich nicht einen Dreck an.
     this concerns you   not   a   dirt   PRT
     'This is none of your business.'

However, as kindly indicated by Manfred Sailer (personal communication), (16) is dubious at best, a judgment confirmed by Christina Behme (personal communication). This may be related to a general tendency to prefer forms like (12a), (13a), and (14a) over those like (12b), (13b), and (14b) independently of minimizers. However, the defect in (16) appears to be much worse than in regular cases.

Fortunately for the present argument, which seeks only to document the existence of the phenomenon of NEG deletion, the status of cases like (16) is of no real significance. We propose that there is NEG deletion in German in the context (17):

(17) A NEG in the context Verb$_x$ [$_{DP}$ ___ einen Dreck/einen feuchten
     Kehrricht] is deleted by Verb$_x$.

Given (17), the only issue raised by the status of (16) is whether the deletion is obligatory or optional. Given the alternation in (15a,b), it must be optional, leaving the analysis of (16) open.

We stress that the possibility of deleting NEG with a minimizer like *einen Dreck* is exceptional. For instance, Manfred Sailer (personal communication) kindly provided further German data specifying the properties of other minimizers including *roter Heller* 'red cent':

(18) Damit   ist kein/*ein roter Heller zu verdienen.
     there.with is no/a   red   cent   to earn
     'You can't earn a red cent with this.'

As (18) indicates, unlike with *einen Dreck*, it is not possible in our terms to suppress the NEG with *ein roter Heller*. Moreover, the latter state of affairs seems to be the general case; that is, other German minimizers behave like *ein roter Heller* and not like *einen Dreck* and do not permit deletion of their associated NEG. This represents no problem for a NEG deletion analysis like that sketched in (17), which explicitly mentions a verb class and particular minimizers.

The claim that forms like *einen Dreck* do not themselves express negation is further supported by another type of example cited by Richter and Sailer (2006:311):

(19) Das geht   niemanden einen Dreck an.
     this concerns no.one   a   dirt   PRT
     'This is no one's business.'

Angehen is one of the verbs that allow NEG deletion with *einen Dreck*. But in this case, *einen Dreck* clearly functions in standard terms as an NPI licensed by the negative indirect object *niemanden*. If *einen Dreck* in (19) were a negator, as in Sailer's analysis, (19) would have a double negative reading like standard English *That concerns NO one in NO sense* equivalent to 'That concerns everyone in some sense'. But no such reading exists for (19).

In present terms, there are a priori various possible analyses of such cases. On one analysis, *einen Dreck* would represent a reversal structure. On another, *niemanden* and *einen Dreck* would share an underlying D of the form [NEG SOME], thus forming a polyadic quantifier along the lines discussed in chapter 6. Each of these analyses raises issues.

As is well-known, observed in Richter and Sailer 2006, mentioned in chapter 6, and stressed to us by Manfred Sailer (personal communication), standard German does not in general allow negative concord. In our terms, German syntax does not permit sharing of Ds of the form [NEG SOME]. That means that a polyadic quantifier analysis of cases like (19), which for us involves shared [NEG SOME] Ds, would be quite exceptional. We do not know enough to say any more about the analysis of (19), which is, we stress, in any event irrelevant to the basic point of this section. It is, however, evidently contraindicated to treat *einen Dreck* in cases like (19) as a "specialized negator." That conclusion supports the most general assumption, namely, that *einen Dreck* lacks the status of a negation in all contexts.

Against this background, we can consider Sailer's (2006:383) discussion of forms like *einen Dreck* arguing that the negation in a Classical NR case is exclusively a main clause constituent. The argument appeals to grammatical pairs like (20a,b), where, however, only (20a) has a grammatical German Classical NR variant, as shown in (21):

(20) a. Das kümmert ihn *(nicht).
　　　 this worries him   not
　　　 'He doesn't care about this.'
　　 b. Das kümmert ihn einen Dreck.
　　　 this worries him a   dirt
　　　 'He doesn't care about this.'

(21) a. Ich glaube nicht, dass ihn das kümmert.
　　　 I   believe not   that him this worries
　　　 'I don't believe he cares about this.'
　　 b. *Ich glaube einen Dreck, dass ihn das kümmert.
　　　 I   believe a   dirt   that him this worries
　　　 'I don't believe he cares about this.'

Sailer sums up the argument from these data as follows:

(22) (Sailer 2006:383)
　　 "Under an analysis in which the surface matrix negation stems from the embedded clause, the ungrammaticality of [(21b)] would be unexpected because the specialized negation is compatible with the verb *kümmern*. If we assume, however, that the negation is part of the matrix clause, the ungrammaticality follows from a violation of the collocational restrictions of the specialized negator."

The argument depends entirely on the view that forms like *einen Dreck* are actually negations, a view we have argued against above. If, as in our proposal, they are simply minimizers, with their associated NEGs deleted in what would be the complement clause in (21b), the ungrammaticality of the latter is entirely expected. The reason that (21b) is ungrammatical is that *einen Dreck* is not NEG and so nothing permits it to raise from the embedded clause. Furthermore, *glauben* 'believe' is not one of the verbs that permits the minimizer *einen Dreck*. Thus, the exceptional German minimizers raise no issue for a syntactic view of Classical NR as applied to German and fail to support a nonsyntactic conception.

7.4 *Too* + Infinitive Cases

Consider complements of an adjectival phrase modified by *too*:

(23) a. Dana is too cynical to do a fucking thing to help Kyle.
　　 b. Dana is too cynical to lift a finger to help Kyle.

Several factors suggest the presence of covert NEGs in these complements. First, each of the sentences is essentially equivalent to a corresponding case with a finite complement clause in which a complement NEG is explicit (Pullum and Huddleston 2002:837):

(24) a. Dana is so cynical that she would not do a fucking thing to help Kyle.
　　 b. Dana is so cynical that she would not lift a finger to help Kyle.

Second, in light of the discussion in chapter 3, the presence of the strict NPIs represented by *a fucking thing* in (24a) and *lift a finger* in (24b) also supports the conclusion that the complements in (23) contain NEGs. That is, the relevant structure of (23b) would be as follows, where we posit as well a covert instance of the sort of modal found in the corresponding finite complements of (24):

(25) Dana is too cynical [COMP [[<NEG> a finger]$_1$ [<Modal> [to lift DP$_1$ to help Kyle]]]]

We assume that the highest complementizer (or perhaps *too*) in the infinitival complements of *too* phrases is the needed NEG deleter, again a lexically marked one. We state the relevant rule informally as follows:

(26) A NEG in an infinitival clause C that is complement to an adjective introduced by *too* is deleted by the COMP of C.

On this analysis, the interpretation of *too* is equivalent to that of *so*, but *too* is only used when there is a deleted NEG in the associated complement clause.

The argument for NEG deletion associated with adjectival modifier *too* is strengthened by examples like (27a):

(27) a. Rachel is too nice not to help people in need.
　　 b. Rachel is so nice that she won't fail to help people in need.

Here, curiously, although the complement of (27a) contains an overt NEG, it is understood positively, that is, as roughly equivalent to (27b). The structure of (27a) can be represented in our terms as in (28):

(28) Rachel is too nice [COMP [<NEG$_2$> Modal [NEG$_1$ to help people in need]]]

Here too, the complementizer would be the lexical NEG deleter for NEG$_2$, again, as in (25), deleting a nonreversal NEG. The resulting meaning would correctly be essentially equivalent to that of (29a), in turn essentially equivalent to that of (29b):[4]

(29) a. Rachel is so nice that she would help people in need.
　　 b. Rachel is so nice that she would not not help people in need.[5]

7.5 Summary

In summary, we have presented the following cases of lexical NEG deletion from French, German, and English, respectively.[6] They will form a core database for the following chapter.[7]

(30) a. A NEG in the context Verb_x ___ is deleted by Verb_x only if $\text{Verb}_x =$ *pouvoir, cesser, oser,* or *savoir.*

   b. A NEG in the context Verb_x [$_{DP}$ ___ einen Dreck/einen feuchten Kehrricht] is deleted by Verb_x.

   c. A NEG in an infinitival clause C that is complement to an adjective introduced by *too* is deleted by the COMP of C.

8   Elements of a General Conception of NEG Deletion

For the purpose of this monograph, we will treat NEG deletion as a phenomenon based on a primitive binary relation between occurrences notated NDEL(X, Y), where X is the deleter and Y is the deleted element. For English, NEG deletion manifests as the lack of pronunciation of forms normally spelled *not*, *n't*, *n-*, *no*, and *non-*. Even though the deleted NEG is not pronounced, it is visible for semantic interpretation. What follows summarizes various properties we take to be characteristic of the NDEL relation.

The basic reflection of the NDEL relation is the following:

(1) *The NDEL Interpretation Condition*
    If NDEL(X, Y), then Y = NEG and Y is not pronounced.

Condition (1) states that NDEL is a relation that determines the covertness or nonphonetic realization of a NEG. Inherent in our view is that NEGs only delete when they stand in certain relations to other phrases, their NEG deleters. That is, underlying the NDEL relation is an assumption that each case of NEG deletion requires determination of some specific phrase that is the deleter of the NEG.

We further assume that the NDEL relation is irreflexive (A does not delete A), asymmetric (if A deletes B, B doesn't delete A), intransitive (if A deletes B and B deletes C, then A does not delete C), and injective (if A deletes C, and B deletes C, then A = B). However, we do *not* assume that if A deletes B and A deletes C, then B = C. Therefore, we do not assume that NDEL is a function. See chapter 6 for earlier discussion of NEG deletion in polyadic structures.

We recognize two basic types of the NDEL relation. As noted earlier, all of the cases in the previous chapter are instances where an element X is specified lexically to be a NEG deleter. We refer to this as *lexical NEG deletion*. It denotes NEG deletion unpredictable by any *general* grammatical conditions.

The second basic type of the NDEL relation was encountered in chapters 4 and 6. The deletion described in chapter 4 involved deletion of both NEGs of a nominal reversal structure. That described in chapter 6 involved deletion of every NEG belonging to the copy Ds we posited in the polyadic structures treated there. In such cases, the NEG deleter is not lexically determined but meets a set of general criteria to be laid out below. We refer to NEG deletion in these cases as *general NEG deletion*, in contrast to lexical NEG deletion. These distinctions yield the following deletion type typology:

(2) A. Lexical NEG deletion   (chapter 7)
    B. General NEG deletion
        i. Polyadic cases   (chapter 6)
        ii. Nonpolyadic cases
           a. Reversals   (chapter 4)
           b. Nonreversals   (chapter 16)

General NEG deletion of nonpolyadic cases of nonreversals has not yet been illustrated but will be extensively appealed to in chapter 16.

We address the properties of lexical NEG deletion by first repeating the specific lexical NEG deletion cases cited in the previous chapter:

(3) a. A NEG in the context Verb_x ___ is deleted by Verb_x only if $\text{Verb}_x =$ *pouvoir, cesser, oser,* or *savoir.*
    b. A NEG in the context Verb_x [$_{DP}$ ___ einen Dreck/einen feuchten Kehrricht] is deleted by Verb_x.
    c. A NEG in an infinitival clause C that is complement to an adjective introduced by *too* is deleted by the COMP of C.

In all these cases, we describe the deletion in terms of a concept we refer to as a *NEG deletion chain* (see (23) for its precise definition). The NEG deletion chains (hereafter always written in angled brackets) for the three cases in (3) are given in (4):

(4) a. <V, NEG>
    b. <V, NEG>
    c. <COMP, NEG>

In all these cases of lexical NEG deletion, exactly one NEG is deleted. In terms of the chain notation, this suggests the following condition:[1]

(5) *The Lexical NEG Deletion Condition*
    If C is a NEG deletion chain whose initial element is a lexical NEG deleter, then C contains one NEG (equivalently, C is of length 2).

In each of the cases in (3) that we considered, an occurrence of the NEG deleter c-commanded the deleted occurrence of NEG. We suggest this is non-accidental. While these cases are all instances of lexical NEG deletion, we boldly suggest that the same holds for the relation between general NEG deleters and the NEGs they delete:

(6) *The NDEL C-Command Condition*
    If NDEL(X, Y), then X c-commands Y.

Note that the c-command requirement determines that NDEL is an irreflexive relation, as no form c-commands itself.

Return to the three lexical NEG deletion cases cited in (3). In (3a), the deleted NEG starts off as sister of V or VP—namely, [NEG V/VP]—and in this position the NEG deleter c-commands the NEG. In (3b), we assume that the minimizer [NEG einen Dreck] is a VP-internal constituent, and hence c-commanded by the verb, which is the NEG deleter. In (3c), the relevant NEG deleter COMP clearly c-commands the NEGs we have taken it to delete.

A further issue is whether a locality relation must hold between NEG deleters and the NEGs they delete. In the lexical NEG deleter cases we have considered, a close locality relation evidently holds between the NEG deleter and the deleted NEG. The strictest possible locality relation is sisterhood (see Postal 2005). A less strict relation is that the NEG deleter and the NEG are clausemates.

For the French *pas* deletion case in (3a), sisterhood seems to obtain. The underlying structure we posited was [NEG V/VP], where V/VP is lexically marked as the NEG deleter, and so the sisterhood condition trivially holds.

For (3b), the verbal NEG deleter and the NEG (contained in the minimizer) are clausemates.

Consider (3c), and the following structure:

(7) Jane is too cynical [COMP to NEG_1 believe in God]

Here, we claim that the infinitival COMP deletes NEG_1; and NEG_1 and COMP are obviously clausemates. If we adopted the sisterhood requirement posited in Postal 2005, the NEG_1 would raise from its underlying position to be a sister of the COMP. In the Principles and Parameters tradition, this would involve adjunction of NEG_1 to COMP, forming the structure [$_{COMP}$ NEG_1 COMP], where COMP could then delete NEG_1.

Because the domain we are studying is largely terra incognita, we wish to adopt for the purposes of this monograph only the most robustly defensible locality condition on NDEL. We therefore posit a condition considerably weaker than sisterhood:

(8) *The NDEL Clausemate Condition*
    If NDEL(X, Y) and Y is a unary NEG, then X and Y are clausemates.

This necessary condition does not preclude the possibility that the correct locality constraint on NDEL is even stricter, even to the level of the sisterhood requirement. But (8) suffices for the present monograph. Condition (8) imposes the clausemate requirement only on unary NEGs, allowing reversal NEGs to be subject to long-distance deletion. The motivations for this restriction are discussed further below.

Having briefly considered the functioning of NDEL in various cases of lexical NEG deletion, we turn to general deletion cases and consider, in particular, whether the same conditions apply. Consider first NEG deletion in reversals:

(9) a. At most half of the students in the class know any physics.
    b. At most half of the students in the class know [[<NEG$_2$> [<NEG$_1$ >
       SOME]] physics]

In standard views of NPI licensing, the NPI *any physics* is licensed by a c-commanding decreasing operator. We further posit that the c-commanding NEG deleter in (9) is the occurrence of *at most half of the students* in scope position.

Actually, it is more accurate factually to make reference to nonmonotonic operators, because of sentences like the following:

(10) a. Most people who know any physics are engineers.
     b. Exactly three people in this class know any physics.

The restriction of *most* is nonmonotonic, not decreasing, yet it licenses NPIs. The phrase *exactly three people* is also nonmonotonic, and it also licenses NPIs for some speakers. With this in mind, a condition is needed that restricts the sort of phrases that can be the initial elements of NEG deletion chains whose first elements are not lexically marked as NEG deleters. Let us use the term *general NEG deleter* to mean a NEG deleter phrase that is not lexically marked as a NEG deleter. We can then propose the following condition:

(11) *The General NEG Deletion Condition*
     If C = <A, NEG$_1$, . . . , NEG$_n$> is a NEG deletion chain and A is a
     general NEG deleter, then A defines a function that is nonincreasing
     with respect to the origin position of each NEG in C.

Consider again example (9a). Given condition (11), one might assume that the following deletion relations are established: NDEL([at most half of the students], NEG_2) and NDEL([at most half of the students], NEG_1). Both NEGs would be deleted by the decreasing DP *at most half of the students in the class*, defining two distinct NEG deletion chains.

But there is a logical alternative, where the relevant relations are NDEL ([at most half of the students], NEG_2) and NDEL(NEG_2, NEG_1). Under this possibility, each element deletes only a single NEG, yielding a single NEG deletion chain, as defined in (23) below. For various reasons that will become clear in the rest of this monograph, we choose the latter alternative. Such an analysis yields the NEG deletion chain in (12):

(12) <[at most half of the students], NEG_2, NEG_1>

In this chain, both NEGs of the reversal structure are deleted, and each deleted NEG is c-commanded by its NEG deleter, as condition (6) requires.

Now consider condition (6) in relation to reversals. Condition (6) might seem to successfully distinguish pairs like these:

(13) a.   At most three students know any professors.
      b.   *Any students know at most three professors.

However, given that we are assuming that the DPs that are NEG deleters are in scope positions, nothing prevents *at most three professors* from having scope wider than *any students* in (13b). We do not pursue this issue here; but see note 5 of chapter 15.

There are well-known cases that show that an NPI does not have to be c-commanded on the surface by its licenser. One example is (14a):

(14) a.   That Arthur ever went to Venus was not proven.
      b.   That Arthur [NEG_2 [NEG_1 ever]] went to Venus was [not proven]

In this case, *ever* is a reversal structure and the NEG deleter is [not proven], and so the NEG deletion chain we recognize is <[not proven], NEG_2, NEG_1>. C-command does not hold between [not proven] and NEG_2 in the output structure. However, in this case, the passive subject clause originates in a direct object position, where c-command does hold. So we suggest that the c-command condition is met if *any occurrence* of the reversal structure is c-commanded by the NEG deleter. Such an account is supported by the unacceptability of examples like the following:

(15) a.   *That Arthur ever went to Venus did not make me angry.
      b.   *That Arthur ever went to Venus did not cause me to lose money.

In these examples, where the *that* clause is an underlying subject, it has no occurrence c-commanded by [not make] or [not cause]. Given the c-command condition (6), that accounts for their ungrammaticality.

We have yet to consider locality constraint (8) on NEG deletion with respect to examples with reversals like (9a). In (9b), the subject DP and NEG_2 are clausemates, and NEG_2 and NEG_1 are clausemates. However, some reversal NEGs are separated from their NEG deleter by island boundaries:

(16) a. At most half of the students in the class accepted the claim that Jermaine was ever here.
    b. At most half of the students in the class accept the claim that Jermaine knows any physics.

In (16a), *ever* is a reversal structure separated from the subject quantifier by a complex NP island. Similarly for *any physics* in (16b). Given these facts, there are two different ways to incorporate reversals into our system.

The approach one of us favors is that deletion of reversal NEGs is not subject to the clausemate locality restriction. This is why the stipulation "Y is a unary NEG" is included in (8). Therefore, reversals can be deleted long-distance by the appropriate deleters and show no sensitivity to islands, because no NEG raising is involved. The approach the other of us favors is that the outer, reversal NEG in a reversal structure must raise to be deleted but that such raising is not blocked by weak islands. The reversal NEG in (16a,b) moves over the island boundaries into a local configuration (sisterhood or clausemate) with the negated verbs. Resolution of this disagreement is complicated and difficult. It requires surveying subtle data involving a range of NPIs potentially analyzable as reversal structures. This would have to be done minimally for English—involving, in particular, study of forms like *yet*, *much*, and *anymore*, which would have to be considered with respect to a wide variety of weak and strong island constraints. We cannot pursue this matter even for English in the current monograph.

Now consider the following question: can a general NEG deleter yield a NEG deletion chain containing only one NEG? We illustrated earlier that *lexical* NEG deletion chains apparently regularly do. Relevantly, example (17a) cannot have structure (17b), since that yields interpretation (17c), which is not in fact an interpretation of (17a):

(17) a. At most half of the class knows any physics.
    b. At most half of the class knows [NEG SOME physics]
    c. At most half of the class does not know any physics.

In this example, according to our assumptions, the NEG deletion chain is <[at most half of the class], NEG>. Such NEG deletion chains must then be ruled out.

To address this issue, we adopt the following constraint (based on Szabolcsi 2004:42), modifying the oversimplified version we gave in (13) of chapter 4:

(18) *The NEG Deletion Evenness Condition (second and final version)*
If G is a NEG deletion chain whose initial element is not a lexical NEG deleter, and whose deleted NEGs are not copies (in a polyadic quantification structure), then G contains an even number of NEGs.

We explicate the reference to copies just below. The single NEG in the NEG deletion chain for (17b) given in (19) violates this condition, correctly blocking the nonexistent reading of the example:

(19) <[at most half of the class], NEG>

Finally, we reconsider the NEG deletion in standard English polyadic quantification structures with *any*. Such NEG deletion is also general (not lexical) NEG deletion. We repeat the principle given in chapter 6:

(20) *The Standard English Negative Concord Reduction Principle*
Let $DP_1, DP_2, \ldots, DP_n$ be a maximal sequence of $n > 1$ DP occurrences in scope position (in a single clause) sharing a D = [NEG SOME], where DP_1 c-commands each of $DP_2, \ldots, DP_n$. And for all i, $1 \le i \le n$, let D_i be the copy of D in DP_i and let NEG_i be the NEG of D_i. For each occurrence of DP_i (i ≠ 1), NEG_i is deleted.

We assume here that DP_1 is the initiator of the NEG deletion chain. Therefore, such deletions satisfy the c-command condition in (6). And since all the DP occurrences are in the scope positions of a single clause, the clausemate condition in (8) is satisfied as well. However, (20) leaves open the question of which NEG deletion chains are formed.

Consider the following concrete example:

(21) a. Nobody saw anybody in any bar.
b. [[NEG_1 SOME] body] saw [[NEG_2 SOME] body] in [[NEG_3 SOME] bar]

What we have said so far is consistent with two scenarios. On one, [[NEG_1 SOME] body] is the initial element of a single NEG deletion chain: <[[NEG_1 SOME] body], NEG_2, NEG_3>. On this analysis, [[NEG_1 SOME] body] would delete NEG_2, which would delete NEG_3. On this analysis, NEG_2 would have to undergo raising first in order to c-command NEG_3 and thus meet the c-command requirement of (6). The other scenario would recognize two separate shorter NEG deletion chains: $<[[NEG_1$ SOME] body], $NEG_2>$ and $<[[NEG_2$ SOME] body], $NEG_3>$. We cannot currently cite any evidence to distinguish these views, so we leave the choice open in the definition of NEG deletion chain given in (23).

However, no matter what view of deletion chains is adopted for English-type polyadic quantification cases, a completely general NEG deletion evenness condition cannot systematically hold. On the short-chain theory, each of the chains contains only one NEG, evidently not consistent with the evenness requirement. On the long-chain theory, while it is true that the NEG deletion chain for (21) contains two deleted NEGs, that is merely a fortuitous consequence of an arbitrary choice of example. Whether evenness holds or not *in general* for such chains is entirely a function of the number of scopal DPs sharing a D:

(22) a. No boy saw any girl. (one deleted NEG)
    b. No boy saw any girl at any time. (two deleted NEGs)
    c. No boy saw any girl at any time at any party. (three deleted NEGs)

This is the reason why our formulation of the NEG Deletion Evenness Condition in (18) excludes copy NEGs (in polyadic quantification structures) from consideration.

We now give a general definition of the notion of NEG deletion chain that we have assumed in our treatments of the various cases of NEG deletion. Then we provide a condition determining which NEGs appear in such chains. The latter is necessary since merely defining the concept in (23) does not force any NEG to be in such a chain.

(23) *Definition:* NEG deletion chain
    A sequence of constituent occurrences $C = <a_1, \ldots, a_n>$ is a *NEG deletion chain* if and only if
    a. a_1 (which we hereafter call the *initiator*) is not NEG;
    b. for all i $(1 \leq i < n)$, $NDEL(a_i, a_{i+1})$; and
    c. there is no m such that $NDEL(a_n, m)$.

We leave open here whether multiple chains can share an initial element (as in the short-chain analysis of the *any* polyadic quantification cases).

Everything in this definition should be familiar except for (23a). Consider the example in (24a), with structure (24b):

(24) a. Lucille didn't see anybody.
    b. Lucille did NEG_1 see [$<NEG_1>$ SOME body]

In this example, NEG$_1$ has raised, yielding two occurrences (the post-Aux occurrence, and that modifying SOME). The lower occurrence is deleted, as is generally the case with occurrences due to raising. That is, the deletion of NEG occurrences that exist as a function of raising falls under whatever principles are taken to ground the nonpronunciation of the launching positions of raised constituents generally. Therefore, it would be redundant to invoke NEG deletion here, so we recognize no NEG deletion chain formation in such contexts.

The fact that every NEG deleted as a function of NDEL is in a NEG deletion chain is imposed by the following condition:

(25) *The NEG Deletion Chain Condition*
    If N is a NEG, then there is a NEG deletion chain containing N if and only if there is an X such that NDEL(X, N).[2]

9 Confounding Cases: Strict NPIs and Scope

9.1 Scope Issues and Nonfinite Complement Clauses

Consider examples like (1a,b) and (2a,b):

(1) a. Andrea doesn't believe/think that Carl said jackshit$_A$ about compilers.
   b. *Andrea doesn't accept/grasp that Carl said jackshit$_A$ about compilers.

(2) a. No expert believes/thinks that Carl said jackshit$_A$ about compilers.
   b. *No expert accepts/states that Carl said jackshit$_A$ about compilers.

Similar pairs with analogous judgment markings play a key role throughout this monograph. By *analogous judgment markings*, we mean that cases like (1a) and (2a), with CNRP main verbs, are taken to be grammatical, while those like (1b) and (2b), with non-CNRP main verbs, are taken to be ungrammatical. By *similar pairs*, we mean that both (a)- and (b)-type examples have a strict NPI in the complement clause.

However, such examples manifest certain complexities and raise various issues. These require clarification in order to justify the heavy weight we place on pairs like (1a,b) and (2a,b). These complexities will require discussion of quantifier scope as well as the behavior of a range of strict NPIs distinct from the type in the examples above.

To begin, consider the following observation:

(3) (Kempson 1985:236)
   "The final datum about *any* and its construal is that *any* in negative polarity environments is ambiguous, *any* in a non-negative polarity environment is not. That is, any case where an 'existential' interpretation of *any* is available can always be over-ridden by a focusing device such as contrastive stress, giving rise to ambiguity."

Kempson's invocation here of contrastive stress has pointed us to the fact that stress contrasts are relevant to the ambiguities of NPI *any* forms as well as to those of other nominal NPIs. Consider:

(4) Vaughn didn't accept to write anything about radiation.

Example (4) has two readings involving the differential scope of the DP represented by *anything*. On one reading, associated with weak stress on this form, its scope is internal to the complement. On this reading, (4) paraphrases (5):

(5) Vaughn didn't accept to write something about radiation.

In our terms, (4) is a reversal case; the initiator of the NEG deletion chain involved in the covertness of the two NEGs underlying *any* is taken to be the negated main verb [NEG accept]. A scenario where such an interpretation is natural is one where the chief editor of the paper is handing out topics for people to write on. She asks Vaughn to write something about radiation, but he refuses. Later on, she reports his reaction using (4).

A second reading of (4) is associated with strong stress on *anything*; the scope of the quantifier is in the main clause. On this reading, (4) is equivalent to (6):

(6) There is nothing about radiation that Vaughn accepted to write.

In terms of the assumptions and notations adopted in this monograph, the relevant aspects of this reading of (4) would be represented most fully as follows:

(7) Vaughn did NEG_1 [<[[<NEG_1> SOME] thing]$_5$> [accept to write DP_5]]

The key observations about (4) on the reading represented in (7) are the following: (i) *accept* is not a CNRP, (ii) no reversal structure is involved, and (iii) the surface position of the DP with main clause scope is in the complement clause. Despite these properties, a structure like (7) nonetheless yields an output with the NEG raised to a position immediately adjacent to the matrix clause Aux from the higher occurrence of DP_5. On its reading equivalent to (6), the structure of (4) thus involves no raising of a NEG out of the complement clause. This is possible because under our assumptions, the main clause NEG in (7) starts out in the DP in a main clause scope position. The NEG can then raise out of the DP in the high-scope position internal to the main clause. No Classical NR is present in (7) or required to account for its properties.

In examples like (8), analogous to (4) except that the main verb is replaced by a CNRP, the situation is slightly more complex:

(8) Vaughn didn't want to write anything about radiation.

Presumably, such cases have a pair of readings of the type seen for (4) (which are rather difficult to get) but also a distinct one that involves Classical NR. In this case, there can be a low-scope, unary-NEG DP, with the NEG that originates in the complement clause scope position raising into the main clause. That is, (8) can paraphrase (9):

(9) Vaughn₁'s wish was that he₁ write nothing about radiation.

Now we turn to cases of infinitival complements containing strict NPIs:

(10) a. *Virginia forced/ordered/told Carmen to say jackshit$_A$ about compilers.

b. Virginia didn't force/order/tell Carmen to say jackshit$_A$ about compilers.

At first glance, perfectly grammatical examples like (10b) might appear to reduce our claim that strict NPIs like *jackshit$_A$* require *local* licensers to non-sense.[1] In these examples, the putatively strict NPI occurs in a complement clause, while the NEG, shown by (10a) to be the critical licensing element, is in the main clause. And, independently of NPIs, these verbs of course show no equivalences of the sort typical of Classical NR cases:

(11) a. Virginia didn't force/order/tell Carmen to sing.

b. Virginia forced/ordered/told Carmen not to/to not sing.

Since (11a,b) represent entirely distinct propositions, there is no basis for invoking Classical NR in (11a) or (10b).

Despite these uncontroversial facts, it nonetheless makes sense to speak of forms like *jackshit$_A$* as requiring a *local* licenser, although the predictions of that claim need to be adjusted to take account of recent discussion of nonstrict NPI cases like those in (4). That is, since the main verbs in (11) are not CNRPs, a unary NEG associated with the NPI quantifier could only appear in the main clause if the scope position of that quantifier were in the main clause. Reversals are, in this case, irrelevant since we argued in chapter 4 that strict NPIs like *jackshit$_A$* do not permit reversal structures. So if *jackshit$_A$* is a strict NPI, the claim is derived that in cases like (10b), the scope of the quantifier DP must be in the main clause, as it is. In other words, to the extent that (10b) is acceptable, it means that there is nothing about compilers that Virginia ordered Carmen to say.

But in analogs of (10b) involving main clause CNRPs, the prediction is that both main clause and complement clause scope is possible. Consider then:

(12) Virginia didn't want Carmen to say jackshit$_A$ about compilers.

As predicted, we believe that this has not only the high-scope reading parallel to that of (10b), that is, one paraphrasable as 'There was nothing Virginia wanted Carmen to say about compilers', but also a low-scope reading paraphrasable as 'Virginia wanted there to be nothing that Carmen said about compilers'. On the latter reading, the NEG can achieve its main clause position by raising out of the DP in a complement clause scope position into the main clause. NEG raising from the complement clause poses no problem, since the matrix verb is a CNRP.

9.2   The Moral

For present purposes, the moral from this discussion of scope and NEG raising is the following. Any attempt to diagnose the presence or absence of Classical NR must always take into account the possibility of NEG raising out of main clause scope positions. More precisely, suppose one finds cases of the schematic form [NEG Verb$_x$ . . . [$_A$ . . . [strict NPI]$_a$ . . .]], where there is no NEG in the complement clause A and Verb$_x$ is *not* a CNRP. Such a case does not falsify our claims that the strict NPI requires a local (clausemate) licenser, because there is an analysis not invoking Classical NR consistent with the locality requirement of the strict NPI. But that analysis generates a testable consequence: namely, the scope of the quantifier corresponding to NPI$_a$ must be in the main clause, so that the NEG originating in the NPI structure can raise out of the high-scope position.[2] That alone allows the situation to be described without any raising of NEG out of the complement of a *non*-CNRP.[3]

9.3   Applying the Moral to Finite Complements

The discussion in this chapter so far has involved nonfinite complement clauses. However, many cases where the issue of high-scope confounds arise in this monograph involve finite complements. We stress, then, that the same considerations yield the same conclusions as those reached so far for nonfinite complement cases. There is one important proviso, though. In some (perhaps many) cases for some (perhaps many) speakers, the high-scope reading of a negative quantifier DP in a finite complement clause is difficult to accept.

Consider first an example involving a nonstrict NPI:

(13) Rodney did not claim that Evelyn owned any cheetahs.

This example has two structures, which we represent as (14a,b):

(14) a. Rodney [NEG$_6$ claim] [that [<[[<NEG$_5$> [<NEG$_4$> SOME]] cheetahs]$_i$> [Evelyn owned DP$_i$]]]

    b. Rodney did NEG$_4$ <[[<NEG$_4$> SOME] cheetahs]$_i$> [claim that [Evelyn owned DP$_i$]]

Structure (14a) is the now familiar reversal case in which the surface NEG in the main clause originates on the matrix V/VP, and both NEGs of the reversal structure are deleted, with the main clause negative verb being the initiator of the relevant NEG deletion chain. Structure (14a) specifies the reading of (13) on which it is equivalent to (15), where the scope of *some* is internal to the complement:

(15) Rodney did not claim that Evelyn owned some cheetahs.

A natural context for (13) on interpretation (15) is as follows. One speaker says, "Rodney claimed that Evelyn owned some cheetahs." The addressed speaker denies this by saying, "No, Rodney didn't claim that Evelyn owned any cheetahs, and Frank didn't claim that either." Here, the antecedent of *that* appears to be *Evelyn owned any cheetahs*, where *any cheetahs* is a reversal.

Structure (14b) gives the high-scope reading on which (13) is equivalent to (16):

(16) There were no cheetahs which Rodney claimed that Evelyn owned.

Such an interpretation is brought out by putting stress on *any* in (13). It is consistent with a scenario where one speaker says, "Rodney claimed that Evelyn owns the cheetahs Simba and Nala." The addressed speaker denies the claim by uttering (13). On such an interpretation, it is awkward to continue with "… and Frank didn't claim that either." On the awkwardness of the continuation, see the paragraph following (18).

The interpretations in (15) and (16) are not logically equivalent. For example, (16) is true if there are no instances of a cheetah x, where Rodney claims that Evelyn owns x. However, even if (16) is true, it may also be the case that Rodney has steadily maintained that Evelyn does in fact own cheetahs, but there is no specific cheetah that he claims that she owns. Since (16) can be true, while (15) is false, they are not logically equivalent.

Return then to the real focus of the issue being addressed, represented by pairs like (1a,b), repeated here:

(17) a. Andrea doesn't believe/think that Carl said jackshit$_A$ about compilers.

    b. *Andrea doesn't accept/realize that Carl said jackshit$_A$ about compilers.

Given the preceding discussion, we can be precise about our view of purported contrasts like (17a,b). Since the occurring NPI does not permit a reversal analysis, we recognize only two a priori possibilities in such cases: a low-scope analysis of the [[NEG SOME] jackshit$_A$] quantifier DP, or a high-scope one. But the former analysis is only possible in (17a) given the main clause locations of the NEGs, since that locus requires that a NEG raise out of the complement clause. And that requires the main verb to be a CNRP, which leaves only a high-scope reading as a possibility for (17b). We must then ask, what is the status of that reading, and how does it relate to our placement of a star on (17b)?

Our partially historical answer is this. We now believe that the high-scope reading is in general grammatical for cases like (17b), although at one time we were of a different opinion and affixed stars to them without explication. When the high-scope reading is excluded, as we have just observed, the result is indeed ungrammatical. The confounding factor then is that grasping high-scope readings is often not clear in finite clause cases, especially with NPIs like *jackshit$_A$*, a fact for which we have no account. But to evaluate the status of examples like (17a,b) and of putative contrasts between them, the scope factor can never be ignored.

Since, as just indicated, scope intuitions relevant to the present issues are often rather subtle, showing that a particular example has only main clause scope for a complement quantifier DP is not straightforward. That difficulty is, we suggest, the key reason why judgments of grammaticality for cases like (17b) have proven to be wavering and difficult over time, and not only for us.

In support of the wide scope reading of the quantifier in (17b) (to the extent that it is acceptable), consider the following contrast:

(18) a. Andrea didn't claim that Carl said jackshit$_A$ about compilers, *but Mary did claim that.
     b. Andrea didn't claim that Carl said anything about compilers, but Mary did claim that.

In (18a), *jackshit$_A$* needs to have scope in the main clause, as discussed above. But then, the embedded clause (whose semantics contains a free variable) cannot serve as the antecedent of *that*. However, in (18b), *anything* as a reversal takes scope in the embedded clause, and the embedded clause is a legitimate antecedent of *that*.

We observe, though, that there are strict NPIs for which the considerations discussed above are irrelevant, because the relevant NPIs do not scope out of finite clauses. For such NPIs, we can safely affix stars without complications. The NPI series *in ages/days/weeks/months/years* . . . is of this type. Consider the following:

(19) a. Anthony hasn't visited his mother in ages.
     b. Not in ages has Anthony visited his mother.
     c. Gloria doesn't believe/think that Anthony has visited his mother in ages.
     d. *Gloria doesn't know/realize that Anthony has visited his mother in ages.

In cases like (19c,d), for whatever reasons, there is no issue of high scope for *in ages*. Therefore, the contrast between the grammatical CNRP main clause cases in (19c) and the non-CNRP main clause cases in (19d) argues directly that the NEG associated with and required by *in ages*, seen in the main clauses in (19a,b), has raised out of the complement clause in (19c). It follows that Classical NR is licit in (19c) but not in (19d), because the main clause is based on a CNRP only in the former.

A second example of a strict NPI for which confounding scope factors are irrelevant is provided by the expression *so good/great/hot*:

(20) a. Virginia is *(not) feeling so hot.
     b. Luke doesn't believe/think that Virginia is feeling so hot.
     c. *Luke doesn't know/realize that Virginia is feeling so hot.

Again, since a high-scope analysis is impossible, the clausal separation of the NEG and the NPI in (20b) must depend on Classical NR. Since that is also impossible in (20c) owing to the lack of a main clause CNRP, the relevant examples are predictably ungrammatical.

A third and last example of a strict NPI not subject to the confounding scope issue is the adjectival modifier *all that*:

(21) a. Arnold is *(not) all that intelligent.
     b. Lucinda doesn't believe/think that Arnold is all that intelligent.
     c. *Lucinda doesn't know/realize that Arnold is all that intelligent.

So far, we have discussed confounding high-scope issues only for cases in which a strict NPI quantifier DP is associated semantically with an overt NEG located in the post-Aux position in the main clause. But (2), which we repeat here, presented the distinct case where the forms permitting complement clause strict NPIs are main clause quantifier DPs:

(22) a. No expert believes/thinks that Carl said jackshit$_A$ about compilers.
     b. *No expert accepts/states that Carl said jackshit$_A$ about compilers.

We believe that exactly the same considerations just discussed pertain here, except that ascertaining the scopes is complicated by the possibility of forming a polyadic quantifier combination of the main clause quantifier DP and complement clause NPI DP. But abstracting away from difficulties in perceiving such readings, characteristic for at least some speakers, other speakers find that (22a) has both a low-scope, Classical NR reading and a high-scope one for *jackshit$_A$*. The former is equivalent to 'Every expert thinks Carl said nothing about compilers' (this reading is discussed at length in chapter 16). The latter is equivalent to 'There is no pair <x, y>, x an expert and y a thing, such that x thinks Carl said y about compilers'.

But allowing for the hedges just above, (22b) has only the analog of the high-scope, polyadic reading, since Classical NR is unavailable with the main clause non-CNRPs. So a star like that on (22b) should, strictly, only mark the low-scope reading for those who accept the high-scope possibility.[4]

9.4 Classifications of NPIs

It is appropriate at this point to reconsider the terminology for NPIs we have adopted and its relation to other terminologies found in the massive NPI literature.

In the framework of this monograph, NPIs are classified according to whether they represent unary- or binary-NEG structures. For example, the NPI variant of *jackshit$_A$* can only represent a unary-NEG structure. The NPIs *anybody* and *ever* can, in distinct environments, represent either type of structure. There are certain contexts where *anybody* can only represent a unary-NEG structure (e.g., Horn clauses; see chapter 13) and others where it represents only a binary-NEG structure.

There are subdivisions in the class of unary-NEG NPIs. For example, we claimed earlier in this chapter that certain unary-NEG NPIs can take matrix scope out of a finite clause, and others (such as *in ages, until, so good/great/ hot, all that,* and *half bad*) resist taking scope out of a finite clause. There are also divisions in the class of binary-NEG DPs, which we have not discussed in this monograph for reasons of space.

In chapter 1, we introduced the term *strict NPI* for those NPIs that need a local licenser. This induces a classification of NPIs into strict and nonstrict NPIs. An obvious problem with this definition of strict NPIs is that the present framework does not actually incorporate a notion *licenser*. Instead, it maintains the view that NPIs originate with at least one NEG, that NEGs often raise away from particular NPIs, and that many NEGs originating in NPIs are deleted by NEG deleters. In other views of NPIs, the cases we differentiate in these terms are normally conflated. Specifically, we know of no other view of NPIs in which a NEG can raise from its associated NPI, since in these views no NEG originates in an NPI. Rather, nominal NPIs are standardly treated as indefinites, under the scope of a decreasing or at least nonincreasing operator.

The question then arises of how the notions *unary/binary-NEG NPI* map onto the notions *strict/nonstrict NPI*. There are three cases to consider:

(23) a. NEG raising from a unary-NEG structure,
      b. deletion of the NEG of a unary-NEG structure, and
      c. deletion of the two NEGs of a binary-NEG structure.

The possibility in (23a), the raising of NEG from a unary-NEG structure, is highly restricted. NEG raising cannot cross either an island boundary or a non-CNRP. In most cases, such NEG raising is clause-bounded; CNRPs are the exception since these permit Classical NR and hence the raising of NEGs out of clauses. Apparent counterexamples of raising over a non-CNRP discussed in earlier sections of this chapter were analyzed such that the NPI takes matrix scope. Hence, the relevant NEGs can raise from the matrix scope position of the NPI. We need not repeat justification for those conclusions here.

Case (23b) involves three subcases: lexical NEG deletion, NEG deletion in polyadic quantification, and a last possibility discussed at length in chapter 16. Such examples are narrowly constrained by the fact that systematically, the NEG deleter and the NEG it deletes must be clausemates.

Finally, consider (23c). The deletion of the NEGs of a binary-NEG structure is fundamentally different from the other cases. Such deletion is in a sense nonlocal. We described two alternative views of this in chapter 8. One possibility is that the NEGs of a reversal structure never undergo raising, but are simply deleted long-distance. Another possibility is that the outer NEG of a reversal structure does undergo raising, but that such raising is not subject to all island constraints and is not subject to condition (4) of chapter 1, that limiting NEG raising to dominating clauses based on CNRPs. Under either analysis, it is clear that the deletion of the NEGs of a reversal structure is nonlocal in a sense that the deletion of other kinds of NEGs is not.

Given this asymmetry between unary- and binary -NEG structures, we make the following identification, linking terms previously used in the literature on NPIs with our present theoretical framework:

(24) Strict NPIs   = Unary-NEG structures
      Nonstrict NPIs = Binary-NEG structures

Of course, much more needs to be said here, especially concerning the classification of binary-NEG structures. But to a first approximation, (24) appears to us to be correct. NPIs that require a local licenser (in the traditional conception) are all unary-NEG NPIs.

We can also relate our views to the very influential division of NPIs into weak, strong, and superstrong, given by Zwarts (1998):

(25) (Zwarts 1998:233)
    "Laws of Negative Polarity
    a. Only sentences in which a monotone decreasing expression occurs
       can contain a negative polarity item of the weak type.
    b. Only sentences in which an anti-additive expression occurs can
       contain a negative polarity item of the strong type.
    c. Only sentences in which an antimorphic expression occurs can
       contain a negative polarity item of the superstrong type."

Putting aside (25c), this classification maps neatly onto our classification of NPIs into unary-NEG structures and binary-NEG structures. Consider the following examples:

(26) a. At most half of the students know anything/*jackshit$_A$ about
       physics.
    b. No student knows anything/ jackshit$_A$ about physics.

Given such data, Zwarts's conceptual framework would classify *jackshit$_A$* as a strong NPI, since it is only possible with an antiadditive such as *no student*, and hence is not possible with the decreasing but not antiadditive *at most half of the students*. In the present framework, *jackshit$_A$* is a unary-NEG NPI analyzed underlyingly as [[NEG SOME] jackshit]. The NEG cannot be deleted in (26a) because of the evenness requirement represented by condition (18) of chapter 8 and the Antiadditive NEG Deletion Condition of note 6 of chapter 16. Furthermore, no polyadic quantification structure is possible in (26a), since no determiner can be shared. In (26b), the NEG is deleted because *no student* and *jackshit$_A$* form a polyadic quantification structure, as described in chapter 6.

Given these considerations, we postulate the following:

(27) Weak NPIs = Binary-NEG structures
     Strong NPIs = Unary-NEG structures

The only category left out is superstrong NPIs. We are not aware of a clear case of such an NPI in English. But any existing superstrong NPI in any language would be characterized in present terms as a unary-NEG structure that prohibits determiner sharing (and is hence unable to enter into polyadic quantifier formation). The NEG of any such unary-NEG structure would raise away from the NPI, giving the appearance of an NPI licensed only by NEG (and hence giving the appearance of an NPI licensed only by an antimorphic expression).

Putting (24) and (27) together and glossing over many issues yields the following linking of our unary/binary distinction with terms that have been used by others in the literature (*strict/nonstrict* and *weak/strong*):

(28) Unary-NEG NPIs = Strict NPIs   = Strong NPIs
      Binary-NEG NPIs = Nonstrict NPIs = Weak NPIs

9.5 Unexpected Contradictions

In this section, we briefly consider certain contradictions at first sight unexpected under the high-scope analyses of various strict NPIs we have appealed to in the first sections of this chapter.

Consider the following:

(29) She didn't ask me to do anything.

In the present framework, (29) can have two structures, neither of which can invoke Classical NR since *ask* is not a CNRP:

(30) a. She did NEG_1 $[<[[<NEG_1>$ SOME] thing$]_5>$ [ask me to do $DP_5]]$
      b. She did NEG_1 $[<NEG_1>$ ask] me $[<[[<NEG_2>$ $[<NEG_3>$ SOME]]
          thing$]_4>$ to do $DP_4]$

These structures have the following rough paraphrases:

(31) a. There is nothing that she asked me to do.
      b. She didn't ask me to do something.

These interpretations are not logically equivalent. For instance, in a workplace scenario, (31a) is true if there is no specific task (among those in my job description) that I have been assigned on day X. But even so, I may have been asked to keep busy on day X by choosing some task on my own. So (31a) can be true, while (31b) is false. The relevant interpretation of (29) is brought out by adding *in particular* to *anything*: *She asked me to keep busy, but she did not ask me to do anything in particular.*

Our assumptions predict, though, that if the nonstrict NPI *anything* in (29) is replaced by a strict NPI, there can only be one interpretation:

(32) She didn't ask us to do jackshit$_A$.

Under our view, only a structure parallel to (30a), with an interpretation like (31a), should be possible in (32). That follows from the claim that strict NPIs like *jackshit$_A$* are incompatible with reversal structures, which is what are found in (30b). Recall from section 4.8 the independent evidence for the conclusion that strict NPIs like *jackshit$_A$* cannot represent binary-NEG structures:

(33) a. *If you do jackshit$_A$, you will be in trouble.
     b. *Everybody who knows jackshit$_A$ will pass the exam.
     c. *Less than half of the class did jackshit$_A$.

Since only binary-NEG NPIs are possible in contexts like (33a–c) and since *jackshit$_A$* is disallowed in all of them, we concluded that *jackshit$_A$* can never manifest a binary-NEG structure.

Consider next the following example, illustrating what we will call the *contradiction test* (suggested to us by Dylan Bumford):

(34) Although he did suggest we do something, he didn't ask us to do jackshit$_A$.

Limiting attention to the first-clause scope order *suggest > something*, this sentence seems to express a contradiction. The problem is that our views do not predict that fact. If the main clause in (34) is assigned a structure parallel to (30a), hence the interpretation in (31a), no logical contradiction should exist.

This result seems to suggest that the only structure for the main clause of (34) is parallel to (30b). Then the contradiction in (34) would follow straightforwardly (since the whole would reduce to an instance of P contradicting ¬P). But assigning the main clause of (34) a reading parallel to (30b) is evidently inconsistent with our conclusion that NPIs like *jackshit$_A$* are limited to unary-NEG structures.

Furthermore, even if (contrary to our analysis) *jackshit$_A$* could have a binary-NEG structure, nothing should block (34) from *also* having a structure parallel to (30a), where *jackshit$_A$* has a unary-NEG structure, with wide scope. On that structure, (34) should not be a contradiction.

Although we cannot give a full account of these facts, we suggest that there is a strengthening (perhaps an implicature) operating in cases such as (34) that can be characterized somewhat as follows: (i) [[NEG SOME] jackshit$_A$] in (34) has wide scope over *ask*; (ii) [[NEG SOME] jackshit$_A$] is interpreted as a quantifier with a maximally inclusive restriction (the set of all individuals in any model), yielding a strong statement; (iii) that statement is taken to be strengthened even further to 'He made no request that we do something'.

The pragmatic basis of the extralogical strengthening in (iii) might be found in the fact that while on strictly logical grounds, cases like (34) are consistent, the circumstances that would permit a true model of them are quite rare.

There is evidence for the sort of pragmatic strengthening just alluded to outside the domain of NPIs. Consider:

(35) Although there is nothing he suggested we drink, he did suggest we
       drink something.

In this case, the *there* construction guarantees the high scope of *nothing*. On purely logical grounds, given that *something* in the second clause can have low scope, this too should be consistent. But a consistent reading does not seem like a normal use of the expression; making it consistent again requires assuming an extremely unlikely model. Genuine acceptability, or at least real naturalness, for a consistent version of something like (35) seems to demand expanding *nothing* with forms such as *in particular* or *specific*.

While (34) seems worse than (35), perhaps this is related to the fact that restrictive phrases like *in particular* cannot be appended to *jackshit$_A$*. This could suggest that (35) is more easily taken as consistent than (34) because it involves a marginal *covert* version of one of the restricting expressions, a possibility not existing for the strict NPI under a hypothesis that such phrases reject both overt and covert versions of restrictive phrases.

10 Strict NPIs and Locality

10.1 Strict NPIs and Antiadditivity

In this monograph, we have distinguished between strict NPIs, claimed in the previous chapter to all be unary-NEG structures, and nonstrict NPIs. In this chapter, we argue that the commonly suggested semantic condition that a strict NPI occur in the scope of an antiadditive operator (see Jackson 1995, Zwarts 1998, Szabolcsi 2004:426–427, Gajewski 2007:302) is not sufficient to account for the distribution of strict NPIs.

We first exhibit a context that is antiadditive (hence decreasing) but nonetheless does not allow strict NPIs. Consider the following cases:

(1) a. I didn't find a person who ate vegetables.
    b. I didn't find a person who ate green vegetables.

Example (1a) clearly entails (1b), indicating that the context 'I didn't find a person who ate ___' is decreasing. A similar deduction goes through if the subject of the main clause is a negative quantifier DP:

(2) a. Nobody found a person who ate vegetables.
    b. Nobody found a person who ate green vegetables.

Once again, (2a) entails (2b), so we conclude that the context 'Nobody found a person who ate ___' is decreasing.

But a stronger statement is justified since the above two contexts are in fact antiadditive. Recall first the definition of *antiadditive* (from Zwarts 1998:222):

(3) *Definition:* Antiadditive
    Let B and B* be two Boolean algebras. A function f from B to B* is said to be *antiadditive* if and only if for each two elements X and Y of the algebra B:
    $F(X \cup Y) = F(X) \cap F(Y)$

From left to right, $F(X \cup Y) \Rightarrow F(X) \cap F(Y)$ represents the decreasing property shown to hold in (1) and (2). So we focus on the right-to-left entailment: $F(X) \cap F(Y) \Rightarrow F(X \cup Y)$.

Consider then the following examples:

(4) a. I didn't find a person who sang and I didn't find a person who danced.

    b. I didn't find a person who sang or danced.

(5) a. Nobody found a person who sang and nobody found a person who danced.

    b. Nobody found a person who sang or danced.

Since (4a) entails (4b) and (5a) entails (5b), we conclude that both the contexts 'I didn't find a person who ___' and 'Nobody found a person who ___' are antiadditive.

The two antiadditive contexts just cited allow some NPIs:

(6) a. I didn't find a person who knows any physics.

    b. I didn't find a person who had ever been to France.

    c. Nobody found a person who knows any physics.

    d. Nobody found a person who had ever been to France.

However, significantly, these contexts disallow strict NPIs:

(7) a. *I didn't find a person who feels all that well.

    b. *I didn't find a person who knows jackshit$_A$ about that.

    c. *I didn't find a person who told a living soul about his dreams.

    d. *I didn't find a person who had seen Mary in ages.

Similar facts hold when the subject is a negative quantifier:

(8) a. *Nobody found a person who feels all that well.

    b. *Nobody found a person who knows jackshit$_A$ about that.

    c. *Nobody found a person who told a living soul about his dreams.

    d. *Nobody found a person who has seen Mary in ages.

These examples indicate that the distribution of strict NPIs cannot be accounted for simply in terms of a requirement to appear in an antiadditive context. In the cases in (7) and (8), the ungrammatical strict NPIs and the form determining the antiadditive context (post-Aux NEG or *nobody*) are separated by a clause boundary—moreover, one that is an island boundary. Given that, a syntactic approach to such data suggests itself.

Consider first (7b). Three possible analyses are given in (9):

(9) a. *I did NEG$_1$ find a person who knows [<NEG$_1$> SOME jackshit$_A$]
         about that
     b. *I did [NEG$_1$ find] a person who knows [<NEG$_2$> [<NEG$_3$> SOME
         jackshit$_A$]] about that
     c. *I did [NEG$_1$ find] a person who knows [<NEG$_2$> SOME jackshit$_A$]
         about that

In (9a), NEG$_1$, originally associated with the strict NPI, raises from the relative clause to the matrix clause. But NEG raising here violates the Complex NP Constraint and hence is ruled out (see chapters 11 and 12 for a more detailed account of Classical NR and islands).

In (9b), the matrix clause V/VP is negated by NEG$_1$. (9b) conveys the intended interpretation of (7b) ('I did not find a person who knows anything about that'). However, it is impossible since *jackshit$_A$* cannot have a reversal structure (see chapter 4). In the terms elaborated in chapter 4, all the strict NPIs in cases like (7) and (8) are unary-NEG DP structures.

In (9c), the matrix V/VP is negated by NEG$_1$ and NEG$_2$ is covert. Therefore, NEG$_2$ must have a NEG deleter—but there is none internal to the relative clause. Furthermore, raising NEG$_2$ to the matrix clause (to be deleted by NEG$_1$) would once again violate the Complex NP Constraint. Finally, formation of the NEG deletion chain <[NEG$_1$ find], NEG$_2$> would violate condition (18) of chapter 8, the NEG Deletion Evenness Condition.

The logic just advanced for analyses (9a–c) of example (7b) would yield the same result for (8b). There, too, the only possible analyses would require the analog of NEG$_2$ in (9c) to raise out of the restrictive relative clause island (see chapter 16 for a detailed analysis of similar cases).

To be fully accurate, though, we observe that for some speakers, some examples like (7b,c) and (8b,c) may nonetheless be grammatical to the extent that such speakers find it possible to interpret the relevant NPIs, *jackshit$_A$* and *a living soul*, as taking scope external to the restrictive relative clauses at issue. That is, the high-scope confound issue discussed in chapter 9 arises once again. Then, in (7b), the analog of NEG$_2$ would raise from the high-scope position of [[NEG SOME] jackshit$_A$] external to the relative clause island, yielding no violation of the Complex NP Constraint.

The Web suggests the reality of the high-scope possibility just alluded to:

(10) I'll try that, thanks. By the way, EA support didn't have anyone that
      knew squat and they sent me here ...
      (social.bioware.com/. . ./Run-for-the-Conduit-timer-issue-1772739-1.
      html)

We stress, though, that for the one of us who is most comfortable with high-scope cases like (10), the other NPIs in (7) and (8) are impossible, because those NPIs cannot scope out of finite clauses.

A complication relevant to our conclusion from data like (7) and (8) arises from observations by Schmerling (1971:202), who noted the existence of grammatical cases like (11):

(11) There was no one in the huge lecture hall who uttered a peep when . . .

While we have not previously cited *utter a peep* as a strict NPI, it is. Moreover, the possibility in (11) is reproduced with strict NPIs we have cited:

(12) a. There was no doctor there who felt all that well.
 b. There was no doctor there who knew jackshit$_A$ about tropical diseases.
 c. There was no doctor there who told a living soul.
 d. There was no doctor there who had seen Mary in ages.

The contrast between cases like (11)–(12) and (7)–(8) is the relevant problem. If the NDEL Clausemate Condition of chapter 8 blocks the latter, how does it fail to block the former, in which strict NPIs also seem to be separated from their licensers by a restrictive relative clause boundary?

Following McCawley (1998:460–463), we believe that these cases represent a construction different from restrictive relative clauses, one whose elements just look like relative clauses. McCawley called this grammatical phenomenon *pseudo-relative clause* and presented several pieces of evidence for the distinction between it and standard restrictive relatives. One of these was the observation that extraction from pseudo-relative clauses is not nearly as acceptability-reducing as extraction from true relative clauses. We accept McCawley's view.

While we are far from having a full account of these sentences, we are led to the conclusion that the strict NPI is licensed internal to the pseudo-relative clause. We propose that in this atypical construction, *no doctor* raises from the subject position of the pseudo-relative clause. So a schematic of the structure of (12a) would be [There was [no doctor] here [who <no doctor> felt all that well]]. Since one occurrence of *no doctor* occupies the subject position of the pseudo-relative clause, it is in a local relation to the strict NPI. We assume this is sufficient for NEG deletion, although we cannot pursue the matter here.

Schmerling (1971:202) made another important observation that supports the previous sketchy remarks. Examples otherwise parallel to (12) in which the pseudo-relative clause is itself negated are ungrammatical:

(13) *There was no one in the huge lecture hall who didn't utter a peep when . . .

This observation generalizes to the strict NPIs we have repeatedly cited:

(14) a. *There was no doctor there who didn't know jackshit$_A$ about tropical diseases.

b. *There was no doctor there who hadn't seen Mary in ages.

This state of affairs can be taken to be a consequence of our proposal that in such cases *no doctor* originates inside the pseudo-relative because under that assumption, the ill-formedness in (13) and (14) falls under whatever constraints block the simpler (15a,b):

(15) a. *No doctor didn't know jackshit$_A$ about tropical diseases.

b. *No doctor hadn't seen Mary in ages.

We conclude that, despite first impressions, pseudo-relative clause cases like those discovered by Schmerling do not threaten our argument from data like (7) and (8).

10.2 Gajewski's Proposal

Our results here have important implications for conclusions drawn in Gajewski 2007. The main thrust of that work is the development of a Bartsch-style approach to Classical NR that can account for the fact that strict NPIs are licensed in the complement of negated CNRPs (as shown in chapter 1). Gajewski (2007:303) pursues this goal by showing that "strict NPIs are allowed under negated NR predicates because these are in fact Anti-Additive." He continues (p. 306), "[I]t is neither necessary nor sufficient for a strict NPI to be a clause-mate with its licenser. What is crucial . . . is the semantic properties of the environment of the strict NPI." By *semantic properties*, Gajewski refers to antiadditivity.

The actual principle he gives is (16a):

(16) a. (Gajewski 2007:302)
"A strict NPI a is licensed in a sentence S if there is a constituent b containing a such that b is Anti-Additive with respect to the maximal F-projection* of a."

b. (Gajewski 2007:302)
"They [strict NPIs] are not licensed by merely DE [downward entailing] contexts, but instead require a context that is Anti-Additive."

Condition (16a) says in effect that if a strict NPI is in an antiadditive environment, it is grammatical. Moreover, it is clear that (16a) is erroneously stated without a needed *only* before the word *licensed*. Without *only*, (16a) fails to indicate that a strict NPI is *not* grammatical when occurring in a *non-antiadditive* context. That such a claim is nonetheless intended is clear from statement (16b), which, in the article itself, precedes Gajewski's statement of (16a).

To clarify, we begin with the following example (Gajewski 2007:293):

(17) Bill doesn't think Mary will leave until tomorrow.

Gajewski shows that negated CNRPs like *think* are, given the excluded middle presupposition, antiadditive for their complement clauses. That is supposedly why, in his terms, the strong NPI *until tomorrow* is licensed.

But the previous section showed that antiadditivity does not suffice and that a necessary condition on strict NPIs is that they stand in a local relation to their licensers. Hence, Gajewski's condition (16a) is insufficient and would, in particular, fail to block all the ungrammatical cases of (7) and (8).

Of course, one could complicate Gajewski's condition to make it sensitive to islands, rendering it consistent with data like those in (7) and (8). But such a move would be otiose. Least significantly, it would not satisfy Gajewski's goal of a purely semantic account of NPI licensing. Further, it would raise the issue of why a semantic property such as licensing by an antiadditive DP would be sensitive to islands. This issue does not arise in our framework, since such cases involve a syntactic phenomenon, NEG raising, that provides independent motivation for the relevance of islands. The following two chapters develop and justify this view in detail.

Further, consider the following data:

(18) a.   Jane forgot to eat or drink.
      b.   Jane forgot to eat and Jane forgot to drink.

Example (18a) entails (18b), showing that the verb *forget* is decreasing with respect to its infinitival complement. Moreover, (18b) also entails (18a), showing that *forget* in such cases is antiadditive. Therefore, Gajewski's principle (16a) predicts that such complements can contain grammatical strict NPIs. But in fact, they cannot:[1]

(19) a.   *Jane forgot to do a fucking thing.
      b.   *Jane forgot to do jackshit$_A$.
      c.   *Jane forgot to drink a drop.

The failure of strict NPIs to occur in the infinitival complements of *forget* may relate to island conditions since there is some ground to think that such complements are weak islands. But as this issue is not strongly relevant to present concerns, we will not consider that possibility.

Next, we observe that the problems with Gajewski's principle (16a) go far beyond issues of islands. In particular, the claim that antiadditivity is a sufficient condition for the grammatical occurrence of strict NPIs is false even for simple clauses in which no question of islands arises. So strict NPIs are not grammatical if their potential licenser is a *zero* form, although these define antiadditive contexts:

(20) a. *Zero doctors lifted a finger to help her.
   b. *Zero doctors felt all that well.
   c. *Zero doctors did jackshit$_A$ on Thursday.
   d. *Zero doctors did a single thing about that.
   e. *Zero doctors have seen Mary in ages.

This conclusion is strengthened because phrases that are both increasing and decreasing like *zero or more NP* are also antiadditive:

(21) a. Zero or more people sang and zero or more people danced. ⇔
   b. Zero or more people sang or danced.

But such forms also do not permit strict NPIs even in simple clauses:[2]

(22) a. *Zero or more people lifted a finger to help her.
   b. *Zero or more people contributed jackshit$_A$.

The earlier evidence in (7) and (8) showing the insufficiency of a pure antiadditive account of strict NPIs based on the relative clause island facts and that in (19) showing the insufficiency based on the infinitival complements of *forget* thus expands independent grounds showing that occurrence in an antiadditive context is not a sufficient condition for the grammaticality of a strict NPI.

Finally, Gajewski's proposal faces problems distinct from the mere insufficiency of the antiadditive condition argued so far. Consider:

(23) a. They didn't tell Ted to sing or dance.
   b. They didn't tell Ted to sing and they didn't tell Ted to dance.

Example (23a) entails (23b), since negated *tell* is decreasing with respect to its infinitival complement. But (23b) does not entail (23a). That follows because although they might not have instructed Ted about singing in particular or dancing in particular, they might have told him to do one or the other.

So the infinitival complement of negated *tell* is not an antiadditive context and according to Gajewski's account (16a) (interpreted in line with (16b)) should not allow strict NPIs. But it actually allows those NPIs seen to be ungrammatical in the (nonetheless) antiadditive context of (19):

(24) a. They didn't tell Ted to do a fucking thing.
   b. They didn't tell Ted to do jackshit$_A$.
   c. They didn't tell Ted to drink a drop.

The facts in (24) are direct counterexamples to Gajewski's proposal that only antiadditive contexts are suitable hosts for strict NPIs. While Gajewski's proposal might be able to be modified to cover (24) by taking into account the issue of scope position, we note that there is no actual proposal to consider.

10.3   Implications

Gajewski's principle (16a) is clearly not viable, and we have shown that part of what it gets wrong, the failure of antiadditive contexts like those in (7) and (8) to permit strict NPIs, argues for the relevance of island conditions. That follows since in standard terms the legitimate NPI licensers in those contexts are separated from the strict NPIs they fail to license by island boundaries. In present terms, this means that the structures could only arise via the raising of unary NEGs out of islands. The fact that such raising is blocked with respect to the islands in (7) and (8) is simply a foretaste of a much more general blockage of (unary) NEG raising out of islands discussed in detail in the following two chapters.

Gajewski's condition (16a) was a major element in his overall attempt to reduce Classical NR to a purely semantic phenomenon, within the tradition initiated by Bartsch's (1973) work. If successful, the general logic would have undermined a syntactic view of Classical NR by showing that appeal to syntax was a useless complication. That is, the exceptional grammaticality of strict NPIs in the complements of CNRPs, critical in attempts to support a syntactic view of Classical NR, would have been shown to follow from independently supported semantic conditions, in particular, from (16a). But the untenable character of (16a) reveals that Gajewski's attempt to use it to account for the grammaticality of strict NPIs in CNRP complement clauses like (17) must fail as well.

We have briefly indicated, though, how a NEG-raising view combined with the fact that ungrammatical cases like (7) and (8) would require raising out of syntactic islands argues, contrary to Gajewski's view, for the syntactic nature of what is called the licensing of strict NPIs. The next two chapters develop this line of argument from syntactic islands for a syntactic view of Classical NR at length with respect to a wide range of island types.

The bottom line is that far from undermining a syntactic view of Classical NR, Gajewski's condition (16a) represents a clear failure of nonsyntactic ideas to properly account for this phenomenon.

Arguments

11 Islands: Preliminaries

11.1 Goal

In this chapter and the next, we will argue that Classical NR is subject to island constraints. This result does not follow from any known semantic/ pragmatic approach to Classical NR, and we see no way it can be made to follow.

In this chapter, we discuss in some detail the islands resulting from clausal passivization and topicalization. In chapter 12, we will provide a somewhat more cursory survey of various other island types.

Previous discussion (that we are aware of) of a role for island constraints in constraining Classical NR phenomena consists largely of remarks in Seuren 1974a:185, 1974b:122. There, Seuren explicitly claimed that cases like (1a,b) showed that Classical NR was subject to the island constraints posited in Ross 1967 [1986] involving complex DPs and coordinate structures:[1]

(1) a. *I don't believe the rumor that Tom has found the solution yet.

    b. *I don't think Tom has found the solution yet and is a reliable chap.

However, in our view, (1a) does not provide a straightforward argument for the relevance of island constraints. The problem is that the verb *rumor* itself is not a CNRP, and it could be argued that (1a) fails simply for that reason. We in effect address this objection in chapter 12 by considering cases where the noun with a clausal complement corresponds to a verb that *is* a CNRP.

Even though the issue suggested by coordinate cases like (1b) of whether Classical NR is constrained by the Coordinate Structure Constraint deserves much further study, we will focus on different island types in this monograph.[2]

Despite the early invocation of the role of island constraints in constraining Classical NR, other works from that period and later ones say little or nothing about islands. Horn's (1978) encyclopedic paper on Classical NR does state:

(2) (Horn 1978:153)
"If NR is a rule of grammar, it is not surprising that it shares with other extraction rules (as well as other syntactic processes) the property of sensitivity to weak and strong island constraints."

Oddly, though, this strong claim is justified hardly at all. It is illustrated and supported not by citation of any standard island constraints from English or other languages but exclusively by reference to a single pair of related facts about Classical Greek:

(3) (Horn 1978:152)
"For now, it suffices to mention that the only Classical Greek verb of saying which governs the infinitive (rather than finite clauses introduced by complementizers *hoti* and *hōs*) is also the only one permitting 'anticipatory negatives.'"

Here, the term *anticipatory negatives* is in effect a reference to a Classical NR reading. These limited observations would, however, support the need to appeal to islandhood specifically for finite complements as islands. That is an entirely nonstandard assumption and one that does not hold for English. Moreover, Horn (1978) did not attempt to support it. Thus, while stating (2), Horn gave no actual justification for it.

Perhaps the extreme weakness of the 1978 database supporting (2) explains why, despite the extensive discussions of Classical NR in Horn's (1989 [2001]) mammoth and extraordinarily wide-ranging and detailed study of negation, neither the term *island* nor the term *movement (constraint)* occurs in the index of that work.

11.2   Strict NPIs

Some CNRPs allow their clausal complements to be passivized or topicalized.[3] One is the verb *believe*. When a clausal complement of *believe* contains a strict NPI whose NEG has undergone Classical NR to the matrix clause, then passivization or topicalization is impossible. Several examples illustrate this generalization:

(4) a.   Wanda does not believe that Kevin would breathe a word about it.
    b.   *That Kevin would breathe a word about it, Wanda does not
          believe.

   c. *That Kevin would breathe a word about it was not believed by
      Wanda.

   d. It was not believed by Wanda that Kevin would breathe a word
      about it.

(5) a. Victor did not believe that a fucking thing had gone wrong.
   b. *That a fucking thing had gone wrong, Victor did not believe.
   c. *That a fucking thing had gone wrong was not believed by Victor.
   d. It was not believed by Victor that a fucking thing had gone wrong.

(6) a. Laura does not believe that Sheila has prayed in years.
   b. *That Sheila has prayed in years, Laura does not believe.
   c. *That Sheila has prayed in years is not believed by Laura.
   d. It is not believed by Laura that Sheila has prayed in years.

Striking in paradigms (4)–(6) is that the strict NPIs are grammatical in the
simple active cases and in those passives where the complement clause is
extraposed. These are exactly the cases where the complement clause is *not*
an island.[4]

Similar examples with *expect* and *anticipate* are given in (7) and (8):

(7) a. They did not expect that Kevin would leave until midnight.
   b. *That Kevin would leave until midnight, they did not expect.

(8) a. They did not anticipate that Sandra would stop at anything to screw
     over Larry.

   b. *That Sandra would stop at anything to screw over Larry, they did
     not anticipate.

Moreover, parallel grammaticality facts are associated with clauses in
subject position even without passivization or topicalization:

(9) a. It is not likely that Mary will lift a finger to help.
   b. *That Mary will lift a finger to help is not likely.

In (9b), the *that* clause is the subject, and it cannot contain a strict NPI
whose NEG has raised to the matrix clause.

Facts like those in (1)–(9) are highly problematic for nonsyntactic views
of Classical NR for the following reason. As we have indicated, such views
take the phenomenon to be based on the possibility of constructing inferences
from the wide scope reading of negation in host main clauses based on a
CNRP to the reading where the negation scopes internal to the complement.
Such a possibility depends on the semantic properties of the CNRPs and the
excluded middle property. In particular, as noted in chapter 10, Gajewski
(2007) claims that given an excluded middle presupposition, the clause

embedded under a negated CNRP is an antiadditive context, and hence strict NPIs are licensed.

But as far as we can see, the relevant semantic properties of CNRPs in (4)–(9) do not vary depending on whether the complement clause is postverbal, a topic, a passivized subject, or a nonpassive subject. Nor, given the same main clause predicate in each set of cases, would one expect any variation in the excluded middle property. The conclusion is, then, that if the excluded middle property holds in any of these cases, it holds in all of them. The nonsyntactic approaches would therefore appear to wrongly predict that Classical NR interpretations should be found in all of them and thus that strict NPIs should be licensed in their complements. So, minimally, such approaches need to be supplemented with some complicating further conditions blocking strict NPIs in these cases.

Of course, any syntactic view of Classical NR also needs to block the ungrammatical cases. But while mysterious from currently popular nonsyntactic vantage points, from a syntactic point of view the facts in (4)–(9) are approachable by noting well-known syntactic facts. Namely, Classical NR in the ungrammatical cases would have to take place from complements that end up as topics or subjects, *both known to be syntactic islands*, while the posited raising in the grammatical original examples like (4a,d) is raising from non-island object or extraposed complement clauses.

Suppose that, on the basis of the evidence so far, we posit the following constraint:

(10) *The Island Sensitivity of NEG Raising Condition (first version)*
    A NEG cannot extract from an island.

A revised, more adequate version will be provided and justified in section 13.4, motivated inter alia by facts concerning Horn clauses.

11.3 Remnant Movement

A further important issue clouds the status of our claim that island boundaries interfere with otherwise potentially grammatical Classical NR examples. This is relevant specifically to islands formed by the topicalization of a clause or the presence of a clause in subject position in passives or unaccusatives. In such cases, which arguably involve the origin of the clauses in nonisland object positions, topicalization yields a fronted topic position that is an island. Consider (4a,b), repeated here:

(11) a. Wanda does not believe that Kevin would breathe a word about it.
    b. *That Kevin would breathe a word about it, Wanda does not believe.

Suppose, though, that in (11b) the NEG was extracted from the complement clause's pretopicalization base position and not from the induced topic position. The result would then not be an island violation given the standard way island constraints are conceived, since the base position does not represent an island. This means that there remains a so far unblocked way to analyze ungrammatical cases like (11b) under Classical NR *even if island constraints correctly block one analysis.*

In other words, analyses like the following (presented informally) need to be blocked:

(12) a. Wanda believes that Kevin would not breathe a word about it →
    (via Classical NR)
    b. Wanda does not believe that Kevin would breathe a word about it →
    (via Topicalization)
    c. *That Kevin would breathe a word about it, Wanda does not believe.

In this schema, Classical NR is not blocked by the fact that topics are islands since raising of the NEG from the clausal object position is not raising out of an island. In a now common terminology, the step from (12b) to (12c) would be an instance of *remnant movement* of the finite clause from which NEG has raised. We will present two possible approaches to this issue.

The first approach appeals to a constraint on remnant movement related to a proposal in Postal 2004b. The second approach proposes a partially novel way of stating island constraints that has the effect of treating cases like (12c) as island violations.

The first approach posits the following condition:

(13) *The NEG Remnant Movement Condition*
    If NEG raises out of a clause C, then C cannot itself be raised.

Condition (13) is related to proposals in Postal 2004b:122, which are concerned with examples like the following:

(14) a. Something quite trivial is likely to be eating Gilbert.
    b. *How likely to be eating Gilbert is something quite trivial?

Postal proposes that (14b) is unacceptable because the raising source position is antipronominal, meaning that it is incompatible with weak definite pronouns. As he states:

(15) (Postal 2004b:13)
"[A]ny grammatical phenomenon that brings about a raising remnant clause not being both c-commanded and linearly preceded by the raisee requires that the instance of raising involve a resumptive pronoun. This will inter alia generate ungrammaticalities in cases where the raising site is an antipronominal context."

Clearly, the source position of any raised NEG cannot be conceived of as a pronominal position, in particular, not as one occupied by a resumptive pronoun. Therefore, condition (13) can be taken to follow from (15).

An alternative to condition (13) would reformulate the island condition (10) in a way referencing all the occurrences of an extracted element. In these terms, island condition (10) would be reformulated as in (16):

(16) If I is a clausal island node and dominates an occurrence of a node Q that is NEG, then every occurrence of Q is dominated by an occurrence of I.

Consider again (11b). Because of the NPI in the embedded clause, the NEG originating in *breathe a word* must have undergone Classical NR. Since the embedded clause occurs in the overall structure both in the object position of *believe* and in the topic position and since the NEG has an occurrence inside of the clause in topic position, which is an island, condition (16) requires all instances of the NEG to be inside an occurrence of the clause. But the occurrence of NEG following the finite Aux is obviously not internal to any occurrence of the complement clause, accounting for the ungrammaticality.

11.4   C-Command

In the previous section, we claimed that examples involving Classical NR from a topicalized or passivized clause are blocked because such complement clauses are islands. Consider (5) again, repeated here:

(17) a.   Victor did not believe that a fucking thing had gone wrong.
     b.   *That a fucking thing had gone wrong, Victor did not believe.
     c.   *That a fucking thing had gone wrong was not believed by Victor.
     d.   It was not believed by Victor that a fucking thing had gone wrong.

In (17c), NEG cannot raise from the *that* clause subject, because it is an island. But (17c) also violates an additional syntactic constraint. In such a case, the NEG must raise from the subject position to the Aux position to its right. Such movement violates the Principles and Parameters/Minimalist constraint on movement in (18), repeated from chapter 5:

(18) *The C-Command Condition on Movement*
     If X moves from P_1 to P_2, then X's occurrence in P_2 c-commands X's occurrence in P_1.

From the point of view of this constraint, the *that* clause in (17c) is in subject position, which, in the Principles and Parameters/Minimalist framework, is Spec,TP. But the NEG appears to the right of the finite Aux *was*. Therefore, the *that* clause asymmetrically c-commands the surface position of NEG. So it is then impossible for the surface position of NEG (following *was*) to c-command the base position of NEG contained in the *that* clause.

Parallel considerations hold of (17b), which involves a topic position rather than a subject position. Therefore, examples such as (17b,c) are blocked by the C-Command Condition on Movement (putting aside the illicit remnant movement derivations described above). The implication is that even if topicalized and passivized *that* clauses were not islands, the movement in (17b,c) would be blocked by an independent syntactic constraint. Hence, this alternative syntactic constraint is equally problematic for the semantic/pragmatic view outlined in chapter 1.

In the next chapter, we consider many other islands, for which the C-Command Condition on Movement in (18) plays no role.

12 Islands: Survey

12.1 Preview

In this chapter, we survey a range of cases where island constraints block Classical NR. At issue are examples invoking the Complex NP Constraint, clause-internal topics, truth predicates, *wh*-islands, clause-internal clefts, pseudoclefts, and Negative Inversion. The clear generalization is that Classical NR is never possible from an island. Such a generalization is especially striking for cases where all known semantic conditions on Classical NR are met (e.g., for truth predicates), but Classical NR is still not possible.

As known since Ross's (1967 [1986]) establishment of the notion *island*, syntactic raising phenomena are subject to island constraints. Therefore, it is possible to account naturally for the above generalization under the assumption that classical NR is a syntactic raising phenomenon, as outlined in chapter 1.

12.2 Complex NP Constraint Cases

Consider first clausal complements of nouns. Such nominal complement clauses are islands and therefore, on our syntactic account, these complements cannot be origins for Classical NR.

The islandhood of clausal complements to nouns is illustrated in (1):

(1) a.   When do you believe that the moon will vanish?
    b.   *When do you hold the belief that the moon will vanish?

The following sentences indicate that when a strict NPI appears in a clause embedded under *belief*, its NEG cannot raise to the matrix clause:

(2) a.   I don't believe that the moon will vanish until Thursday.
    b.   I hold the belief that the moon will not vanish until Thursday.
    c.   *I don't hold the belief that the moon will vanish until Thursday.

Similar facts hold for the complement of *expectation*:

(3) a.   What town do you expect that they will find rebels in?
    b.   *What town do you have the expectation that they will find
         rebels in?

(4) a.   I don't expect that they will find a living soul in that town.
    b.   I have the expectation that they will not find a living soul in that
         town.
    c.   *I don't have the expectation that they will find a living soul in that
         town.

That is, just as noun complements preclude interrogative extraction, they
also do not allow strict NPIs whose licensers are outside of the complement
clause.[1] Other examples illustrating the same constraint are given in (5):

(5) a.   *Deborah did not have the expectation that Ted would stop at
         anything to get promoted.
    b.   *Deborah did not entertain the thought that Carolyn would breathe a
         word about it.
    c.   *Deborah did not hold the belief that Carolyn had told a living soul.
    d.   *Deborah did not have the expectation that a damned/fucking thing
         would go wrong.
    e.   *Deborah did not entertain the thought that Karen would lift a finger
         to help Sidney.
    f.   *Karen did not hold the belief that Ted would learn squat$_A$ about
         Turkish politics.

12.3   Clause-Internal Topics

As is well-known, topicalization internal to an embedded clause turns that
clause into an island:

(6) a.   When does Leslie believe that Jim should call Irene?
    b.   *When does Leslie believe that Irene, Jim should call?

    Correspondingly, Classical NR is blocked in such cases:

(7) a.   Leslie doesn't believe that Jim should call Irene until tomorrow.
    b.   *Leslie doesn't believe that Irene, Jim should call until tomorrow.

(8) a.   Leslie doesn't believe that a damned thing upset Lester.
    b.   *Leslie doesn't believe that Lester, a damned thing upset.

(9) a.   Leslie doesn't believe that Carl said squat$_A$ to the chairman.

    b.   *Leslie doesn't believe that the chairman, Carl said squat$_A$ to.

Since (6a,b) indicate that internal topicalization renders the complement clause an island, the fact that (7b), (8b), and (9b) containing strict NPIs are ungrammatical then argues that Classical NR is impossible out of that kind of island as well.

12.4   Truth Predicates

In chapter 1, we outlined Bartsch's (1973) pragmatic approach based on the excluded middle property. Truth predicates are particularly problematic for such an approach. In this section, we develop a criticism of a pragmatic or semantic account of the relevant properties of truth predicates, specifically *true* or *the case*.

The discussion begins with key observations from Horn 1975:291–292, 1978:203:

(10) a.   It is not true/the case that 2 plus 2 is 8.

    b.   It is true/the case/that 2 plus 2 is not 8.

Despite the distinct positions of the negations in these cases, the (10a) examples are logically equivalent to the (10b) examples. Recall that on Bartsch's (1973) analysis, the excluded middle property ensures that a sentence (based on a CNRP) with negation in the matrix clause entails the corresponding sentence with negation instead in the embedded clause. With truth predicates, such an entailment is guaranteed independently of the excluded middle property by the semantics of the predicate. Therefore, on the semantic/pragmatic analysis, the main clause predicates in (10) should be CNRPs.

However, when these predicates are negated, embedded clause strict NPIs are impossible:

(11) a.   It is true that Carolyn will not breathe a word about it.

    b.   *It is not true that Carolyn will breathe a word about it.

(12) a.   It is true that I didn't do a fucking thing.

    b.   *It is not true that I did a fucking thing.

(13) a.   It is true that Karen didn't lift a finger to help Sidney.

    b.   *It is not true that Karen lifted a finger to help Sidney.

(14) a.   It is true that Teresa has not been seen in days/years.

    b.   *It is not true that Teresa has been seen in days/years.

The strict NPIs in the (b) cases are ungrammatical. This is a simple indication that the hope of a purely semantic or pragmatic treatment of Classical NR based on logical equivalence is untenable.

Truth predicates also raise a problem for the pragmatic account of the class of CNRPs given by Horn and Bayer (1984:402). These authors state, "What is common to all NR predicates is the relative slimness of the functional difference between the preraised form with lower negation and the logical form with the upstairs negative taking wide scope." However, since with truth predicates, the form with lower negation and the form with higher negation are logically equivalent, this characterization determines that truth predicates should be CNRPs. But we have shown that they are not. See Gajewski 2007:308 for an unconvincing account of this fact in terms of presupposition projection with truth predicates.

While semantic/pragmatic approaches would expect truth predicates to be CNRPs, in our framework the fact that they are not CNRPs reduces to the fact that the complements of truth predicates are islands, as illustrated in (15)–(17):

(15) a. It is true that he can fix your engine in that way.
     b. *In what way is it true that he can fix your engine <in what way>?

(16) a. It is true that James can stand on his head for a long time.
     b. *How long is it true that James can stand on his head <how long>?

(17) a. It is true that he left for that reason.
     b. *the reason why it is true that he left <why>

So where nonsyntactic views of Classical NR appear to wrongly predict that truth predicates should be CNRPs, a syntactic view appealing to island constraints correctly predicts that they cannot be.

12.5 *Wh*-Islands

The syntactic approach to Classical NR predicts that it should be constrained by *wh*-islands. The prediction is difficult to test since most Classical NR verbs do not take interrogative complements:

(18) a. I think that it will rain.
     b. *I think whether it will rain.
     c. I believe that it will rain.
     d. *I believe whether it will rain.
     e. It seems that it will rain.
     f. *It seems whether it will rain.

    g. I want to leave.

    h. *I want what to eat.

However, the verb *plan* takes interrogative complements, as in (19), and it is also a CNRP, as seen in (20):

(19) a. I always plan what to eat on a trip.

      b. I did not plan whether I should tell Joan the whole story.

(20) a. I plan not to leave early.

      b. I don't plan to leave early.   (interpretation identical to (20a))

Furthermore, strict NPIs are possible with *plan* when Classical NR is found (supporting the classification of *plan* as a CNRP):

(21) a. I plan not to leave until tomorrow.

      b. I don't plan to leave until tomorrow.

Given the above data, the verb *plan* can be used to test the prediction that Classical NR cannot extract NEGs from *wh*-islands:

(22) a. I plan what not to eat on a long trip.

      b. I do not plan what to eat on a long trip.

Examples (22a,b) have clearly different interpretations. While (22a) involves some planning about what people should not eat on a long trip, (22b) involves no planning at all. Rather, it affirms the absence of any kind of planning with regard to trip food consumption. So (22a,b) lack the kind of semantic equivalence characteristic of Classical NR cases.

But that lack of equivalence follows from the assumption that Classical NR is subject to island constraints. Since the complement of *plan* in (22b) is a *wh*-island, Classical NR is then predictably impossible. Hence, (22b) can only be understood with matrix clause scope for the negation.[2]

The conclusion from (22) is reinforced by data on strict NPIs:

(23) a.   I planned how not to tell a living soul about the money.

      b. *I did not plan how to tell a living soul about the money.

A matrix clause NEG cannot license a strict NPI in the embedded clause in (23b).

Under the syntactic approach, the data in (22) and the strict NPI data in (23) both follow from island constraints. Since embedded interrogatives are *wh*-islands, it is impossible for NEG to raise out of the embedded *wh*-clause into the matrix clause, as illustrated in (24):

(24) *I did NEG_1 plan how to tell [<NEG_1> a living soul] about the money

On the Minimalist conception of Classical NR outlined in section 3.8, the NEG in Classical NR moves through Spec,CP. Since the specifier of the embedded CP is filled by *how* in (24), such movement is impossible. Furthermore, movement of NEG$_1$ directly to the main clause from the embedded clause, without passing through Spec,CP, violates the island constraint.

12.6 Clause-Internal Clefts

Just as clause-internal topics block Classical NR, so do clause-internal clefts:

(25) a. I think that it's Ted who didn't say a goddamn thing.
 b. *I don't think that it's Ted who said a goddamn thing.

(26) a. I think that it's Ted who didn't tell a living soul.
 b. *I don't think that it's Ted who told a living soul.

(27) a. I think that it is Ted who has not spoken to his mother in ages.
 b. *I don't think that it is Ted who has spoken to his mother in ages.

 Clearly, clefting blocks standard cases of movement:

(28) a. *What do you think that it's Ted who said?
 b. *Who did you think that it's Ted who told?
 c. *How long ago do you think that it's Ted who has spoken to his mother?

12.7 Pseudoclefts

It is impossible for Classical NR to extract from the clause of a pseudocleft construction (see also Bošković 1997:241):

(29) a. I don't think that Ted knows shit about Turkish.
 b. *What I don't think is that Ted knows shit about Turkish.

(30) a. I don't think that the movie was half bad.
 b. *What I don't think is that the movie was half bad.

(31) a. I don't think that Ted will be here until 6:00.
 b. *What I don't think is that Ted will be here until 6:00.

 Although it is difficult to embed a pseudocleft construction, it is clear that the clausal part is an island:

(32) a. You said that what you think is that Ted talked to Mary.
 b. *Who did you say that what you think is that Ted talked to?

12.8 Negative Inversion

Negative Inversion foci also create islands (see chapter 13 for a detailed treatment of Negative Inversion):

(33) a. You said that under no circumstances would John fix his car in that way.
 b. *How did you say that under no circumstances would John fix his car?

Therefore, it is unsurprising to find that Negative Inversion foci also block Classical NR. First, note that *no fewer than* does not license strict NPIs:

(34) *No fewer than three people said a fucking thing about those dogs.

However, *no fewer than* phrases, although defining increasing functions, do license Negative Inversion, since they have the property SYNNEG introduced and motivated in chapter 14:

(35) No fewer than three dogs did Tod not say a fucking thing about.

In light of these facts, consider the following contrast:

(36) a. I think that no fewer than three dogs did Tod not say a fucking thing about.
 b. *I don't think that [$_A$ [no fewer than three dogs] [$_B$ did Tod say a fucking thing about]].

Given the strict NPI in (36b), NEG must have raised from the embedded clause, since the increasing negative phrase based on *no fewer* could not license the strict NPI. But then the main clause NEG must have extracted from the island created by the Negative Inversion focus, which is barred because of the island, accounting for the ungrammaticality of (36b).

12.9 Intervention and Islands

Having surveyed a number of island constraints in the above sections, we now consider the possibility that some of those constraints might be subsumed under a general intervention constraint, due to Seuren:

(37) (Seuren 1974a:192)
 "There is, furthermore, the fact that the negative can only be raised out of an embedded S when it [the negation *not*] is *the highest operator*." (our emphasis)

Seuren did not give a fully explicit statement of the principle he was alluding to here, and because he was a supporter of the exclusively clausal/propositional level view of negation that we rejected in chapter 3, our formulation could not have followed his in any event. We propose the following revision consistent with our theoretical framework:

(38) *The Highest-Operator Constraint (on Classical NR)*
If a NEG raises from clause B to clause A, and NEG originates in a unary-NEG structure W = [NEG X], then W is the highest operator in B.

Seuren motivates his proposed constraint on Classical NR with observations like the following. A Classical NR example like (39a) can only have the interpretation of (39b), not that of (39c):

(39) a. I don't suppose Fred always falls asleep during meetings.
b. I suppose that Fred doesn't always fall asleep during meetings.
c. I suppose that Fred always doesn't fall asleep during meetings.

In our terms, in cases like (39a) the NEG originates in [NEG always], while in (39c) NEG originates in a position lower than *always*, specifically in [NEG fall], consistent with the meanings of these sentences. Under these assumptions, condition (38) properly blocks reading (39c) for (39a) while allowing reading (39b).

Another example that falls naturally under Seuren's constraint is (40b):

(40) a. Carol didn't see many people.
b. I don't think that Carol saw many people.

As noted in chapter 3, (40a) is ambiguous (NEG > *many*, or *many* > NEG). However, (40b) is not similarly ambiguous and only means (41a), not (41b):

(41) a. I think that Carol saw few people.
b. I think that many people, Carol didn't see.

This fact follows from Seuren's constraint. Example (40b) with interpretation (41b) would have the representation in (42):

(42) I do NEG_1 think that <[many people]$_2$> Carol [<NEG_1> see] DP_2

But clearly, *many people* in scope position is a higher operator than NEG and hence Classical NR is blocked by Seuren's constraint.[3]

Seuren does not define the concept *operator*. And we will not try to give a precise definition either except for the following remarks. We assume that this concept covers quantificational DPs and adverbs as well as modal auxiliaries. We assume that for quantificational DPs and adverbs, the Highest-Operator

Constraint is defined in terms of scope positions (so a DP in its scope position blocks NEG raising from a lower constituent). Definite DP subjects never have any consequences for Classical NR. We assume that they are not operators, and thus are always irrelevant for condition (38), or else that in any case where a definite DP might seem to otherwise wrongly invoke (38), the NEG involved raises from a higher position than the definite DP, yielding no detectable truth-conditional difference. As Larry Horn (personal communication) notes, some quantificational elements, including *usually*, do not block Classical NR. We have no current account of how to weaken (38) to allow such cases.

Some of the island constraints we have invoked might follow from Seuren's Highest-Operator Constraint. For example, consider the fact that a Negative Inversion focus creates an island for Classical NR:

(43) *I don't think that [$_A$ [no fewer than three dogs] [$_B$ did Tod say a fucking thing about]].

As noted in section 12.8, since Negative Inversion has taken place, the embedded clause B is an island, and a NEG cannot escape from it under Classical NR. But (43) with NEG raising from the embedded clause also violates Seuren's Highest-Operator Constraint on the plausible assumption that *no fewer than three dogs* is an operator.

A number of the island constraints we discussed above could perhaps be covered by Seuren's constraint. These include clause-internal topics, *wh*-islands, clause-internal clefts, and pseudoclefts. However, it is less clear how Seuren's constraint would apply to topic islands (see chapter 11), the Complex NP Constraint, or truth predicate cases.

12.10 Islands and Nonstrict NPIs

In this section, we very briefly show that most of the island types considered in chapter 11 and earlier in this chapter that block strict NPIs do not block nonstrict NPIs, that is, reversal structure NPIs. The general procedure is to substitute nonstrict NPIs for strict ones in a relevant subset of earlier examples, making only minimal other revisions if any.

The following examples illustrate nonstrict NPIs in topic and subject clauses:

(44) a. Wanda does not believe that Kevin would ever discuss it.
   b. That Kevin would ever discuss it, Wanda does not believe.
   c. That Kevin would ever discuss it was not believed by Wanda.

(45) a. It is not likely that Mary would ever go to France.
   b. That Mary would ever go to France is not likely.

(46) a. It is not likely that Mary knows any physics.
   b. That Mary knows any physics is not likely.

These examples show that nonstrict NPIs are acceptable in the relevant contexts. This suggests that the ungrammaticality of strict NPIs in topic and subject clauses is due to their unary-NEG structure, as we have suggested in the preceding sections.

Examples (47)–(51) illustrate nonstrict NPIs in complex noun phrases:

(47) a. I don't expect that they will find anyone there.
   b. I have the expectation that they will not find anyone there.
   c. I don't have the expectation that they will find anyone there.

(48) a. I don't believe that he has ever been to France.
   b. I hold the belief that he has never been to France.
   c. I don't hold the belief that he has ever been to France.

The next set of examples illustrates nonstrict NPIs with clause-internal topics:

(49) a. Leslie doesn't believe that Jim should call Irene at any time.
   b. Leslie doesn't believe that Irene, Jim should call at any time.

(50) a. Leslie does not believe that Jim taught any physics to the first-year students.
   b. Leslie does not believe that to the first-year students, Jim taught any physics.

(51) a. Leslie does not believe that Jim ever spoke harshly to the first-year students.
   b. Leslie does not believe that to the first-year students, Jim ever spoke harshly.

Examples (52) and (53) show nonstrict NPIs in the complement of a truth predicate:

(52) a. It is true that Carolyn will not say anything about it.
   b. It is not true that Carolyn will say anything about it.

(53) a. It is true that he won't ever go to Paris.
   b. It is not true that he will ever go to Paris.

Cases (54)–(55) document nonstrict NPIs in *wh*-islands. As opposed to their behavior in the islands considered above, nonstrict NPIs are ungrammatical in *wh*-islands:

(54) a. I plan how not to teach any physics again.
   b. *I don't plan how to teach any physics again.

(55) a.   I plan how not to ever set foot in there.
     b.   *I don't plan how to ever set foot in there.

The following examples illustrate nonstrict NPIs in embedded clauses containing a cleft construction:

(56) a.   I think that it is Ted who doesn't know any physics.
     b. ??I don't think that it is Ted who knows any physics.

(57) a.   I think that it is Ted who has never been to France.
     b.   *I don't think that it is Ted who has ever been to France.

Further, the data sets in (58) and (59) show nonstrict NPIs in pseudocleft constructions:

(58) a.   I don't think that Ted knows anything about Turkish.
     b.   What I don't think is that Ted knows anything about Turkish.

(59) a.   I don't think that Ted has ever been to France.
     b.   What I don't think is that Ted has ever been to France.

Finally, the following examples illustrate nonstrict NPIs in a clause manifesting Negative Inversion:

(60) a.   I think that no fewer than three dogs has Tod not ever loved.
     b.   *I don't think that no fewer than three dogs has Tod ever loved.

(61) a.   I think that during no fewer than three semesters has Tod not
             taught any physics.
     b.   *I don't think that during no fewer than three semesters has Tod
             taught any physics.

The conclusion is that most island types shown earlier to block strict NPIs have essentially no blocking effect on nonstrict ones. The exceptions are the cases of clauses with *wh*-islands, cleft constructions, and clauses with Negative Inversion. We will consider these briefly. But first we turn to the logic of what should be concluded from the general acceptability of nonstrict NPIs in most islands even when their licensers are external to the island.

The basis of the island context contrast between the two NPI types is a function of the interaction of the NDEL Clausemate Condition of chapter 8 with the Island Sensitivity of NEG Raising Condition given so far as (10) of chapter 11 (a revised version is provided at the end of chapter 13). We repeat these conditions here:

(62) *The NDEL Clausemate Condition*
     If NDEL(X, Y) and Y is a unary NEG, then X and Y are clausemates.

(63) *The Island Sensitivity of NEG Raising Condition (first version)*
     A NEG cannot extract from an island.

We pick one context containing an ungrammatical strict NPI and a corresponding grammatical nonstrict NPI to indicate how conditions (62) and (63) have the consequences just described:

(64) a. Leslie does not believe that Jim ever spoke harshly to the first-year students.
     b. Leslie does not believe that to the first-year students, Jim ever spoke harshly.
     c. Leslie does [NEG$_3$ believe] that to the first-year students, Jim [[NEG$_2$ [NEG$_1$ SOME] ever]] spoke harshly

(65) a. Leslie doesn't believe that Jim should call Irene until tomorrow.
     b. *Leslie doesn't believe that Irene, Jim should call until tomorrow.
     c. *Leslie does NEG$_1$ believe that Irene, Jim should call [<NEG$_1$> until tomorrow]

The structure of (64b) is given in (64c). In this structure, [NEG$_3$ believe] deletes NEG$_2$ and NEG$_2$ deletes NEG$_1$. There is no need for either NEG$_1$ or NEG$_2$ to raise to the matrix clause because long-distance deletion of NEG$_2$, a reversal NEG, is consistent with (62).

But in (65), *until tomorrow* is a unary-NEG structure. Therefore, a structure parallel to (64c) is not possible. Rather, the correct structure is given in (65c), where NEG$_1$ raises away from *until tomorrow* into the matrix. However, this raising violates (63), so the structure is ruled out.

The remaining issue is the unacceptability of examples involving nonstrict NPIs in the (b) examples of (54)–(57) and (60)–(61). First, we need to say that the distribution of nonstrict NPIs in these contexts requires much more investigation. We have found quite a bit of variability in grammaticality judgments in the examples we have looked at, especially for the cleft cases. Second, nothing in our framework predicts these sentences to be ungrammatical. All nonstrict NPIs in islands should be acceptable according to the principles of our analysis. We suggest that some other principle, independent of the ones we have presented, is responsible for the ungrammaticality of these examples. Plausibly, Linebarger's (1987) Immediate Scope Constraint is at issue. In the case of (54b) and (55b), the *wh*-phrase would be the intervener. In (56b) and (57b), the clefted constituent would be the intervener, while in (60b) and (61b), the intervener would be the increasing negative phrase. Such a view raises many questions that we are not able to pursue here.

12.11 Summary

We have presented a body of evidence supporting the view that Classical NR is blocked when the origin and host sites of the relevant NEG are separated by syntactic island boundaries. This fact threatens nonsyntactic views of Classical NR because the semantic/pragmatic alternative depends on the semantic properties of CNRPs and some version of the excluded middle property. The claim of the semantic/pragmatic approach is that the Classical NR reading (and the licensing of strong NPIs) can be derived by logic from the combination of the excluded middle property and the meaning associated with a NEG scoping over the main clause. It is then difficult to discern any reason why the construction of Classical NR *inferences* should be controlled by island boundaries determined by topicalization of clauses, subject clauses, and so on. This conclusion is strengthened by the fact that the same environments that block strict NPIs in the relevant cases do not in general block nonstrict NPIs. That makes it difficult to see how the strict NPI facts can be attributed to some general semantic facts relevant to NPI licensing.

To avoid possible misunderstanding, we have not claimed that it is *impossible* for such strict NPI sensitivity to islands to be incorporated into semantic/pragmatic approaches to Classical NR. But the burden of proof clearly lies with defenders of such views to show how the latter can provide a principled basis for the Classical NR island facts. While there is a literature claiming a semantic basis for certain so-called weak island effects (see Szabolcsi and Zwarts 1990, 1993, Szabolcsi 1992, 2007, Honcoop 1998, Szabolcsi and Den Dikken 1999), we know of no attempt to extend such ideas to islands generally nor any work addressing the distribution of Classical NR in such terms.

13   Horn Clauses: Preliminaries

13.1   Fronted NPIs

The examples in (1) represent standard cases of the *Negative Inversion* construction:

(1) a. Never has he visited Madrid.
    b. They proved that never had he visited Madrid.
    c. No student did she manage to convince of that.
    d. They determined that no student had she managed to convince
       of that.
    e. Not every student/Not many/Few students did they convince
       of that.

The most obvious characteristic of the construction is that the extracted non-*wh*-constituent in the clause-initial position, hereafter the *Negative Inversion (NI) focus*, cooccurs with subject-Aux inversion, which is obligatory, as the following examples indicate:[1]

(2) a. *Never he has visited Madrid.
    b. *They proved that never he had visited Madrid.
    c. *No student she managed to convince of that.
    d. *They determined that no student she had managed to convince
       of that.

We are aware of only a quite modest-sized literature on this construction, including Jackendoff 1972:364–369, Progovac 1994:99–102, McCawley 1998:582–586, Haegeman 2000, and Büring 2004. It is important to distinguish NI foci from fronted phrases without associated inversion in constructions usually referred as topicalization (see chapter 15).

Classical NR issues related to Negative Inversion arise from Horn's (1975:283) attestation of (3), which he had heard on a news broadcast:

(3) I don't think that ever before have the media played such a major role in a kidnapping.

That work cited no other examples of the construction involved and provided no analysis beyond advancing that the Aux inversion in the embedded clause "would perhaps similarly have been triggered by a pre-transported negative below *think*." The current relevance is that *think* is of course a CNRP and Horn added that analogs of (3) are impossible with non-CNRP main verbs, specifically *assume* and *realize* (but see sections 14.5 and 16.5 for apparent contra-indications), a conclusion endorsed by McCawley (1998:598). In other words, Horn (1975) assumed that the possibility of constructions like that in (3) depends on Classical NR.

Since we repeatedly refer to *that* clause complements like that in (3), with fronted NPI phrases and subject-Aux inversion word order, we need a term for them. Let us honor Horn for what we take to be a genuinely important discovery by referring to them as *Horn clauses*. What follows provides a more systematic characterization of this construction.

Horn repeated (3) in a later work (1978:168), but again provided no other examples. However, other cases (like these, from McCawley 1998:598) are not hard to come by:

(4) a. I don't suppose that under any circumstances would he help me.
    b. We didn't anticipate that at any time would our work create difficulties.

Furthermore, it is easy to find examples on the Web:

(5) a. and I don't believe that at any time did I have to resort to the 'always available' items that I sometimes did in the past. (boards.cruisecritic.com/archive/index.php/t-970352.html)
    b. I don't believe that at any time did traffic come to standstill. (theragblog.blogspot.com/.../police-state-amerikkka-right-in-my -own...)
    c. I don't believe that at ANY time did Rockstar consider closing shop. (www.destructoid.com/.../offended-by-hot-coffee-rockstar-will -give-y...–)

We offer as well the following, which are perfect for us:

(6) a. I don't believe that in any sense were those actions decisive.
    b. I didn't expect that for any reason would she agree to that.

   c. I don't guess that any of your friends have they yet interviewed.

   d. I didn't imagine that either of them would she be anxious to marry.

   e. I don't suppose that in any of his classes has he actually made such statements.

   f. I didn't think that at any previous point in my life had I been a real socialist.

   g. I didn't think that carvings of any respected deity had he destroyed.

Horn went on to add the following remarks about (3):

(7) (Horn 1978:168–169)

"In this sentence, Subject-Auxiliary Inversion has not only applied in a subordinate clause, it has apparently been triggered by a negative which appears in the surface structure in the clause above that where the inversion has taken place. In a theory with a syntactic rule of neg-raising, we might posit as an intermediate string in the derivation of (96) [= (3)] something of the form:

   I believe that NEG [the media have (at) some time before played such a major role in a kidnapping]

Whatever might be the details of the rules involved, *(at) some time* is realized as *ever* (triggered by the presence of NEG) and optionally fronted within its clause. If fronting applies, the result is approximately:

   (97′) I believe that $_S$[not ever the media have played . . .]

At this point Subject-Aux Inversion obligatorily applies, reversing the order of *the media* and *have*; inversion is triggered by the sentence negative in the downstairs clause. The negative element can now either raise over *believe*, resulting in the newsman's (96), or incorporate into *ever*, yielding:

   (98) I believe that never before have the media played such a major role . . .

If the higher predicate is not an NR-governor, only the latter possibility, Negative Incorporation, is available:

   (99) a. I {claim/?*regret} that never before have the media played . . .[2]

        b. *I don't {claim/regret} that ever before have the media played . . .

        c. I don't {claim/*regret} that the media have ever before played . . .

As (99c) shows, it is not *ever* which triggers inversion, since *ever*, a relatively lenient NPI, is triggered by negation over *claim*—although not over factive *regret*—but no inversion is possible in the lower clause [as (99b) shows]."

Horn's remarks in (7) recognize that Horn clause–containing sentences like (3) involve syntactic raising of a NEG from the embedded clause, a conclusion accepted by McCawley (1998:598).

But, oddly, Horn's later work, which ended up *denying* the syntactic nature of Classical NR, did not attempt to indicate how a nonsyntactic treatment of Classical NR handles cases like (3). Contrast the following remarks:

(8) a. (Horn 1975:284)
"The subj-aux inversion case of (16) [= (3)] is even more problematical for an interpretive approach, since the syntactic nature of this rule [= Classical NR] is presumably beyond reproach."
b. (Horn 1989 [2001:315])
"As it happens, there are ample grounds to doubt both the feasibility and the desirability of a grammatical treatment of the NRP [= Classical NR]."

More generally, we know of no nonsyntactic treatment of Classical NR since 1978, regardless of author, that treats such facts.[3] So, works like Tovena 2001, Klooster 2003, to appear, Gajewski 2005, 2007, Sailer 2005, 2006, Homer 2010, and Romoli 2012, 2013a, 2013b simply do not mention examples like (3)–(6).[4]

13.2 The Present Analysis in a Nutshell

We propose for Horn clause cases like (3) an analysis that treats an example like (9d) as resulting from the raising via Classical NR of the NEG in structures like (9c):

(9) a. I think that the media have [NEG_1 SOME ever before] played such a major role
b. I think that [NEG_1 SOME ever before] have the media played such a major role
c. I do NEG_1 think that [<NEG_1> SOME ever before] have the media played such a major role
d. I don't think that ever before have the media played such a major role.

A core assumption is that the main clause NEG_1 originates in the embedded clause in a constituent [NEG_1 SOME ever before], an assumption not found in Horn 1975, 1978. In (9a), [NEG_1 SOME ever before] appears in the preverbal adverbial position. The extraction of this constituent via Negative Inversion to the initial position of the embedded clause triggers subject-Aux inversion, as shown in (9b). At that point, NEG_1 raises to the matrix clause, yielding (9c). (9c) is the structure of (9d).

The analysis in (9) must be complicated a bit by the conclusion of chapter 5, where we showed that NEG raising always takes place from a scope position. If the NI focus position (preceding the Aux) were a scope position, then no modifications would be required. But as discussed in chapter 14, it appears that the NI focus position is not the same (or not always the same) as the scope position. Therefore, we claim that in (9c) NEG raising actually originates from a scope position located higher than the NI focus position. So a more accurate representation is as follows (assuming that [NEG_1 SOME ever before] is a PP):

(10) I do NEG_1 think that <[<NEG_1> ever before]$_2$> [PP_2 have the media
      played such a major role]

The raising of NEG_1 into the matrix clause leaves the embedded clause scope of [<NEG_1> ever before]$_2$ unchanged. From the point of view of truth-conditional semantic interpretation, Classical NR is invisible. This is, we believe, a key property of all Classical NR cases.

The three crucial assumptions in the above account are (i) *ever before* is underlyingly analyzed as the unary-NEG structure [NEG_1 SOME ever before], (ii) Negative Inversion is triggered by negative XPs, and (iii) Classical NR raises NEG_1 out of the embedded clause. Assumption (i) was outlined in chapter 3, and it constitutes one of the main assumptions of our framework for analyzing NPIs. Assumption (ii) will be discussed in detail in chapter 14. Assumption (iii) is the main conclusion argued for in this monograph.

Significantly, not all NPIs give rise to Negative Inversion. In particular, the reversal NPIs discussed in chapter 4 do not:

(11) a. If you think that Melissa would leave at any point, let me know.
      b. *If you think that at any point would Melissa leave, let me know.

(12) a. Do you think that Melissa would leave at any point?
      b. *Do you think that at any point would Melissa leave?

(13) a. Exactly three people think that Melissa knows any physics.
      b. *Exactly three people think that any physics does Melissa know.

(14) a. Everyone who thinks that he will surrender at any time is
         mistaken.
     b. *Everyone who thinks that at any time will he surrender is
         mistaken.

Unlike the NPI in the Horn clause in (9d), none of the NPI DPs in (11)–(14) can be interpreted as underlying [NEG SOME] quantifier DPs. Rather, they are all interpreted as reversal structures [NEG$_2$ [NEG$_1$ SOME]], that is, as semantically equivalent to indefinites. We discuss the reasons that reversals do not trigger Negative Inversion more fully in chapter 14.

The NPIs in Horn clauses are unary-NEG NPIs and hence, by section 9.4, they are strict NPIs. This conclusion is supported by the sensitivity of Horn clauses to CNRPs (see (7)).

13.3 Horn Clauses and Islands

Preliminary support for our analysis of Horn clauses as involving NEG raising comes from island data. We showed in chapters 11 and 12 that Classical NR is subject to island constraints. Specifically, then, Classical NR out of Horn clauses is subject to the same set of island constraints holding for non–Horn clause island structures.

First, Horn clauses are systematically excluded from topicalized clauses:

(15) a. Wanda does not believe that on any occasion had Kevin lied.
     b. *That on any occasion had Kevin lied, Wanda does not believe.
     c. *That on any occasion had Kevin lied was not believed by Wanda.

Second, Horn clauses are excluded from complex noun phrases:

(16) a. I don't believe that at any point did Sandra steal money.
     b. I hold the belief that at no point did Sandra steal money.
     c. *I don't hold the belief that at any point did Sandra steal money.

Third, Horn clauses are excluded from the complement of truth predicates:

(17) a. It is true that never before had Sandra agreed to the proposal.
     b. *It is not true that ever before had Sandra agreed to the proposal.

Finally, Horn clauses are excluded from pseudocleft constructions:

(18) a. I don't think that under any circumstances would he agree.
     b. *What I don't think is that under any circumstances would
         he agree.

13.4   An Apparent Island Paradox

The claim of chapters 11 and 12 that Classical NR obeys island constraints supports the view that Classical NR is a syntactic phenomenon. In the preceding section, we showed that the NEG raising involved in Horn clauses also obeys islands. Our analysis of Horn clauses then creates a serious conceptual problem, since it assumes that Classical NR is possible out of the scope position of an NI focus.

It is unclear to us whether DPs in scope positions should be taken as islands or not. However, it is clear that left-extracted DPs are islands, as shown in (19) and (20):

(19) a.   They photoshopped no photos of Graham.
      b.   It was Graham that they photoshopped no photos of.
      c.   No photos of Graham did they photoshop.
      d.   *It was Graham that no photos of did they photoshop.

(20) a.   They photoshopped some photos of Graham.
      b.   It was Graham that they photoshopped some photos of.
      c.   Some photos of Graham, they photoshopped.
      d.   *It was Graham that some photos of, they photoshopped.

If DPs in scope positions were islands in the same way as left-extracted DPs, that would pose a dilemma for our account. The solution to this dilemma requires a nontraditional view of the force of island constraints, one differentiating that force in terms of the nature of the constituents extracted from. Where, traditionally, islands have been assumed to restrict all extractions regardless of constituent type, we propose that NEG raising is limited by island boundaries only for clausal islands, as follows:

(21) *The Island Sensitivity of NEG Raising Condition (second and final version)*
      If K is a clause and an island, then a NEG cannot extract from K.

The innovative (21) claims that island boundaries bar NEG raising, hence Classical NR, only if they are clausal, where the ban on extraction across island boundaries is much more general for the extraction of DPs, PPs, and so on (see also the discussion following (4) of chapter 3).

14 Horn Clauses: Negative Inversion

14.1 Properties of the NI Focus

After formulating key necessary syntactic and semantic conditions on Negative Inversion, we show that given those conditions, the analysis of Horn clauses presented in chapter 13 is essentially inevitable.

As previously indicated, Negative Inversion is characterized by the leftward displacement of a phrase, as in topicalization, *wh*-interrogatives, and the like, distinctively combined with obligatory subject-Aux inversion.[1] An additional, subtler characteristic of the construction is the existence of strict syntactic and semantic conditions on the type of phrase that can be fronted. These have been an issue since at least Jackendoff 1972:364–369.

Some researchers have appealed to a condition requiring the NI focus to be a monotone decreasing operator with respect to its scope:

(1) a. (May 1985:10)
   "[A]pparently only quantifiers that are monotone decreasing for Y can be moved to COMP in S-structure."
   b. (Haegeman 2000:32)
   "The semantic contrast between neg_1 and neg_2 is reflected in their monotonicity. Neg_1 is monotone decreasing, while neg_2 is not." (*neg_1* is in effect Haegeman's term for NI foci, while her *neg_2* denotes fronted negative phrases that do not cooccur with subject-Aux inversion.)

That is, it is claimed that for a phrase P to be a legitimate NI focus, P needs to satisfy the semantic condition of being a monotonically decreasing DP. Then suppose that, on the basis of claims like (1a,b), one takes NI foci to be subject to a semantic condition representable as in (2). In this condition and ones to follow, the notation $[\![Q]\!]$ represents the semantic value of Q. S represents a sentential node excluding focus and topic positions (in Principles and

Parameters work, S would be TP or IP). FocP is the category immediately dominating the NI focus.

(2) *The Negative Inversion Condition (first version)*
    In a structure K = [$_{FocP}$ Q Aux S], where Q is an NI focus,
    [[Q]] is a monotone decreasing function.

Condition (2) rightly permits decreasing phrases like those in (3) to be NI foci, whether those phrases manifest overt negatives or not:

(3) a.   Not many unions has the government proposed that to.
    b.   Not every union has the government proposed that to.
    c.   No union has the government proposed that to.
    d.   Few unions has the government proposed that to.
    e.   Less than four unions has the government proposed that to.
    f.   Scarcely any of the students were they able to query about that.
    g.   Rarely have I found such people to be very helpful.

Moreover, condition (2) properly blocks the following ungrammatical examples:

(4) a.   *Every one/All of the gorillas did they teach French to.
    b.   *Certain/Lots/Some of the gorillas did they teach French to.
    c.   *The/Those/These gorillas did they teach French to.
    d.   *Jason did they teach French to.

Condition (2) thus has the virtue of making a wide range of correct predictions.

Nonetheless, condition (2) is factually inadequate. First, to the best of our knowledge, all speakers allow Negative Inversion with *only* phrases:

(5) Only three gorillas have we trained.

But, as is well-known, *only* phrases are not decreasing, because of the positive presupposition with which they are associated. So in (6a) it is presupposed that Nancy ate vegetables, which does not entail that she ate spinach. Hence, the inference from (6a) to (6b) fails:

(6) a.   Only Nancy eats vegetables.
    b.   Only Nancy eats spinach.

However, von Fintel (1999) proposes that even though *only* phrases are not monotone decreasing, they satisfy a property called *Strawson decreasingness*. In (6), (6a) entails (6b) under the assumption that the presupposition of (6b) (Nancy eats spinach) is satisfied. One could then keep the condition on Negative Inversion consistent with cases like (5) by modifying condition (2) to appeal to the Strawson decreasing property rather than decreasingness tout court.

A similar issue is raised by the following examples involving exceptive phrases:

(7) a. None of the students but/except Barbara did they flunk.
     b. None of the students but/except Barbara did they flunk twice.

Like the *only* DPs in (5) and (6), the fronted DPs in (7a,b) are nonmonotonic, not decreasing. Thus, (7a) does not entail (7b). But the exceptive expressions nevertheless yield fine NI foci. An approach based on Strawson decreasingness can also work here—that is, can allow the strictly nondecreasing (nonmonotonic) DPs *none of the students but/except Barbara* to be legitimate NI foci.

Nonetheless, the basic idea of condition (2) is just wrong. For despite data like (3a–g), direct counterexamples to condition (2) are provided by examples (8a–c). To our knowledge, such cases have not previously been discussed in the literature:

(8) a. No less than three gorillas were they able to teach French to.
     b. No fewer than three gorillas were they able to teach French to.
     c. No fewer than three gorillas were they able to teach both French
         and German to.

The phrases *no fewer/no less than three gorillas* in (8a–c) are increasing.[2] (Similar remarks hold about the phrases *not fewer* and *not less*.) That is, (8c) entails (8b) and not conversely. As briefly illustrated in (4), most increasing phrases cannot be NI foci—that is, cannot be phrases in clause-initial position linked to subject-Aux inversion. Nonetheless, cases like (8a–c) are entirely grammatical. Such examples show that if an increasing phrase is formed with a negative determiner, then it will trigger Negative Inversion.

However, internal to our framework of assumptions, not all negative phrases trigger Negative Inversion. Consider again the reversal data presented in chapter 13:

(9) a. If you think that Melissa would leave at any point, let me know.
     b. *If you think that at any point would Melissa leave, let me know.

(10) a. Do you think that Melissa would leave at any point?
     b. *Do you think that at any point would Melissa leave?

(11) a. Exactly three people think that Melissa knows any physics.
     b. *Exactly three people think that any physics does Melissa know.

(12) a. Everyone who thinks that he will surrender at any time is
mistaken.

    b. *Everyone who thinks that at any time will he surrender is
mistaken.

These examples show that reversal phrases do not trigger Negative Inversion, even though they have, in our terms, the form DP = [[NEG_2 [NEG_1 SOME]] NP]. Putting these observations together, we propose the revision of (2) in (13b), based on the definition in (13a):

(13) a. *Definition:* SYNNEG
    An XP Z is *SYNNEG* if and only if there is a unary-NEG structure
    V = [NEG X] and
    i. Z = V, or
    ii. V is the D of Z.

    b. *The Negative Inversion Condition (second version)*
    In a structure K = [$_{FocP}$ Q Aux S], where Q is an NI focus,
    i. Q is SYNNEG, or
    ii. ⟦Q⟧ is a monotone decreasing function.

Case (13ai) can be taken to cover NI foci in all the cases in (14a–f). Case (13aii) straightforwardly covers NI foci like those in (3a,c), (8a–c), and (14g,h):

(14) a. Not unless she is late will we miss the film.
    b. Not (just) because he is a vampire did Sandra hesitate to
marry him.
    c. Not since Lucy met Carl has she paid any attention to Mike.
    d. Not until Thursday/I finish this manuscript can I think about going
to the beach.
    e. Not after next week will he be available for consultation.
    f. Not willingly did he become a pamphleteer.
(books.google.com/books?id=PwgwAAAAYAAJ)
    g. Not one/a single manuscript did they neglect.
    h. Not a damn thing did they accomplish.

Consider again (8a). Negative Inversion is possible there because *no less than three gorillas* is SYNNEG, satisfying (13aii). In (12b), the phrase *any time* is a reversal structure and of the form [[NEG_2 [NEG_1 SOME]] time]. The reversal form is (by definition) not SYNNEG and also not decreasing. Rather, such a reversal structure has an increasing semantic value since SOME does. Therefore, (12b) satisfies neither (13bi) nor (13bii), and Negative Inversion is impossible.

In the remainder of this section, we consider various difficulties for condition (13b). First, there are certain decreasing phrases that to our knowledge no speakers accept as grammatical inputs to Negative Inversion:

(15) a. A human can know a finite number of primes.
     b. *A finite number of primes can a human know.

(16) a. We will look for a group consisting of zero students.
     b. *A group consisting of zero students will we look for.

In (15) (assuming *zero* is finite number), *a finite number* is decreasing, but (15b) is still ungrammatical. One way that (13b) could be modified to handle these cases would be to change (13bii) to "For the determiner D of Q, [[D]] is a monotone decreasing function in its second argument." Since the indefinite determiner [[a]] is not decreasing in its second argument, the examples in (15) and (16) would be ruled out.

We next consider a range of expressions with decreasing semantic values for which speakers differ with respect to whether Negative Inversion can be triggered. First, consider the following examples from Adger and Svenonius 2011:47:

(17) a. On no more than three occasions in history has there been a land
         bridge connecting Asia with North America.
     b. *On at most three occasions in history has there been a land bridge
         connecting Asia with North America.
     c. On at most three occasions in history, there has been a land bridge
         connecting Asia with North America.

One of us agrees with the star on (17b) but one does not. Adger and Svenonius comment that "[t]his suggests that the expression *no more than* bears a formal feature, call it NEG, which is not present in the expression *at most*, despite logical equivalence." In the present context, condition (13b) does not block (17b), since *on at most three occasions in history* is a decreasing phrase with respect to its scope.

Similar cases of decreasing expressions that do not systematically form legitimate NI foci involve the numeral *zero*, which forms decreasing (in fact, antiadditive) DPs. One of us rejects the following sentences but the other does not:

(18) a. I looked at their last 80 games and zero times have they given up
         that many points and that many yards.
         (www.sportsnet.ca/football/cfl/.../mcmaster_kyle_quinlan
         _draft...)

    b.   But *on zero occasions have* I found myself held up, delayed, late to my destination or in any other way inconvenienced by cyclists on the roads.
(westseattleblog.com/2010/09/admiral-way-restriping)

Similarly, *up to* phrases do not trigger Negative Inversion for all speakers:

(19) a.   Deborah will eat up to three hotdogs.
      b.   *Up to three hotdogs will Deborah eat.

While *up to* in (19b) is logically equivalent to *no more than*, Negative Inversion is nevertheless ungrammatical for both of us.

There is also variation with respect to *exactly* phrases (see also Büring 2004:2). Consider (20), from Atlas 1996:301:

(20) Exactly one feature did I notice in the landscape.

Condition (13b) rules out example (20), and for some speakers, including one of us, this is the correct result. For other speakers cited in Büring 2004, including Atlas, and for the other of us, (20) is acceptable.

A bolder, more speculative formulation that might address some of the weakness of (13b) would be the following:

(21) *The Negative Inversion Condition (third version)*
      In structure $K = [_{FocP}\ Q\ Aux\ Z]$, where Q is an NI focus, Q is SYNNEG.

This purely syntactic condition relies only on the presence of a unary NEG to pick out NI foci. From this statement, the facts in (15)–(20) (for speakers who do not allow Negative Inversion in these cases) can be taken to follow directly. However, an account of Negative Inversion based on (21) would need to be buttressed by many additional assumptions determining that a range of forms including *only, rarely, few, hardly,* and *less than* contain a syntactic NEG, as motivated by the grammaticality of the following examples:

(22) a.   Only Michael did they feel free to talk to.
      b.   Rarely had they experienced such a great performance.
      c.   Very few people would they admit to their club.
      d.   Hardly ever had he talked to somebody so enlightened.
      e.   Less than half the class has Michael actually spoken to.

While instances of NEG are obviously not overt in such forms, there is a case to be made for analyses that assign them covert instances of NEG. For *only*, the idea that it contains a syntactic NEG is supported by the fact *only Michael* is equivalent to *nobody but/except Michael*, and the equivalence covers both the asserted and presupposed aspects of meaning. This suggests an analysis of [only DP_x] as a reduction of [no Y but/except DP_x]—say, via raising of the exceptive phrase or its DP to a higher position in the larger DP (such an analysis would have to guarantee the case-marking facts: *No one except *I/me *am/is; Only I/*me am/*is*).

For speakers who allow inversion with *zero*, we speculate that they have the representation [<only> zero], and hence it is really the covert *only* and not *zero* (an antiadditive) that permits Negative Inversion.

Along the same lines, *Few people run* means 'For some contextually specified small number n, there is no set g of people with cardinality greater than n such that all members x of g run'. On this semantic analysis, it is plausible to claim that syntactically *few* involves NEG, and hence is SYNNEG.

We leave it to future work to see if similar approaches are viable for cases like (22b,d,e).

The variation between speakers seen in all these cases where we speculate about covert instances of NEG would be attributable to syntactic differences between the grammars of speakers depending on the distribution of null *only* in their grammars; see Horn 2001 for discussion of distinct grounds for recognizing covert instances of *only*.

If these highly speculative remarks are on the right track, then a completely syntactic account of Negative Inversion (independent of any properties like decreasingness or antiadditivity) might be within reach. Such an account, as opposed to a purely semantic one, could be able to account for the cited speaker variation and also for ungrammatical cases, such as (15) and (16), involving clearly decreasing expressions for which Negative Inversion is impossible.

While we have taken the space to formulate condition (21) and have sketched speculative analyses that would be consistent with and supportive of it, we stress that the no doubt controversial aspects of the discussion of (21) are not necessary for our argument from the properties of Negative Inversion for a Classical NR analysis of Horn clauses. For that, it will suffice to appeal to condition (13b)—more precisely, to further modifications of (13b) provided in what follows.

14.2 Scope and Negative Inversion

Neither condition (13b) nor condition (21) distinguishes contrasting pairs of the type probably first noted in Klima 1964:300 and illustrated in (23a,b) from Jackendoff 1972:364, 365:

(23) a. In no clothes does Bill look attractive.
     b. In no clothes, Bill looks attractive.

While (23b) looks like it might be a counterexample to the claimed requirement of subject-Aux inversion with Negative Inversion, arguably the conditions for Negative Inversion are not even met.[3] One notes the sharp difference
in intonation represented by the absence of a comma in (23a) and its presence
in (23b). Furthermore, *no clothes* in (23b) cannot license an NPI in the rest of
the clause:

(24) In no clothes, Bill might (*ever) shock the audience.

We speculate that the initial phrase in (23b) is a kind of reduced adverbial
clause something like *while wearing no clothes*, with the scope of the quantifier phrase *no clothes* internal to that constituent. Then the reason for the
contrast between (23a) and (23b) is, as we will show, that *no clothes* has scope
over the matrix clause in (23a), but not in (23b).

The relevance of scope to (23) and (24) motivates incorporating reference
to scope into the condition on Negative Inversion. Setting aside the speculative
condition (21), we therefore propose the following revision of the more con-
servative (13b):[4]

(25) *The Negative Inversion Condition (fourth and final version)*
      In a structure $K = [_{\text{FocP}} \; Q \; \text{Aux} \; S]$, where Q is an NI focus,
      a. Q is (or dominates) a DP V such that V's scope position is higher
         than the position of any other element of K; and
      b. i. V is SYNNEG or
         ii. $[\![V]\!]$ is a monotone decreasing function.

Return then to (23a). We assume the NI focus position is not the scope
position of the fronted constituent. Rather, the scope position of *no clothes* is
higher than the NI focus position, adjoined to the highest clausal constituent
(in this case, FocP):

(26) $[_{\text{FocP}} <[\text{no clothes}]_1> [_{\text{FocP}} [\text{in DP}_1]_5 \text{ does Bill look attractive} <PP_5>]]$

Since <X> denotes an unpronounced occurrence of X, the only visible occurrence here is the one dominated by the PP in the NI focus position. In (23b),
on the other hand, the scope position for *no clothes* is internal to the reduced
adverbial clause. That determines that *no clothes* in (23b) cannot qualify as an
NI focus and hence explicates the impossibility of the subject-Aux inversion
characterizing Negative Inversion.[5]

Many other examples illustrate the importance of scope in the statement of
the Negative Inversion Condition. Consider first:

(27) a. Karen's carvings of none of the goddesses were they willing to buy.
      b. Karen's carvings of not less than three goddesses were they willing
         to buy.

In (27a), the DP triggering Negative Inversion (*none of the goddesses*) is decreasing—in fact, antiadditive—and thus cannot fail to satisfy condition (25). In (27b), the DP triggering Negative Inversion (*not less than three goddesses*) is increasing, but it contains an overt unary NEG (and hence, is SYNNEG) and thus satisfies (25) despite the increasing property. The structure of (27b) in such terms is roughly as in (28):

(28) $[_A$ <$[_B$ not less than three goddesses$]_1$> $[_C$ [Karen's carvings of DP$_1]_2$
      were they willing to buy <DP$_2$>]]

In this structure, phrase B has scope higher than any other element of C but only the lower occurrence of *not less than three goddesses* (dominated by the NI focus) is pronounced.

Condition (25) also rightly predicts that (29a) will only have reading (29c), and not reading (29b):

(29) a. Your belief in no god were the authorities willing to tolerate.
      b. The authorities were willing to tolerate your not believing in
          any god.
      c. No god x is such that the authorities were willing to tolerate your
          believing in x.
      d. The authorities were willing to tolerate your belief in no god.

On one reading, represented in (29b), the scope of *no god* in (29a) is lower than that of *your belief*, hence not the highest in the matrix clause. In that case, (29a) is ungrammatical because the whole fronted DP then represents an increasing function with respect to the clause and the required negative DP fails to have highest scope. On a distinct reading, represented in (29c), the scope of *no god* is higher than that of *your belief* and indeed higher than anything else in the clause. That reading is compatible with Negative Inversion because the phrase with highest scope, *no god*, is then decreasing with respect to the entire clause. Finally, for the non–Negative Inversion case (29d), condition (25) is obviously irrelevant, and, notably, (29d) has both reading (29b), blocked for (29a), and reading (29c).

14.3   Horn Clauses Revisited

Returning to Horn clauses, we can now say that if analyzed *without* appeal to syntactic NEG raising, the fronted NPI phrases could not satisfy the Negative Inversion Condition (25). Consider the following example:

(30) I don't think that under any circumstances would he commit larceny.

Semantic approaches almost universally take nominal NPIs to be increasing indefinite DPs (see, e.g., Ladusaw 1996b:334). And on that analysis, since they would contain no NEG, they could not be SYNNEG. Hence, on these approaches *any circumstances* in (30) would not satisfy condition (25). But under a syntactic analysis of Classical NR and the analysis of strict NPIs as unary-NEG structures, the fronted phrase in (30) reduces to a legitimate SYNNEG and decreasing NI focus under condition (25). That follows since we have analyzed the NI focus in (30) as underlyingly identical to that in (31):

(31) I think that under no circumstances would he commit larceny.

And of course the overtly negative decreasing NI focus in (31) satisfies condition (25).

The ability of our syntactic approach to Horn clauses to explain how they can satisfy a necessary general condition on Negative Inversion is a critical piece of evidence for a syntactic view of Classical NR. And we know of no nonsyntactic view of Classical NR that has even tried to provide an adequate analysis of Horn clauses. One response that advocates of semantic/pragmatic views of Classical NR might make would simply deny that cases like (30) and Horn clauses generally instantiate Negative Inversion. This is hardly a conceptually desirable conclusion, though, as it forces the complication of positing some distinct fronting condition limited largely to Horn clauses.

But the situation is worse for the hypothetical rejection of a Negative Inversion analysis of Horn clauses: namely, there is direct factual evidence that despite the lack of an *overt* instance of NEG, the fronted phrases in Horn clauses do represent NEG-containing NI foci. This evidence involves a range of contexts where DPs apparently satisfying condition (25) nonetheless, for reasons that need not concern us, cannot trigger Negative Inversion. Strikingly, these same contexts preclude the formation of Horn clauses.

First, Negative Inversion of the phrase *nothing* in the idioms *stop at nothing* in (32) and *think nothing of* in (33) is impossible. Similarly, no corresponding Horn clause is grammatical:

(32) a.   Carla will stop at nothing (won't stop at anything) to get that job.
     b.   *Nothing will Carla stop at to get that job.
     c.   I believe that Carla will stop at nothing to get that job.
     d.   *I don't believe that anything will Carla stop at to get that job.

(33) a.   Vernon thinks nothing (doesn't think anything) of drinking nine beers.
     b.   *Nothing does Vernon think of drinking nine beers.

    c. I believe that Vernon thinks nothing of drinking nine beers.
    d. *I don't believe that anything does Vernon think of drinking nine beers.

Second, expressions that impose indefinite interpretations (*there is* and *have*) on DPs also do not allow Negative Inversion of those DPs, and corresponding Horn clauses are also impossible:

(34) a. There is no (is not any) gorilla in that SUV.
      b. *No gorilla is there in that SUV.
      c. I believe that there is no gorilla in that SUV.
      d. *I don't believe that any gorilla is there in that SUV.

(35) a. Sally has no money with her.
      b. *No money does Sally have with her.
      c. I believe that Sally has no money with her.
      d. *I don't believe that any money does Sally have with her.

Third, predicative expressions cannot trigger Negative Inversion, and once again the corresponding Horn clauses are equally ungrammatical:

(36) a. Boris will be no Einstein/will not be any Einstein.
      b. *No Einstein will Boris be.
      c. I figured that Boris would be no Einstein.
      d. *I didn't figure that any Einstein would Boris be.

Since Horn clauses and Negative Inversion cases systematically manifest the same constraints, these data argue strongly that Horn clauses involve Negative Inversion and not some distinct, hitherto unknown left extraction.[6]

This fact must count against any approach that cannot incorporate the fundamental unity of Negative Inversion and Horn clauses. But the complication of regarding Horn clauses and Negative Inversion as distinct phenomena is inherent in any nonsyntactic treatment of Horn clause Classical NR cases. That follows because although the main clause dominating a Horn clause contains a NEG, the essence of nonsyntactic accounts of Classical NR eliminates any possibility of syntactically associating that NEG with the fronted NPI. And without that NEG, the fronted phrases in Horn clauses cannot qualify as legitimate NI foci under condition (25) and hence such clauses cannot be taken to instantiate Negative Inversion.

On the contrary, we have sketched how a syntactic view of Classical NR can associate the NEG in the main clause with the fronted phrase in a Horn clause, reducing that phrase to an unexceptional NI focus. This clear clash between the consequences of syntactic and nonsyntactic views of Classical

NR relative to Horn clauses thus provides a strong argument in favor of the syntactic view.

Our syntactic analysis of Horn clauses incorporating condition (25) and syntactic NEG raising is nonetheless significantly different from the syntactic view assumed in Horn 1978:168–169 and reiterated in McCawley 1998:598. As already noted, that analysis did not take the raised NEG to originate in the NI focus, that is, in the fronted NPI DP. While in our view, NEGs arise in various distinct positions including internal to DPs, these authors essentially accepted the assumption made in Klima 1964 that most syntactic negation, even that of negative DPs, arises as a so-called sentence negation. Two strong objections to such a view are highlighted by the existence of Horn clauses.

First, under the sentential negation view, negative DPs of the type subject to Negative Inversion must involve *lowering* sentence negations into DPs, indefinitely deeply as indicated in (37):

(37) No doctor's assistant's cousin's home mortgage payment's suspension had Karen predicted.

But unbounded lowering is arguably otherwise unknown and hence its invocation for negative phrases is theoretically suspicious at best. That structures like (37) satisfy condition (25) follows from the independent semantic fact that no matter how deeply the initial DP in recursive possessive cases is embedded, that DP has the highest scope in the clause.

Second, under the assumption that the NEGs of NI foci originate in a high sentential negation position, the fronted DPs in Horn clauses are systematically not decreasing phrases, since they are not taken as sources for Classical NR. Nor are they increasing phrases meeting the SYNNEG condition in (25); hence, nothing like (25) could be appealed to. We take this to be another reason for rejecting the idea that negation in general arises in some single high clausal position, or indeed, in any unique position at all.

14.4 A Condition on Horn Clauses

Despite the previous discussion, not all cases of Negative Inversion yield corresponding well-formed Horn clauses. In (38a), each fronted negative DP in the Negative Inversion examples corresponds to a Horn clause in (38b):

(38) a. I believed that no gorilla/not a single gorilla/neither gorilla could they teach to speak Mohawk.

　　　 b. I didn't believe that any gorilla/a single gorilla/either gorilla could they teach to speak Mohawk.

But the well-formed Negative Inversion examples in (39a) do not correspond to well-formed Horn clauses in (39b):

(39) a. I believed that not all gorillas/not every gorilla/not many gorillas/ not a lot of gorillas could they teach to speak Mohawk.
   b. I didn't believe that *all gorillas/*every gorilla/*many gorillas/*a lot of gorillas could they teach to speak Mohawk.

Such contrasts are replicated in cases where the DP that triggers Negative Inversion is embedded internal to the NI focus:

(40) a. I believed that male offspring of not a single gorilla did they teach to speak Mohawk.
   b. I didn't believe that male offspring of a single gorilla did they teach to speak Mohawk.

(41) a. I believed that male offspring of not a lot of gorillas/not many gorillas did they teach to speak Mohawk.
   b. *I didn't believe that male offspring of a lot of gorillas/many gorillas did they teach to speak Mohawk.

While the negative DP in (40a), which has a grammatical Horn clause correspondent, defines an antiadditive function and the negative DPs in (41a) don't, the condition governing the above examples is nonetheless not reducible to a semantic condition invoking antiadditivity. That is shown by the facts in (42):

(42) a. I think that no fewer than three students did they admit.
   b. I don't think that any fewer than three students did they admit.

Here, even though (42a) involves a DP defining an increasing, and hence non-antiadditive, function, it yields a good NI focus that corresponds to an equally good fronted phrase in the Horn clause in (42b).

The relevant condition seems to be that Classical NR of the NEG of an NI focus is only possible when that DP involves an existential quantifier like SOME (or the closely related *a*). For example, in (38a) the relevant DP is *no gorilla*, which we analyze as [[NEG SOME] gorilla]. It is possible to extract NEG away from SOME in this example. However, in (39a) it is impossible to extract NEG away from [not every gorilla], or from the other quantifiers cited there. We suggest, then, that the following condition governs the phenomenon:

(43) *The Condition on Classical NR from Negative Inversion Foci*
   If Q is the highest-scoping element of an NI focus and NEG raises from Q into the next higher clause, then Q = [[$_D$ NEG SOME/A . . .] NP].

Condition (43) permits particular cases like (42b) since in that case the NEG is raising from a scope position occurrence of [[NEG SOME fewer than n] NP], which satisfies the condition on Q in (43).

Condition (43) also correctly allows cases like (44b), in which the NI focus is analyzable as [[NEG SOME . . .] NP], specifically, [[NEG SOME where near seven] gorillas], although *nowhere near seven gorillas* does not define an antiadditive function:

(44) a. I believe that nowhere near seven gorillas were they able to adequately train.
   b. I don't believe that anywhere near seven gorillas were they able to adequately train.

A serious problem with formulation (43), though, is that Classical NR and the corresponding Horn clauses are generally possible with *even* phrases, which might appear not to involve a [NEG SOME] structure, as in (45b):

(45) a. Not even the assistant manager did they try to contact.
   b. I don't believe that even the assistant manager did they try to contact.

One possibility is that the *(not) even* phrase originates as an intensive on a DP, whose form would be schematically [[NEG SOME] X], [not even Y]]. So the structure of (45a) would be *<Nobody> not even the assistant manager did they try to contact*. But we cannot attempt here to develop a serious analysis of this type.[7]

Data involving conjoined cases with *neither/either* support condition (43), if these occurrences of *neither/either* are analyzed as [NEG SOME [ONE of either [DP or DP]]]:

(46) a. I believe that neither Jane nor Marla have they yet interviewed.
   b. I don't believe that either Jane or Marla have they yet interviewed.

14.5   Quasi–Horn Clauses

As touched on in section 14.2, Horn (1975:283, 1978:169) offered, though with limited data, the generalization that Horn clause complements are only possible in Classical NR environments, that is, only with main predicates that are CNRPs. He supported this generalization in the latter work by contrasting his original Horn clause case, given as our (3) of chapter 13 and repeated in (47a), with that in (47b), whose main verb is not a CNRP:

(47) a. I don't think that ever before have the media played such a major role in a kidnapping.

    b. *I don't claim that ever before have the media played such a major role in a kidnapping.

McCawley (1998:598) added to the class of cases like (47b) the single example (48):[8]

(48) *I didn't say that under any circumstances would he help you.

Our view of the logic of the contrast in (47) is as follows:

(49) a. The fronted phrases characterizing Horn clauses give rise to subject-Aux inversion.

    b. Therefore, there is evidence that those phrases are NI foci.

    c. If the fronted phrases in Horn clauses are NI foci, they must satisfy the Negative Inversion Condition in (25).

    d. Given their overt structure (not involving an overt NEG), the fronted phrases in Horn clauses can only satisfy condition (25) if they originate with a NEG that modifies the SOME of the fronted phrase.

    e. Since the needed NEG is not overt, it must have been either deleted or raised or both.

    f. Since there is no legitimate general NEG deleter in the complement clause, the NEG must have raised.

    g. Since there is an overt NEG in the main clause, it is a candidate to be the raised NEG and that assumption yields the correct meaning for the whole.

    h. Therefore, the main clause NEG is the raised NEG, and Horn clauses are instances of Negative Inversion combined with Classical NR of the NEG that legitimizes Negative Inversion.

The ineluctable consequence of that logic is that Horn clauses can only occur with main verbs that are CNRPs, as Horn originally claimed. Therefore, since neither *claim* nor *say* is a CNRP, the ungrammaticality of examples (47b) and (48) is exactly what the logic in (49) predicts. Another way to put this is that on our view, the NPI in a Horn clause is a unary-NEG structure, and therefore, by the conclusion in section 9.4, it is a strict NPI. Therefore, it should obey the locality constraints on strict NPIs. Hence, NEG raising from the NPI in a Horn clause should be blocked by non-CNRPs. However, this picture of Horn clauses, which appears to strongly support our view that Classical NR is a syntactic phenomenon, runs into apparent difficulties.

First, one of us finds that with the right stress pattern, an example like (48) may well be grammatical and is, in any event, greatly improved. This involves strong stress on the NPI *any*. While this is weak evidence at best for questioning Horn's generalization, which the logic of (49) yields and which is critical to the argument from Horn clauses we have developed, other cases raise the same sort of problem. For instance:

(50) a. I didn't accept that any of those problems had she ever really solved.
   b. The States couldn't provide us with evidence that at any time had there been a request for road closure.
      (share.pdfonline.com/.../GG%20letter.htm)
   c. I have found no evidence suggesting that at any time did the policymakers harbor doubts on the effectiveness of the law of one price to decisively and immediately reduce the rate of inflation of traded goods (Gil, 1980).
      (kellogg.nd.edu/publications/workingpapers/WPS/146.pdf)

A modest inquiry among a New York University class of six people found that two accepted (50a), three rejected it, and one found it marginal at the level of?*. The one of us who does not clearly reject McCawley's (48) also accepts (50a), as well as the Web examples (50b) and (50c), kindly provided by Vincent Homer (personal communication). And among the students cited above, none of the six rejected (50b) outright and two found it acceptable without doubts (two-OK, three-?, and one-??).

While the complement clauses in (50a–c) have the form of Horn clauses, the main clause in each sentence contains no CNRP. We will refer to clauses involving the fronting of NPI phrases (or NPI-containing phrases) linked to subject-Aux inversion directly embedded under a matrix structure *not* involving a CNRP as *quasi–Horn clauses.*

Given the modest evidence for the assumption that quasi–Horn clause cases like those in (48) and (50) can be grammatical for at least some speakers under the phonological condition described, two alternative conclusions are possible:

(51) a. The assumption that Horn clauses depend on Classical NR is just false.
      or
   b. Some independently motivated mechanism in the grammar of English/Universal Grammar distinct from Classical NR accounts for the existence of quasi–Horn clauses.

If (51a) were correct, our argument for Classical NR from Horn clauses would be undermined. But if the alternative in (51b) can be justified, even the existence of a wide range of grammatical (for many speakers) quasi–Horn clauses would be irrelevant to our argument. Under that possibility, quasi–Horn clauses would not bear on claims about Horn clauses simply because they would not be Horn clauses. To lend (51b) some substance, we need to provide a characterization of quasi–Horn clauses that (i) distinguishes them from Horn clauses, (ii) shows that they do not involve Classical NR, and (iii) accounts for the fact that they nonetheless also involve Negative Inversion of what appear to be NPI phrases.

First, the evidence showing that the fronted phrases in Horn clauses result from Negative Inversion and not some distinct fronting phenomenon (also capable of triggering subject-Aux inversion) can be argued straightforwardly to show the same thing for the relevant phrases in quasi–Horn clauses. That is, quasi–Horn clauses are also Negative Inversion structures.

In particular, the fact that the fronted NPIs in Horn clauses support intensives, taken to argue for the unary-NEG character of DPs in chapter 4, has analogs applying as well to quasi–Horn clauses. So adding intensives (italicized in (52)) to the fronted phrases in (52c,d) no more degrades them than similar additions in (52a,b) degrade the Horn clauses they contain:

(52) a.   I didn't believe that any of those problems, *not one/not any*, had she ever really solved.
   b.   It was not believed that at any time, *not even on Thursday*, had he contacted any of them.
   c.   I didn't accept that any of those problems, *not one/not any*, had she ever really solved.
   d.   It was not proven that at any time, *not even on Thursday*, had he contacted any of them.

Second, recall the argument in section 14.3 that specific contexts satisfying the necessary conditions of the Negative Inversion Condition nonetheless do not form grammatical Horn clauses. That argument applies as well to quasi–Horn clauses. While we give only one example, the reader can verify that the other, similar arguments of section 14.3 hold as well:

(53) a.   Carla will stop at nothing (won't stop at anything) to get that job.
   b.   *Nothing will Carla stop at to get that job.
   c.   I accept that Carla will stop at nothing to get any high-paying job.
   d.   *I don't accept that ANYthing will Carla stop at to get ANY high-paying job.
   e.   I don't accept that ANYthing will Carla place beyond consideration.

Just as Negative Inversion is blocked with the *stop at nothing* construction, so quasi–Horn clauses are similarly blocked, even for the one of us who accepts a wide range of quasi–Horn clauses. The data support the assertion that quasi–Horn clauses also involve Negative Inversion.

We thus conclude that quasi–Horn clauses represent instances of complement clause Negative Inversion of NPI phrases exactly as Horn clauses do. What, then, is the distinction between the two construction types, beyond the sheer difference in main clause predicates? The answer, we believe, is found in our chapter 9 discussion of the confounding factor of high scope. That is, we suggest that quasi–Horn clauses can exist (to the extent that they are acceptable) for exactly the reasons invoked in chapter 9 for the grammaticality in certain cases of strict NPIs in the complements of non-CNRPs.

So we take the crucial factual difference between quasi–Horn clauses and Horn clauses proper to involve quantifier scope. As indicated earlier, in our view the scope of the negative quantifier represented by the fronted NPI-containing phrase in every genuine Horn clause is internal to the complement clause. But for quasi–Horn clauses, we claim that the scope of the relevant quantifiers is the main clause.

First, consider quantifier scope in a Horn clause like the one in (54a):

(54) a. Carol doesn't think that at any time did Stan betray his wife.
     b. Carol thinks that at no time did Stan betray his wife.

This pair shares a low-scope analysis of the *time* DPs, yielding an interpretation where the content of the thought specified by the complement clause is 'at no time did Stan betray his wife'. But one of us finds that (54a,b), with strong stress on respectively *any* and *no*, have distinct readings in which the relevant DPs have high scope. This reading renders (54b) equivalent to (55a), whose meaning can be paraphrased as (55b):

(55) a. At no time did Carol think Stan betrayed his wife.
     b. There is no point in time x such that Carol thinks Stan betrayed his wife at x.

It is not really pertinent to the current argument to argue that such a high-scope reading exists in CNRP cases, so we will not discuss that factual question any further. However, we observe that if high-scope cases like (54a) are real, they do not fit well into our contrastive Horn clause/quasi–Horn clause terminology. We have claimed that in Horn clauses, the scope of the fronted NPI DP is always in the complement clause, and we have defined quasi–Horn clauses in such a way that they can only exist as complement clauses of *non-*CNRPs. Thus, a high-scope version of cases like (54a) would not fit into either category. We will not attempt to refine the terminology to cover the very restricted class of cases at issue.

Consider then a quasi–Horn clause analog of the Horn clause case (54a):

(56) Carol doesn't accept that at any time did Stan betray his wife.

One of us finds (56) acceptable if *any* is strongly stressed. If it were fully parallel to (54a), it would be ambiguous, with both low-scope and high-scope readings of [[NEG SOME] time]. One more potential reading to consider for (56) is one where *at any time* is a reversal, and the matrix NEG negates the matrix V/VP.

Of these three readings, our system determines that (56) can only have the high-scope reading for [[NEG SOME] time], as the only available structure in the current system is (57):

(57) Carol doesn't (= NEG_1) [<[[<NEG_1> SOME] time]$_3$> [accept [that [[at DP_3]$_4$ did [Stan betray his wife PP_4]]]]]]

The present view allows structure (57) for (56) but does not permit a low-scope-plus-Classical-NR analysis. Nor does it permit a reversal analysis of *any time* since reversal phrases do not trigger Negative Inversion.

Given that inference from our system of ideas, the issue is whether that consequence corresponds to the facts about sentences like (56). That is, for those who accept them, is it true that their meanings involve high scope? If so, (56) should mean (58) and only (58):

(58) There is no point in time t such that Carol accepts that Stan betrayed his wife at t.

While this seems correct to us, determining the scope properties of NPIs is difficult and complex and we can only touch on it here (see chapter 9 for discussion).

A suggestive contrast is the following:

(59) a. I did not claim that Evelyn put any cheetahs in a cage, but Bill did claim that.
b. I did not claim that ANY cheetahs did Evelyn put in a cage, *but Bill did claim that.

In (59a), *any cheetahs* is a reversal structure. So the sentence is equivalent to (60):

(60) I did not claim that Evelyn put some cheetahs in a cage.

In (59b), *any cheetahs* cannot represent a reversal structure since we have shown that reversals are not SYNNEG or decreasing and therefore cannot trigger Negative Inversion. Therefore, in (59b) *any cheetahs* must be a strict (unary-NEG) NPI. But since NEG raising is blocked out of the complements of non-CNRPs, the only possible analysis of (59b) is that *any cheetahs* takes matrix scope and that NEG raises from the DP in the high-scope position. But if *any cheetahs* takes matrix scope in (59b), then the embedded clause (containing a free variable) cannot serve as the antecedent of *that*. In (59a), on the other hand, *any cheetahs* as a reversal takes scope in the embedded clause, and the embedded clause can serve as the antecedent of *that*.

An indirect argument that quasi–Horn clauses like that in (56) systematically involve high scope for the quantifier DP forming the fronted DP can be based on the NPI facts in (61):

(61) a. The doctor didn't believe/claim that Audrey would ever again feel well.

 b. The doctor didn't believe/*claim that Audrey would feel all that well afterwards.

The difference between (61a) and (61b) is that while *ever (again)* is not a strict NPI, the modifier *(all) that* is. Strict NPIs do not permit reversal analyses, while others do. Therefore, *ever (again)* in (61a) can have a reversal analysis in the *claim* case, which thus need not invoke Classical NR. That is possible because the NEG deleter of the reversal NEG can be [NEG claim]. The analog involving a strict NPI with a unary-NEG structure [NEG ever] would be possible in the *believe* case of (61a). That follows since with a CNRP, the NEG could simply raise and appear as the overt NEG in the main clause. But in the *claim* case, raising of the unary NEG to the main clause would require a violation of the CNRP condition on Classical NR.

In (61b), we assume that *all that well* cannot take scope outside of the embedded clause. So the NEG in (61b) could not raise away from the NPI *all that well* in a main clause scope position. Therefore, in the current system of ideas there is no grammatical analysis of the *claim* case of (61b).

Since a unary-NEG analysis is impossible in the *claim* version of (61a), only the reversal analysis remains. But a reversal analysis is not possible for *all that*, as shown by the ungrammaticality of this form in typical environments where reversal structures are grammatical:

(62) a. *Everyone who was feeling all that well left early.
 b. *At most three people feel all that well.
 c. *They didn't consider the possibility that he was feeling all that well.

The ungrammaticality of the *claim* variant of (61b) and its contrast (for some speakers) with the quasi–Horn case in (56) is then exactly what is expected if *claim* complements can contain strict NPIs only if those NPIs can take high scope out of the complement clause.

Crucially, the fronted NPIs in NI focus position in both quasi–Horn clauses and Horn clauses must be strict NPIs. We have presented evidence above that reversals (binary-NEG NPIs) do not trigger Negative Inversion, since they are neither SYNNEG nor decreasing. In this light, consider again (56). The phrase *any time* cannot be a reversal since, if it were, it would not trigger Negative Inversion. Therefore, it must be a unary-NEG NPI. But then if [[NEG SOME] time] had scope in the complement clause, the single NEG of [[NEG SOME] time] would have to raise out of the complement of a non-CNRP, which is impossible. It follows that the only possible analysis of (56) is that *any time* has matrix scope, and that NEG raises from [[NEG SOME] time] in its matrix scope position.

This same argument can be made with the strict NPI expression *half bad*. This also cannot take a reversal structure:

(63) a. *Everyone who thought the movie was half bad watched it again.
  b. *If the movie was half bad, why did you walk out in the middle?
  c. *They didn't consider the possibility that the movie was half bad.

Given this fact, and given that *half bad* is subject to a restriction precluding it from scoping out of a complement clause, our system must claim that it cannot occur under negated non-CNRPs, although it can under CNRPs. And that is the case:

(64) a. She doesn't believe/think that the movie was half bad.
  b. *She doesn't claim/realize that the movie was half bad.
  c. I don't imagine/anticipate that the movie will be half bad.
  d. *I don't foresee/suggest that the movie will be half bad.

Our key conclusion is that the occurrence of a strict NPI in the complement of a non-CNRP with its raised NEG or NEG deleter in the main clause is restricted as follows: it is possible only for a strict NPI structure that can have a scope higher than the complement clause. Obviously, that requires minimally that such NPI structures be scope-bearing phrases. But this is only a necessary condition. The logic of our argument entails that any constraint that precludes high scope for a scope-bearing element in the complement of a non-CNRP will evidently also block strict NPIs in such a complement clause.

We observe that the NI focus position in a quasi–Horn clause is always occupied by a scope-bearing DP, since the NI focus in every case of Negative Inversion, whether a simple case like (65a), a Horn clause like (65b), or a quasi–Horn clause like (65c), is a scope-bearing phrase:

(65) a. At no time did Stan betray his wife.
     b. Carol didn't believe that at any time had Stan betrayed his wife.
     c. Carol didn't claim that at any time had Stan betrayed his wife.

Thus, barring specific scope constraints, a high-scope analysis is in principle available in quasi–Horn clauses. We thus expect that speakers who accept some cases of strict NPIs under non-CNRPs will also accept the strict NPIs in NI focus position in quasi–Horn clauses.[9] This remark is in effect an addendum to our discussion of the high-scope confound problem in chapter 9.[10]

We have barely approached the range of data whose study would be necessary to support our claim that quasi–Horn clauses do not conflict with the logic of (3) and thus do not threaten our argument for a syntactic view of Classical NR based on Horn clauses. But we have offered some evidence for the idea that quasi–Horn clauses involve only high-scope analyses for the fronted DPs in NI focus position in their complement clauses. Since, under high-scope analyses, the negative quantifier including the NEG of the NI focus occurs in the main clause in a high-scope position, the separated NEG found in the main clause in cases like (65c) can then achieve its surface position by raising out of the covert negative quantifier phrase in the matrix scope position. This possibility underlies a resolution of what is at first sight a paradox: namely, a NEG that in one sense originates in a complement clause ends up in the dominating main clause without violating the constraints on Classical NR, specifically without violating the claim of Horn's work and the present monograph that Classical NR is impossible except with main clause CNRPs.

To summarize, despite the brevity of our discussion and the limited data analyzed, we regard the conclusions in (66) as reasonably plausible:

(66) a. Quasi–Horn clauses are not Horn clauses, thus cannot directly
        threaten our argument for Classical NR from Horn clauses.
     b. There is a supportable analysis of quasi–Horn clauses appealing to
        no ad hoc assumptions that satisfies the following conditions:
        i.   It yields a high-scope analysis that seems to provide correct
             semantics for the cases discussed.
        ii. It provides a structure for the NI foci in quasi–Horn clauses that
             both satisfies the Negative Inversion Condition and provides a
             motivated mechanism for the covertness of the NEGs in those
             NI foci.
        iii. It accounts both for the presence in the main clause of the NEG
             of the complement clause NI focus and for the ability of that
             NEG to permit the NI focus to satisfy the Negative Inversion
             Condition.

    iv. Finally, all this is achieved with no appeal to Classical NR, which should not be present with non-CNRP main verbs.

These conclusions represent the substance that we have given to alternative (51b), which states that quasi–Horn clauses do not threaten our Horn clause argument for the syntactic nature of Classical NR. And they indicate how the issue that quasi–Horn clauses raise is the same high-scope confound issue discussed in chapter 9.[11]

There is a bit more to be said about quasi–Horn clauses, but we must delay further discussion until section 16.5, since it involves clause types only treated in detail in that chapter.

15 Topicalization

15.1 The Necessary Condition on Topicalization

In the preceding chapter, we formulated a proposal for the necessary general condition on Negative Inversion. In this chapter, we investigate conditions on topicalization and the way topicalization structures interact with Classical NR.

In the overwhelming mass of cases, when Negative Inversion is possible for a particular phrase type, topicalization is impossible, and conversely:

(1) a. Under no circumstances would I agree to such a plan.
    b. *Under no circumstances, I would agree to such a plan.

(2) a. Under those circumstances, I would agree to such a plan.
    b. *Under those circumstances would I agree to such a plan.

Given such facts, the condition on the fronted phrase for topicalization appears to be essentially the negation of the condition on the fronted phrase for Negative Inversion, (25) of chapter 14, repeated here:

(3) *The Negative Inversion Condition*
    In a structure $K = [_{\text{FocP}} \text{ Q Aux S}]$, where Q is an NI focus,
    a. Q is (or dominates) a DP V such that V's scope position is higher than the position of any other element of K; and
    b. i. V is SYNNEG or
       ii. $[\![V]\!]$ is a monotone decreasing function.

Recall that SYNNEG was defined as follows ((13a) of chapter 14):

(4) *Definition:* SYNNEG
    An XP Z is *SYNNEG* if and only if there is a unary-NEG structure V = [NEG X] and
    i. Z = V, or
    ii. V is the D of Z.

Given that, the condition on topicalization can be formulated as follows:

(5) *The Topicalization Condition*
　　In a structure K = [$_{TopP}$ Q S], where Q is a topic,
　　a.　Q is (or dominates) a DP V such that V's scope position is higher than the position of any other element of K; and
　　b.　i.　V is not SYNNEG and
　　　　ii.　⟦V⟧ is not monotone decreasing.

Note that (5b) is the negation of (3b). Conditions (3) and (5) jointly account for the following systematic contrasts:[1]

(6) a.　That fashion magazine/*No fashion magazine, I am sure he read.
　　b.　Those fashion magazines/*Not many fashion magazines, people still buy.
　　c.　Almost everyone/*Not everyone, they plan to interview.
　　d.　Many professors/*Few professors, the dean said were vampires.
　　e.　More than/*Less than thirty-two admission candidates, they did contact.

For example, (6a) with *no fashion magazine* is excluded because *no fashion magazine* is both SYNNEG and monotone decreasing.

Increasing DPs that are SYNNEG also cannot be topics, as illustrated in (7b,d):

(7) a.　Jane invited no fewer than seventy people to her party.
　　b.　*No fewer than seventy people, Jane invited to her party.
　　c.　*Only Louise, Jane is going to exclude from the meeting.[2]
　　d.　*Not only Louise, Jane is going to exclude from the meeting.

The ill-formedness of both (7c,d) illustrates both a desirable consequence of condition (5) and a problem parallel to the one *only* phrases in particular raised for our formulation of the Negative Inversion Condition. Even though the topic in (7d) is a negation of that in (7c), and the former yields an ungrammatical topicalization, so does the latter. The ungrammaticality of (7d) follows from the fact that *not only Louise* is SYNNEG (via (5bi)). But *only Louise* in (7c) is technically nonmonotonic, hence not actually blocked by (5bii). Again, perhaps an appeal to Strawson decreasingness is the proper solution, as *only Louise* in (7c) is Strawson decreasing. Alternatively, our suggestion in chapter 14 that such *only* phrases might be reductions of those like *no one except Louise* offers the possibility that *only Louise* is SYNNEG, hence blocked as a topic by (5bi).

Condition (5) also predicts the following facts concerning the scope of negative quantifiers embedded in other DPs:

(8)   a.   The disbarring of not a single corrupt lawyer, she disapproved of.
            (= She disapproved of the fact that no corrupt lawyers were
            disbarred.)
      b.   Your willingness to interview not one star, Ted was shocked by.
            (= Ted was shocked by the fact that you were unwilling to
            interview any stars.)
      c.   Interrogations of no one, he said took little time.
            (= He said failures to interrogate anyone took little time.)

Example (8a) is grammatical even though the topic contains a decreasing negative DP, because the latter fails to have scope over the matrix clause. Similarly, (8b,c) are grammatical because *not one star* and *no one* do not take scope in the matrix clause.[3]

15.2   Topicalization and NEG Raising: A Puzzle

It is revealing to compare (9a), whose complement involves a Horn clause, and (9b), whose roughly parallel complement arguably manifests topicalization:

(9)   a.   I don't think that in any clothes did Bill look attractive yesterday.
      b.   *I don't think that in any clothes, Bill looked attractive yesterday.[4]

Examples (10a,b) illustrate a similar contrast:

(10) a.   I do not believe that Jerome's enthusiasm for any of the candidates
            did we actually discuss.
      b.   *I do not believe that Jerome's enthusiasm for any of the
            candidates, we actually discussed.

The generalization seems to be this:

(11) Classical NR cannot extract NEG from a topic.

For the remainder of the section, we focus for concreteness on the contrast in (10). Little more need be said about (10a), since it represents a regular Horn clause, corresponding to the Negative Inversion case (12):

(12) I believe that Jerome's enthusiasm for none of the candidates did we
        actually discuss.

Because its NI focus satisfies condition (3), example (12) is grammatical. That is, the NI focus dominates an element (*none of the candidates*) that scopes over the whole clause, and since *none of the candidates* is SYNNEG and decreasing, (12) satisfies condition (3). In our terms, then, (10a) is simply the Classical NR variant of (12) and thus expectedly grammatical.

The key question is why the topicalization case (10b) is *not* grammatical. One might attribute that property to the fact that the topicalized DP is an island out of which a NEG has been extracted by Classical NR. But that view is not consistent with the Island Sensitivity of NEG Raising Condition, (21) of chapter 13, repeated here:

(13) *The Island Sensitivity of NEG Raising Condition (second and final version)*
      If K is a clause and an island, then a NEG cannot extract from K.

Rather than adopting the above ideas based on islands, however, we will argue that (10b) is ill-formed because two independently justified constraints having nothing to do with islands impose contradictory, hence mutually unsatisfiable, conditions on interactions between Classical NR and constituent fronting under topicalization like that in (10b). The first of these is the English Topicalization Condition given in (5). The second is Seuren's (1974a) Highest-Operator Constraint (on Classical NR) already encountered in (38) of chapter 12.

To understand the ungrammaticality of (10b) in present terms, one must consider how our system of ideas forces it to be characterized. The ungrammatical (10b) would relate directly by the relevant NEG raising to (14a), which would seem to be the topicalized version of (14b):

(14) a. I believe that Jerome's enthusiasm for none of the candidates, we actually discussed.
      b. I believe that we actually discussed Jerome's enthusiasm for none of the candidates.

Examples (14a,b) differ in terms of scope properties. Example (14b) has at least two possible scope positions for the negative quantifier DP. One position is internal to the constituent *Jerome's enthusiasm for none of the candidates*, yielding equivalence to (15a). The other position of the negative quantifier is internal to the complement clause but higher than its main verb *discussed*, yielding rough equivalence to (15b):

(15) a. I believe that we actually discussed Jerome's lack of enthusiasm for any of the candidates.
      b. I believe that no candidate x is such that we actually discussed Jerome's enthusiasm for x.

Critically, though, the topicalization example (14a) has only reading (15a). The absence of reading (15b) follows from condition (5) since reading (15b) has a decreasing negative phrase as the highest-scoping element in the complement clause of *believe*, which condition (5) forbids.

What we have shown, then, is this. If (14a) is the source for the ungrammatical (10b) under Classical NR, it can only have interpretation (15a). To explain the ungrammaticality of (10b) without invoking any island violation, it then suffices to find an independently justified condition that blocks Classical NR from (14a) on interpretation (15a).

15.3   Seuren's Highest-Operator Constraint

We propose to explain cases like (10b) in terms of Seuren's (1974a) Highest-Operator Constraint, (38) of chapter 12, repeated here:

(16) *The Highest-Operator Constraint (on Classical NR)*
     If a NEG raises from clause B to clause A, and NEG originates in a
     unary-NEG structure W = [NEG X], then W is the highest operator
     in B.

We have already shown that a Classical NR analysis of the ungrammatical (10b) could only have (14a) as a source under scope analysis (15a). Under that analysis, the negative quantifier DP *none of the candidates* does not occupy a complement clause scope position. Rather, the increasing expression formed by the topic itself has the highest scope position, as required by condition (5). But in that case, condition (16) is not satisfied, and thus there is no legitimate Classical NR analysis of a topicalization example like (10b).

Significantly, (10b) has then been shown to be blocked without appeal to island constraints. Thus, our goal of showing that (10b) does not conflict with our conception of the role of island constraints in constraining Classical NR has been achieved. What examples like (10b) provide evidence for instead is the validity of the claim that the conditions on topicalization—here, (5)—and conditions on Classical NR—specifically, (16)—yield mutually unsatisfiable requirements on Classical NR *from a topic*.[5]

16 The Composed Quantifier Argument

16.1 The Argument

The argument at issue here depends on the existence of a well-documented variant of the Classical NR phenomenon involving not an overt main clause Aux instance of NEG as in (1a) but instead one or another negative quantifier phrase, like those italicized in (1b–f):

(1) a. Graham did not expect that she would arrive until Saturday.
   b. *No one* expected that he would breathe a word about it.
   c. *Not a single linguist* figured that in any sense was he anti-American.
   d. *No linguist* imagined that Carla had told a living soul about her father.
   e. *None of us* thought that he would stop at anything to achieve that.
   f. *Not one linguist* thought that Ralph understood squat$_A$ about gas turbines.

Each of (1b–f) has a CNRP in the main clause and a strict NPI in the embedded clause. We have argued that such a strict NPI needs to be licensed by a clausemate negation. However, none of these examples manifests a matrix clause containing an overt NEG that could have raised from its embedded complement clause. That renders it unclear how one could invoke Classical NR in such cases. So examples like (1b–f) pose a serious problem for the idea that Classical NR is what allows strict NPIs to be separated from negation in (1a), as supporters of a syntactic view of Classical NR including ourselves have claimed. In this chapter, we show how this argument has been elaborated in the literature on Classical NR and then argue that it lacks the force against syntactic views that it has been claimed to have.[1]

The basic argument against a syntactic view of Classical NR based on data like (1b–f) is seen here:

(2) (Horn 1978:170)

"Similarly, the negatives appearing in the quantificational expressions in the sentences below would (on their lower-clause reading) be incorporated after raising from their positions in the corresponding primed examples:

(101) a.   *Nobody would suppose anymore that the war was worth it.*

      a′.   Everybody would suppose {now/%anymore} that the war was not worth it.

      b.   Not everyone thinks I ought to leave you.

      b′.   Someone thinks I ought not to leave you.

      c.   {Only/Nobody but} John intends to vote for Porky Pig.

      c′.   Everybody but John intends not to vote for Porky Pig.

In each of these cases the negative is semantically associated with a clause below the NR [Neg-Raising] predicate(s) (*suppose, think, ought, intend*) although lexically incorporated above it. A plausible alternative to account for this reading is to semantically decompose (e.g. via meaning postulates) *nobody, not everyone,* and *only* into quantifier+neg complexes feeding Neg-Association."

Let us refer to the reasoning based on data like Horn's (101) as the *composed quantifier argument*. In essence, the argument is this: to maintain Classical NR in examples like (1b–f), one would have to assume that there is a raised NEG and that it somehow lexically incorporates into the matrix clause quantifier.[2] Since such an analysis is at best implausible, no NEG can have raised in (1b–f).

Horn and Bayer (1984) restated the argument and Horn (1989 [2001]) restated it once again:

(3) (Horn 1989 [2001:314–315])

"Any coherent transformational program for the NRP [Neg-Raising Phenomenon] must countenance a syntax in which Neg-Raising feeds those incorporation rules which result in the formation of the lexical items in (44) (cf. Horn [1978]: 170–71):

(44) nobody   -er than

      neither . . . nor   few

      {neither/none} of   scarcely (any)

      only   doubt

Thus, the sentences of (44′) are understood with the (italicized) incorporated negative taken in each case as semantically within the scope of the (boldface) neg-raising trigger to its right:

(44′) *Nobody* **supposes** that nuclear war is winnable.
       Neither Mutt *nor* Jeff **think(s)** that Chris has been here in weeks.
       {Neither/ None} of them is (are) **likely** to marry you.
       Only Kim **intends** to seek reelection.
       I spent *more than* I **should** have.
       {Few/Scarcely any} of my friends **believe** you'd lift a finger
       for me.
       I *doubt* that he {**wants/plans**} to resign just yet.

Thus, the first example is taken as suggesting that everybody supposes
nuclear war is not winnable, the second that both Mutt and Jeff think
that Chris hasn't been here in weeks, and so on. . . . For those who
subscribe to the currently received view that rules of word formation (as
opposed to rules of inflectional morphology on some accounts) are not
to be interspersed with rules of syntax, the thesis that a syntactic rule of
NR applies to the output of the lexical formative process involved in the
creation of . . . the operators in (44) amounts to a reductio of the
syntactic program for the NRP."

This version of the argument makes explicit that the conclusion depends on
rejecting the idea that the NEG putatively raised by Classical NR could
become covert in the lexicalization of various quantifiers.

The composed quantifier argument has apparently been broadly convincing.
We know of no past rejection of it in the literature. And variants of it are
restated as definitive by other authors. For instance:

(4) a. (Gajewski 2007:312)
       "Also notice that to explain the licensing of *until* in (83) [= *No one
       thought Bill would leave until tomorrow*], a syntactic account would
       have to decompose the negative subject into negation and a universal
       quantifier:
       (91) a. SS: [every one not thought [that Bill ___ left]]
                       "no one"
             b. LF: [every one ___ thought [that Bill not left]]
       As Horn (1978) has already pointed out, this is problematic. While
       decomposition of negative quantifiers like *no one* is often proposed,
       most evidence supports decomposing it into negation and an
       existential/indefinite, cf. Kratzer (1995), Potts (2000), Penka & von
       Stechow (2001). Having two such different decompositions of a
       single form should be avoided."

b. (Homer 2010:3–4)

"This purely syntactic view is hard-pressed to explain neg-raising with negative quantifiers, e.g. *no one* and *never*:

(3) a. No one wants to help me.

 b. *Paraphrasable as:* Everyone wants not to help me.

(4) a. John never wants to help me.

 b. *Paraphrasable as:* John always wants not to help me.

(3a) and (4a) are preferentially interpreted as meaning (3b) and (4b) respectively. Here again, it seems that negation is interpreted in the scope of the embedding predicate; what is surprising though is that the paraphrases contain positive universal quantifiers (*every* and *always*). If interpreting negation in the embedded clause is all there is to neg-raising, then the facts are inexplicable. The reason is that if negative quantifiers spell out negation and an existential quantifier (as is now standardly assumed, cf. Jacobs 1980, Ladusaw 1992, Geurts 1996, de Swart 2000, Zeijlstra and Penka 2005, Penka 2007), the reading that the negative transportation hypothesis (i.e. syntactic neg-raising) predicts is inadequate. It is given in (5b) below; (5c) is the paraphrase of the result of reconstructing the entire negative quantifier (negation and the existential quantifier). Not only is the actual reading not derived, but the two readings obtained by reconstruction are simply unavailable.

(5) a. NEG_1 someone want [t_1 help]

 b. Someone wants not to help me.

 c. (There) wants no one to help me.

The syntactic accounts are therefore insufficient."

The composed quantifier argument really has at least two aspects. Both depend on the claim that a higher-clause NEG is semantically associated with the lower clause, a claim supported by strict NPI examples like (1b–f), of which Horn (1989 [2001]) gave several. The first aspect of the argument is that even in the clearest cases like Horn's (101a,b) in (2), a syntactic Classical NR–based analysis seemingly requires treating the main clause quantifier DP (e.g., *nobody* in Horn's (101a)) as involving a post–Classical NR composition of some quantifier DP with the putatively raised NEG. This conclusion was based on the assumption that *only that kind of composition* can yield the right meaning. This was considered a strong objection because it requires a view of lexicalization under which it must operate on the output of syntactic operations. And that possibility was not popular in relevant grammatical circles at the time. Perhaps it is no more popular today.

The second aspect of the composed quantifier argument is explicit in Gajewski's and Homer's remarks about the apparently needed composition of a universal quantifier with NEG to yield the right meaning in the type of case cited by Homer:

(5) John never wants to help me.

To achieve the assumed correct meaning 'John always wants not to help me' via Classical NR, the argument is that *never* must be decomposed into [ALWAYS (NEG)]. Then, while the universal part arises in the main clause, the NEG originates in the complement clause, only reaching a point in the main clause where it can be lexically combined with the universal element via Classical NR. The motivated and standard analysis of *never*, on the contrary, is [NEG (SOMETIMES)], with both elements originating in the main clause in a case like (5).

Similarly, consider the following examples:

(6) a. No linguist believes that the columnist knows jackshit$_A$ about the subject.
     b. Some linguist believes that the columnist does not know jackshit$_A$ about the subject.
     c. Every linguist believes that the columnist does not know jackshit$_A$ about the subject.

A syntactic Classical NR analysis of (6a) seemingly requires taking the phrase *no linguist* to be a syntactic composition of the raised NEG and a distinct universal quantifier, *everybody*, since (6a) is equivalent to (6c), not to (6b) (assuming the excluded middle property of *believe*).

However, despite its apparent force and widespread acceptance, what the composed quantifier argument shows is not that syntactic accounts are generally insufficient but rather, at worst, only the inadequacy of certain *particular syntactic assumptions*. But the composed quantifier argument as a *general* attack on syntactic views of Classical NR is flawed, since the assumption that getting the meanings right in cases like (5) and (6a) must depend on post–Classical NR composition of the quantifiers cited *is just not true*. The relevant sentences can be correctly characterized with no post–NEG raising lexical composition of quantifiers and NEG at all. One can avoid wrong meanings and obtain the right ones without lexicalization of raised NEGs. We will show this in the following sections in two ways. First, we will present a viable syntactic analysis of the composed quantifier cases free of the properties underlying the strong criticisms we have just documented. Second, we will provide strong factual support for this analysis drawn principally from island facts of the sort treated in chapters 11 and 12, and from Horn clauses as treated in chapters 13 and 14. Chapter 17 on parentheticals provides independent evidence in support of our syntactic analysis of the relevant cases.

16.2 A Syntactic Alternative to the Composed Quantifier Analyses

Our analysis of the putatively composed quantifier examples is based on triples of examples like those in (7)–(12):

(7)   a.   Each detective thought that the prisoner had not seen his wife in years.
      b.   No detective thought that the prisoner had seen his wife in years.
      c.   *No detective proved that the prisoner had seen his wife in years.

(8)   a.   All of the doctors anticipated that she would not be feeling awful/ so hot after the operation.
      b.   None of the doctors anticipated that she would be feeling awful/so hot after the operation.
      c.   None of the doctors conceded that she would be feeling awful/*so hot after the operation.

(9)   a.   Both of the students imagined [that they would not be expelled until the end of the semester].
      b.   Neither of the students imagined [that they would be expelled until the end of the semester].
      c.   *Neither of the students knew [that they would be expelled until the end of the semester].

(10) a.   Every single one of the patients was likely not to/to not feel so hot at that stage.
      b.   Not a single one of the patients was likely to feel so hot at that stage.
      c.   *Not a single one of the patients was certain to feel so hot at that stage.

(11) a.   Every one of those judges thought that the ringleader would not stop at anything to avoid prosecution.
      b.   None of those judges thought that the ringleader would stop at anything to avoid prosecution.
      c.   *None of those judges recognized that the ringleader would stop at anything to avoid prosecution.

(12) a.   Every professor believes that Mike does not know jackshit$_A$ about physics.

    b. No professor believes that Mike knows jackshit$_A$ about physics.

    c. *No professor claims that Mike knows jackshit$_A$ about physics.

But to keep the discussion within manageable proportions, we focus exclusively on the cases in (12). This engenders no loss of generality for our conclusions since all the example sets share the same relevant properties.

Three things need to be explained about cases like (12). First, why is the strict NPI *jackshit$_A$* licensed in the embedded clause in (12b), in the absence of any overt local licensing negation? Second, how is it that (12a,b) are logically equivalent (a question taken up in section 16.6)? And third, why is (12c) ungrammatical, at least on a nonpolyadic analysis? The latter hedge alludes to possible confounding high-scope readings of strict NPIs in the complement clauses of non-CNRP main verbs, discussed at length in chapter 9. See the discussion of (17) below.

Our answer to the first and third questions hinges on the proposal that (12a,b) are associated with the simplified respective structures (13a,b):

(13) a. Every professor believes that [Mike does know [[NEG$_1$ SOME]
      jackshit$_A$] about physics]

    b. No professor [NEG$_2$ believes] that [Mike knows [[NEG$_1$ SOME]
      jackshit$_A$] about physics]

In both (13a,b), NEG$_1$ originates in the D of the DP *jackshit$_A$*. What is novel in (13b) is the presence of the verbal NEG$_2$, which is the key to our analysis.[3]

Crucially, (13a,b) have the same interpretation, which is determined as follows. First, their complement clauses are identical in structure, and hence in interpretation. Second, *every professor believes p* (with the predicate logic representation $\forall x B(x,p)$) is identical in interpretation to *no professor doesn't believe p* (with the predicate logic representation $\neg \exists x \neg B(x,p)$). In other words, every professor has belief p if and only if there is no professor who doesn't have belief p. We return to these issues in section 16.6.

Before presenting our analysis, however, we observe that the structures in (13) ignore the scope occurrences of *jackshit$_A$*. And given the discussion in previous chapters, it is impossible to consider the relevant sentences without taking those into account. Representations of these structures consistent with previous assumptions would then be as follows:

(14) a. Every professor believes that [Mike does NEG$_1$ [<[[<NEG$_1$> SOME]
      jackshit$_A$]$_3$> [know DP$_3$ about physics]]]

    b. No professor [<NEG$_2$> believes] that [Mike [<[[NEG$_1$ SOME]
      jackshit$_A$]$_3$> [knows DP$_3$ about physics]]]

In (14a), NEG_1 originates as a sister to SOME, raises to the position right-adjacent to the embedded Aux from its scope occurrence in the embedded clause, and is spelled out overtly. In (14b), NEG_1 originates in the same position of the embedded clause, accounting for the presence of the strict NPI. But in addition to NEG_1, there is also a NEG_2. And in (14b), both NEG_2 and NEG_1 are deleted, in ways we touch on presently. The critical element here is the NEG_2 in (14b), whose existence no version of the composed quantifier argument has ever contemplated.

The deletions rendering covert the two NEGs posited for (12b) in structure (14b) satisfy the general conditions on NEG deletion sketched in chapter 8. Since the two NEGs posited in (14b) are, evidently, not pronounced, we naturally invoke two instances of the NDEL relation. We also assume that the pair of NEG deletions required for analysis (14b) yields the NEG deletion chain in (15):

(15) <[No professor], NEG_2, NEG_1>

This sequence satisfies the definition of NEG deletion chain in (23) of chapter 8. That is, as required there, the initiator of the NEG deletion chain is not a NEG, all the other members are, and each member of the chain except the last is the NEG deleter of its successor element. The last member of the chain is properly not a NEG deleter. Moreover, (14b) trivially satisfies the NEG Deletion Chain Condition (25) of chapter 8.

There is an issue, however, in relating (14b) to the NDEL C-Command Condition (6) of chapter 8. While *no professor* evidently c-commands NEG_2, in its original position modifying the verb NEG_2 does not c-command NEG_1. There are two ways to keep the analysis consistent with (6) of chapter 8. The first would invoke the view that NEG_2 raises out of the verb-modifying position to be deleted by *no professor*. In particular, we assume that NEG_2 would raise to the immediate post-Aux position (where Aux is covert). This represents a view not inconsistent with any claim we have made. The second way would adopt the idea that NEG_2 originates higher than the verb level, in a position modifying the VP (containing the complement clause). We need not choose between these for the present argument. The key is that issues of c-command failure do not threaten our proposals.

Next, in (2) of chapter 8 we offered a typology of NEG deletions, dividing them first into lexical and general types, then separating the latter into polyadic and nonpolyadic cases. Then, among the nonpolyadic cases, we distinguished between those involving reversals and those involving nonreversals. Representation (14b) contains no reversal structure.

Clearly, in cases like (12b), represented as (14b), there is no motivation whatever for the complications involved in invoking lexical NEG deletion. The phenomenon is perfectly general and unlinked to particular lexical choices beyond the need for the main verb to be a CNRP. Therefore, in present terms, such cases instantiate general NEG deletion and thus must satisfy the General NEG Deletion Condition, (11) of chapter 8. This requires the initiator of the relevant NEG deletion chain to define a nonincreasing function with respect to the origin positions of the deleted NEGs. And that holds for the form *no professor* in (12b).

Since the NEG deletion chain in (15) does not involve a polyadic structure, nor lexical NEG deletion, the NEG Deletion Evenness Condition, (18) of chapter 8, must hold. It does, since according to (15) two NEGs are deleted.

The conformity of structure (14b) with the various conditions on NEG deletion mentioned so far is largely straightforward and raises no new problems. Specifically, NEG_2 can unproblematically have *no professor* as its NEG deleter in accord with (8) of chapter 8, the NDEL Clausemate Condition.

But an important issue is nonetheless raised by the deletion of NEG_1. In a structure like (14b), NEG_1 and NEG_2 certainly do not originate as clausemates. Therefore, the NDEL Clausemate Condition can only be satisfied if NEG_1 raises into the main clause, which is what we assume. We observe that the raising of NEG_1 to the matrix clause in the case of (14b), an instance of Classical NR, satisfies the C-Command Condition on Movement of chapter 5, requiring the target position of any raising to c-command the origin position.[4]

The issue of the positions to which the deleted NEGs (NEG_1 and NEG_2) in (14b) are raised is nontrivial since the deleted NEGs are covert. We assume that NEG_2 in (14b) raises away from the V/VP to a post-Aux position (in this case the Aux itself is covert). Therefore, NEG_1 cannot raise to the same position. There are various possibilities with regard to the position to which NEG_1 raises in the matrix clause. But we will not make any claims about that here.

A critical remark at this point is that the raising of NEG_1 into the matrix clause in (14b) is only possible with a main clause predicate that is a CNRP. That is, recall that in (4) of chapter 1, Classical NR was stated such that it entails the following:

(16) If NEG raises from clause B into clause A with predicate P, then P is a CNRP.[5]

That requirement is met in (14b) since *believe* is, of course, a CNRP. An evident entailment is that analogs of (14b) in which the CNRP is replaced by a non-CNRP main verb will be ungrammatical. And that is of course the case in (12c), whose underlying structure we take to be (17):

(17) No professor [<NEG$_2$> claims] that [Mike [<[[NEG$_1$ SOME] jackshit$_A$]$_3$> [knows DP$_3$ about physics]]]

Since the main clause architecture in (17) is isomorphic to that in (14b), the deletion of NEG$_2$ by the subject DP is as unproblematic here as in the earlier structure (14b). The complement clause in (17) is fully identical to that in (14b), and again NEG$_1$ finds no appropriate NEG deleter in the complement clause and hence could only find one in the main clause. The fundamental difference between (12b,c) is now apparent. Since the main verb is not a CNRP, NEG$_1$ in (17), unlike its correspondent in (14b), cannot raise into the matrix clause.

We note, however, that our discussion of the ungrammaticality of (12c) ignores the confounding high-scope issue discussed in chapter 9. It is quite possible that for some speakers, with the right lexical choices, cases like (12c) will be grammatical on a reading where *jackshit$_A$* takes main clause scope and forms a polyadic quantifier structure with *no professor*. On that analysis, (12c) would mean 'There is no pair of professors x and things y such that x claims Mike knows y about physics'. The structure underlying such a meaning does not, of course, invoke Classical NR; rather, it invokes deletion of the NEG in the main clause scope occurrence of *jackshit$_A$* by the main clause scope occurrence of *no professors*. We return to such confounding issues in section 16.5.

Now, consider cases where in addition to the strict NPI, there is a quantifier DP subject in the complement clause, as in (18), which we find ungrammatical:

(18) *No professor believes that everybody knows jackshit$_A$ about physics.

Our analysis of the composed quantifier cases like (12b) predicts the ungrammaticality of (18) on a reading for the NPI *jackshit$_A$* where its scope is in the complement clause. To see that, one must consider two possible analyses depending on whether the DP *everybody* has higher complement-clause-internal scope than the NPI phrase or conversely. That is, at issue are two structures of the following form:

(19) a. No professor [<NEG$_2$> believes] that [<[[NEG$_1$ SOME] jackshit$_A$]$_3$> [<[everyone]$_4$> [DP$_4$ knows DP$_3$ about physics]]]

b. No professor [<NEG$_2$> believes] that [<[everyone]$_4$> [<[[NEG$_1$ SOME] jackshit$_A$]$_3$> [DP$_4$ knows DP$_3$ about physics]]]

Consider first possibility (19a). NEG$_1$ in both (19a) and (19b) originates in a scope position, consistent with condition (4) of chapter 5, requiring NEGs raising from scope-bearing DPs to have their scope occurrences as their launching sites. Moreover, in (19a) NEG_1 occurs in the highest operator in the complement clause, and hence its raising into the main clause under Classical NR satisfies the Highest-Operator Constraint, (38) of chapter 12. So far, there is no problem with (19a). But to satisfy that condition, the structure in (19a) must instantiate a situation in our terms where an antiadditive syntactically negative DP in object position scopes over *everybody* in subject position. However, that particular type of so-called *inverse scope* configuration is independently impossible. Compare:

(20) Everybody knows nothing about physics.

This has only *everybody* > *nothing* scope, not inverse scope. The reason is that monotone decreasing quantifiers resist inverse scope over existential or universal quantifiers; see de Swart 1998:109, citing Liu 1990. So structure (19a) cannot yield a grammatical analysis of (18).

In (19b), on the contrary, the nonnegative quantifier has highest scope, avoiding a violation of the relevant inverse scope condition. However, in that case, the presence of Classical NR would violate the Highest-Operator Constraint. Thus, there is no way for (18) to be grammatical on a complement clause scope analysis of *jackshit*$_A$.

Any possible main clause scope analysis of *jackshit*$_A$ in (18) is, we assume, also blocked by the condition on inverse scope involving negative quantifier DPs. That follows since the height of the scope occurrence of *jackshit*$_A$ does not affect the inverse property, which refers to the relation between overt nonscope occurrences.

Our account also properly treats examples of the composed quantifier argument based on coordinate cases like (21) (based on examples in Horn 1978:171–172):

(21) a. Neither Mutt nor Jeff thought that the movie was half bad.
   b. Neither Mutt nor Jeff [<NEG_2> thought] that the movie was
      [<NEG_1> half bad]
   c. <[Neither Mutt nor Jeff], NEG_2, NEG_1>
   d. Both Mutt and Jeff thought that the movie was not half bad.

Here too an analysis with an "extra" covert NEG in the main clause eliminates any motivation for appealing to composition of main clause quantifiers with raised NEGs. NEG_1 can raise and be deleted by NEG_2, and the decreasing form *neither Mutt nor Jeff* can then delete NEG_2, yielding the NEG deletion chain (21c). The equivalence of (21a,d) is determined by the duality of the negative quantifier in (21a) and the universal quantifier in (21d), given that, under our Classical NR analysis, the complement clauses in (21a,d) are identical. We discuss this sort of equivalence in greater detail in section 16.6.[6]

16.3 Island Effects

In chapters 11 and 12, we argued on the basis of data from a variety of island types that Classical NR is subject to island constraints. However, the data in those chapters exclusively concerned the subtype of Classical NR cases that involve an overt main clause post-Aux NEG. In the present section, we show that the same patterns are found in structures of the sort underlying the composed quantifier argument. Because the reader can independently map earlier examples into the type relevant here, we will be very selective about the new data provided. We will also keep running commentary to a minimum.

First, recall from chapter 11 that data involving strict NPIs in topicalized clauses were argued to support the role of island constraints in constraining the distribution of Classical NR:

(22) a.   Laura does not believe that Sheila has prayed in years.
    b. *That Sheila has prayed in years, Laura does not believe.
    c. *That Sheila has prayed in years is not believed by Laura.

The same pattern appears in the type of structures relevant to the composed quantifier argument:

(23) a.   No coworkers believe that Sheila has prayed in years.
    b.   No coworkers [NEG_2 believe] that Sheila has prayed [NEG_1 in years]
    c. *That Sheila has prayed in years, no coworkers believe.
    d. *That Sheila has prayed in years is believed by no coworkers.

We stress that the same logic appealed to in section 12.10 is relevant here. On our analysis, NEG_1 in (23b) is deleted by NEG_2. The NDEL Clausemate Condition determines that the NDEL relation can only exist if NEG_1 raises into the main clause to become a clausemate of NEG_2. This is possible in (23a) since no island boundary intervenes between the main clause and the NPI. But in (23c,d) such boundaries do intervene, accounting for the ungrammaticality of the sentences. So in these cases, the ungrammaticality is a function of the interaction of Classical NR, the NDEL Clausemate Condition, and the Island Sensitivity of NEG Raising Condition ((13) of chapter 15). It also follows that nonstrict (reversal structure) NPIs will be grammatical in the same contexts in all of (23a–d), which is the case. The overall logic of this paragraph holds for all of the following cases in this section.

Next, in section 12.3 we presented island facts related to the presence of complement-internal topics:

(24) a.   Leslie doesn't believe that Jim should call Irene until tomorrow.
     b.   *Leslie doesn't believe that Irene, Jim should call until tomorrow.
     c.   Leslie doesn't believe that Carl said squat$_A$ to the chairman.
     d.   *Leslie doesn't believe that the chairman, Carl said squat$_A$ to.

Again, the cases relevant to this chapter show the same distribution:

(25) a.   No manager believes that Jim should call Irene until tomorrow.
     b.   *No manager believes that Irene, Jim should call until tomorrow.

(26) a.   Not a single observer believes that Carl said squat$_A$ to the chairman.
     b.   *Not a single observer believes that the chairman, Carl said squat$_A$ to.

In section 12.6, we showed that complement-clause-internal clefts, which are islands, block Classical NR:

(27) a.   I think that it is Ted who didn't tell a living soul.
     b.   *I don't think that it is Ted who told a living soul.

(28) a.   I think that it is Ted who has not spoken to his mother in ages.
     b.   *I don't think that it is Ted who has spoken to his mother in ages.

Once more, there is strict parallelism with the main clause quantifier DP cases:

(29) a.   Neither detective thinks that it is Ted who didn't tell a living soul.
     b.   *Neither detective thinks that it is Ted who told a living soul.

(30) a.   Neither detective thinks that it is Ted who has not spoken to his mother in ages.
     b.   *Neither detective thinks that it is Ted who has spoken to his mother in ages.

Earlier chapters treated a large class of island constraints, showing their relevance to constraining Classical NR. Even for the subset of those island constraints discussed here for negative quantifier cases, the diagnostics for the presence of Classical NR (strict NPIs) systematically fail to appear when, in our terms, the relevant NEG raising could only reach the main clause by exiting a clausal island. Notable at this point is that nothing need be added to previous accounts to block the ill-formed cases in this section. The ungrammaticality simply follows from the earlier Island Sensitivity of NEG Raising

Condition, (13) of chapter 15, combined with our analysis outlined in (14b) and (15).

On the contrary, the ill-formed examples in this section seem mysterious from the standpoint of the semantic/pragmatic accounts that have generated the composed quantifier argument. None of them have offered any ground for the fact that the supposedly semantic/pragmatic phenomenon, one claimed to involve nothing more than inferences, systematically obeys varied constraints barring extractions from islands. If there is some way for them to explicate these facts, providing it should be a requirement on the adequacy of future nonsyntactic proposals about Classical NR.

Given these comparative advantages of the syntactic view of Classical NR, the following is clear. Far from *undermining* a syntactic approach, the domain from which the composed quantifier argument draws its evidence actually provides strong support *for* a syntactic view and raises an enormous barrier to the success of any nonsyntactic treatment. Moreover, that barrier has never been addressed in any nonsyntactic view with which we are familiar.

16.4 Composed Quantifier Cases and Horn Clauses

As just shown, island data strongly support our syntactic analysis of the composed quantifier cases. Similarly, the fact that Horn clauses are licensed in composed quantifier structures also strongly supports our syntactic view. Consider the following examples:

(31) a. No officer expected that any sergeant would they promote to
         lieutenant.
     b. No officer expected that at any time would they promote Greg.

These examples appear to involve Horn clauses, whose fronted XPs we have shown in chapter 14 to be instances of Negative Inversion despite the absence of any overt NEG internal to their overt occurrences. In other words, we showed that the fronted phrases in Horn clauses represent disguised NI foci. The fact that such phrases instantiate Negative Inversion led to the conclusion that they represent a unary-NEG analysis since only that analysis could permit them to satisfy the Negative Inversion Condition, (3) of chapter 15. However, the discussion of Horn clauses in chapters 13 and 14 did not treat the specific clause type in (31) with a negative quantifier matrix subject. Rather, we limited attention to Horn clauses whose unary NEG originating in the NI focus ended up as an overt NEG in the main clause.

We can, however, now consider cases like (31a,b) in the light of dual considerations that interact in such examples: those involving the character of

Horn clauses and those involving Classical NR. The first point is that fronted DPs like *any sergeant* and *any time* in (31a,b) must be analyzed as unary-NEG structures to satisfy the Negative Inversion Condition. Since the unary NEGs are not overt, there must be NEG deletion, which must meet the general conditions on that. Let us focus on (31a) for concreteness.

Unary-NEG deletion must satisfy the NDEL Clausemate Condition. Therefore, the NEG of the NI focus in (31a), call it NEG_1, either must have an originally local NEG deleter or must raise into the main clause to be deleted by the only available legitimate NEG deletion chain initiator in that clause, *no officer*. However, if NEG_1 raises into the main clause and is deleted there by *no officer*, a violation of the NEG Deletion Evenness Condition, (18) of chapter 8, ensues.

That problem is, however, circumvented by the assumption central to our treatment above of (14b): namely, there is an "extra" verbal constituent NEG in the main clause. Given that, the relevant structure of (31a) would be (32a), permitting formation of the NEG deletion chain (32b):

(32) a. No officer [<NEG_2> expected] that [<[[<NEG_1> SOME] sergeant]$_4$>
         [DP$_4$ [would they promote DP$_4$ to lieutenant]]]
     b. <[No officer], NEG_2, NEG_1>

The NEG deletions determining (32b) satisfy all of the conditions we have posited. NEG_2 can delete NEG_1 because it c-commands it under one of the assumptions cited earlier; and NEG_1 can raise into the main clause under Classical NR because *expect* is a CNRP, permitting it to be a clausemate of NEG_2. The phrase *no officer* can delete NEG_2 because (i) *no officer* is a decreasing operator, (ii) it c-commands NEG_2, and (iii) it and NEG_2 are clausemates.

Thus, our syntactic analysis of Horn clauses and our syntactic treatment of the composed quantifier cases, each previously developed and supported independently, interact perfectly from a syntactic point of view. Moreover, their interaction appears to yield a correct semantic result, namely, that (31a) has a reading equivalent to (33a), in turn equivalent to (33b):

(33) a. No officer didn't expect that no sergeant would they promote to
         lieutenant.
     b. Every officer expected that no sergeant would they promote to
         lieutenant.

In section 16.6, however, we discuss this semantic result in greater detail, considering its relation to the excluded middle property. That aside, this account evidently achieves these results with no appeal to the kind of quantifier DP + NEG composition that authors like Horn, Gajewski, and Homer have taken to create a decisive refutation of a syntactic view of Classical NR.

To conclude this section on the interaction of the type of Horn clauses found with main clauses not containing overt instances of post-Aux NEGs, we add the following. Nonsyntactic approaches to Classical NR have no more provided a nonsyntactic analysis of Horn clause cases like (31a,b) than they have of the overt post-Aux NEG cases treated in chapter 14. As far as Horn clauses are concerned, then, extant nonsyntactic accounts of Classical NR do not even qualify as competitors of the current syntactic analysis.

16.5 A Confounding Factor: More Quasi–Horn Clauses

There is, however, a potential confounding factor, related to the general discussion of quasi–Horn clauses in section 14.5. The legitimacy of (32a) as a structure for (31a) hinges on the fact that *expect* is a CNRP. One then concludes that otherwise parallel examples in which a non-CNRP is substituted for *expect* should be ungrammatical. Example (34) provides instances of such substitutions:

(34) No officer indicated/proved/reported/stated that any sergeant would they soon promote.

However, for at least some speakers (including one of us), some such sentences seem to be grammatical, provided that the NPI form *any* is strongly stressed. We thus believe there is a contrast between the following two types of complements of main clauses like that in (34):

(35) a. No officer reported that ANY sergeant would they soon promote.
    b. *No officer reported that any SERgeant would they soon promote.

Assuming that the contrast in (35) is real, we suggest that it illustrates the same type of confound discussed in chapter 9. In present terms, (34) has three possible structures. On one, [[NEG SOME] sergeant] takes scope in the embedded clause. This structure is ruled out since it requires raising of a NEG out of the complement clause of a non-CNRP. In the second structure, [[NEG SOME] sergeant] takes matrix scope. In this case, the complement is not a Horn clause but what we have called a quasi–Horn clause. In the third structure, *any sergeant* represents a reversal structure. We assume this is blocked since reversal phrases cannot trigger Negative Inversion.

Quasi–Horn clauses of the type at issue—that is, those without an overt NEG in the main clause—are found on the Web:

(36) a. I have found no evidence suggesting that at any time did the
      policymakers harbor doubts on the effectiveness of the law of one

price to decisively and immediately reduce the rate of inflation of traded goods (Gil, 1980).

(kellogg.nd.edu/publications/workingpapers/WPS/146.pdf)

b. " . . . because there was never any evidence that at any time had he uttered a pro-Fascist, or anti-Semitic remark," Mr. Buckley wrote.

(www.nysun.com/national/case-of-the-nazi-propagandist/18043/)

c. There was no testimony from either Maynard, Sevrans, or Shields that at any time had they relied upon any of these particular items believing . . .

(mi.findacase.com/research/wfrmDocViewer.aspx/xq/fac.../qxShare)

Such cases do not provide any problem for our views of Classical NR if each has an analysis as a quasi–Horn clause, that is, one where the NEG legitimizing the Negative Inversion in the complement clause is part of a negative quantifier DP whose scope is in the main clause. This seems to us a correct conclusion, but there are too many such cases of different types for us to analyze them in detail in the present monograph. There are many complications in particular cases.

For instance, in all of (36a–c) the complement clause manifesting Negative Inversion is embedded inside a nominalization rather than directly inside the main clause, as was the case with the Aux-located NEG type of quasi–Horn cases considered in section 14.5.[7]

Second, nominalization cases like (36a–c) also arguably involve polyadic analyses in which one (or in the case of (36b) possibly two) main clause [NEG SOME]–type DPs share a D with the negative DP NI focus in the complement. For example, a polyadic analysis of (36c) in the terms developed in chapter 6 would yield a meaning for that example of the schematic form in (37):

(37) There is no <x, y>, x testimony, y a point of time, such that x is testimony from either Maynard, Sevrans, or Shields that they had relied on any of these particular items at y.

This seems an accurate account of the interpretation of the example.

The same points made about quasi–Horn clauses in chapter 14 hold for the type at issue here. We suggest that these also instantiate the confound of high-scope occurrences discussed in chapter 9. For a brief illustration, consider the relevant part of (36b):

(38) There was never any evidence that at any time had he uttered a pro-Fascist, or anti-Semitic remark.

In our terms, this would have to have a polyadic structure with the phrase *any time* having a high-scope occurrence just as much as *never* and *any evidence* do, the three sharing the same D. The meaning of the whole would be roughly 'There was no triple $<t_1, x, t_2>$ such that t_1 and t_2 are points in time and x is an element of evidence such that at t_1 x is evidence that he uttered at t_2 a pro-Fascist or anti-Semitic remark'.

It seems clear that the meaning of (38) cannot involve the meaning of 'at no time' under the scope of *evidence*. Thus, even ignoring the lack of a CNRP environment, having the scope of the NEG (needed to legitimize the instance of Negative Inversion) in the complement clause cannot yield a proper interpretation.

Furthermore, *at any time* in (38) could not be analyzed as a reversal, since we have shown in chapter 14 that reversals do not trigger Negative Inversion. However, distinguishing between a wide scope polyadic interpretation of *at any time* in (38) and a narrow scope indefinite (reversal) interpretation is difficult. See section 9.5 for relevant considerations.

Quasi–Horn clauses of the type at issue here represent a rich area for further inquiry into the related areas of NEG raising, NEG deletion, and NPI distribution. But this is a domain beyond the scope of the present monograph.

16.6 Classical NEG Raising and the Excluded Middle Property

In our discussions of the composed quantifier argument, we have so far had very little to say about a semantic equivalence that is central to Horn's (1978) original proposal of the argument and is taken as axiomatic by its later advocates. The issue did arise with respect to the claimed equivalence of (33a,b) above; but in general, we have focused on the issue of NPI licensing in the relevant constructions as well as on Horn clauses. In this section, we will show how the framework we have developed to account for the facts we have concentrated on also accounts for the semantic equivalence that Horn noted.

At issue is the equivalence of pairs like (12a,b), repeated here:

(39) a. Every professor believes that Mike does not know jackshit$_A$ about physics.

 b. No professor believes that Mike knows jackshit$_A$ about physics.

We start from the observation that when *think* (or any other CNRP) is used in a context that blocks the presence of the excluded middle property, strict NPIs are not acceptable in the embedded clause:

(40) a. *I don't think that Vincent knows jackshit$_A$ about physics, because I have never heard of him.

b. *I don't think that Marilyn has seen her mother in ages, because I don't know Marilyn.

c. *I don't think that Michael is feeling so hot, and I don't think Michael is not feeling so hot, because I have no opinion about Michael's health.

The generalization seems to be that if there is a strict NPI in the embedded clause, a negated matrix CNRP cannot have a 'no opinion' interpretation:

(41) If a strict NPI is grammatical in the complement of a negated CNRP verb V, then V has the excluded middle property.

Generalization (41) references strict NPIs, since it is strict NPIs that we have repeatedly appealed to in arguments for Classical NR.

Our framework can explain (41) as follows. There are two cases to consider. In the first case, the NEG in the matrix clause in the examples in (40) modifies the matrix V/VP. In that case, the strict NPI is left without a NEG and is hence ungrammatical. In the second case, in all the examples in (40), the NEG in the post-Aux position in the main clause has raised into the main clause from its origin in the strict NPI of the embedded clause. Therefore, (40a–c) are respectively identical in interpretation to (42a–c):

(42) a. I think that Vincent doesn't know jackshit$_A$ about physics, because I have never heard of him.

b. I think that Marilyn has not seen her mother in ages, because I don't know Marilyn.

c. I think that Michael is not feeling so hot, and I don't think that Michael is not feeling so hot, because I have no opinion.

Each of these sentences is semantically anomalous for the following reasons. Example (42a) asserts the contradiction that I both have thoughts about Vincent and have never heard of him. Similarly for (42b,c). And for the same reason, the examples in (40) are semantically anomalous.

We have therefore shown that on one analysis the structures in (40) are ungrammatical, and on the other they are semantically anomalous.

In this light, consider examples like (43) with main clause negative quantifiers:

(43) None of my friends thought that Bill was gifted.

This example can express either (44a) or (44b):

(44) a. Every one of my friends thought that Bill wasn't gifted.

b. None of my friends had an opinion about whether Bill is gifted.

The latter reading of (43) can be forced by certain expansions of the original:

(45) None of my friends thought that Bill was gifted, since none of them had ever heard of him.

Example (43) entails (44a) if the excluded middle property holds: then everybody had some opinion about whether or not Bill was gifted. So under that condition, if (43) is true, then (44a) must be true.

Against this background, one can see that a generalization very close to (41) holds in these cases as well:

(46) a. *Nobody thinks that John knows jackshit$_A$ about physics, because they have never heard of him.
   b. *Nobody thinks that Mary has seen her mother in ages, because they don't know Mary.
   c. *Nobody thinks that John is feeling so hot, and nobody thinks that John is not feeling so hot, because they have no opinion.

In all cases, the occurrence of the strict NPI seems to force the absence of a 'no opinion' interpretation, a generalization captured in the following variant of generalization (41):

(47) If a strict NPI is licensed in the complement of a CNRP verb V with a negative quantifier subject, then V has the excluded middle property.

Like generalization (41), generalization (47) can be shown to follow from the current system. Take (48a), with the relevant structure in (48b):

(48) a. No one thinks that Alfred knows jackshit$_A$ about physics.
   b. No one [<NEG$_2$> thinks] that [<[[NEG$_1$ SOME] jackshit$_A$]$_3$> [Alfred knows DP$_3$ about physics]]
   c. Everyone thinks that Alfred doesn't know jackshit$_A$ about physics.

Here, the complement clause of (48b) means 'there is nothing that Alfred knows about physics'. Call this meaning M. The main clause then states that no one doesn't think M. Logic alone then determines the wanted equivalence to (48c), given the standard duality of existential and universal quantification represented in (49):

(49) $\sim\exists x \sim P(x) \Leftrightarrow \forall x P(x)$

Now, return to the statement in (47). Recall that the excluded middle property is of the following form:

(50) x think that p or x think that not p

In our terms, the structure of both (48a,c) involves a main verb (plus a complement clause) expressing a definite opinion on the part of the main clause subject: namely, for every x, x has the opinion that Alfred knows nothing about physics. Therefore, there cannot be a 'no opinion' reading. Therefore, (47) holds.

It is worthwhile pointing out why, in contrast to the strict NPI cases, those with nonstrict NPIs in their complements can support the 'no opinion' interpretation. Consider:

(51) a. I don't think that Melissa knows anything about physics, because I have never heard of her.

    b. No one thinks that Melissa knows anything about physics, because no one has ever heard of her.

Example (51a) is grammatical because the NPI can have a low-scope reversal analysis, with the NEG deleter of the reversal NEG being [NEG think] (so there is no Classical NR). There is no contradiction between the main clause and the *because* clause, because the main clause is negative and hence attributes no thought to the speaker.

The NPI in (51b) can also have a reversal analysis where *no one* is the NEG deleter of the reversal NEG. Because the main verb is *think* unmodified by a covert NEG, the structure does not entail that anybody has any opinion. So again the meaning is consistent with the absence of the excluded middle property.[8]

16.7 Meaning Equivalences with Other Quantifiers

So far in this monograph, our discussions of Classical NR cases with main clause negative quantifier DPs (and no overt post-Aux NEG) have almost entirely utilized DPs of the form [no X]. Specifically, this was the case in the argument that examples like (12a,b), repeated here, are equivalent:

(52) a. Every professor believes that Mike does not know jackshit$_A$ about physics.

    b. No professor believes that Mike knows jackshit$_A$ about physics.

While convenient for certain purposes, this artifact should not obscure the point that the logic of such arguments does not depend on this limited choice of data. To show this, we work out a few cases for quantifiers distinct from *every* and *no* showing equivalences of the sort adduced by Horn (1978:170), quoted in (2) and illustrated in (52).

The task is to show that our syntactic analysis of the composed quantifier cases yields the correct interpretation for other quantifier subjects, specifically, that the analysis rightly also predicts the equivalence of pairs like (53a,c):

(53) a. Not many people think that Loretta married Ted.
      b. Not many people [NEG$_2$ think] that Loretta [NEG$_1$ married Ted]
      c. Many people think Loretta did not marry Ted.

We are concerned, then, with pairs like (53a,c) under our assumption that there is a covert NEG in the complement clause and a covert verbal NEG in the main clause, as in (53b). To understand the relations between (53a,c), first consider a sentence with no complement clause and hence no Classical NR:

(54) a. Not many people worry about Loretta.
      b. Not many people didn't worry about Loretta.

In (54a), *not many* is equivalent to *few*. In other words, (54a) means that few people worry about Loretta. Now suppose there is a set of ten people. Let us stipulate that within that set, seven to ten people counts as many, and zero to three people counts as few. In this context, (54a) has the interpretation in (55a), which can be paraphrased as (55b):

(55) a. There is no set of people g, such that |g| > 3, where for every
          member x of g, x worries about Loretta.
      b. No more than three people worry about Loretta.

There is also an implicature that if one says (54a), somebody actually worries about Loretta. The same implicature exists with *few*.

Consider now (54b). Under our analysis of *not many*, its interpretation is equivalent to (56):

(56) No more than three people do not worry about Loretta.

For the set of ten people, this means that zero, one, two, or three people do not worry about Loretta (with an implicature that there is at least one person who does not worry about Loretta). This means that the rest do worry about Loretta (with the implicature that not everybody worries about Loretta). Hence, seven or more people worry about Loretta. Therefore, many people worry about Loretta.

Returning to (53a), if not many people did not think p, then it follows, given the reasoning above, that many people did think p. Therefore, according to our analysis, (53a) with structure (53b) is equivalent to (53c), which is the desired result. Thus, the cases in (53) show that the logic illustrated in earlier sections for the [no X] quantifier cases holds as well for the [not many] type.

Consider next the subject quantifiers *a majority/minority of the class*:

(57) a. A majority of the class believed that the official lied.
     b. A majority of the class [NEG_2 believed] that the official [NEG_1 lied]
     c. A minority of the class believed that the official did not lie.

The relevance of pairs like (57a,c) is, of course, that while neither contains an overt NEG, *minority* is, for quantification over odd-numbered sets (which exclude an equinumerous division), the negation of *majority*.

Focus first on the non–Classical NR case:

(58) a. A majority of the class did their homework.
     b. A majority of the class didn't do their homework.
     c. A minority of the class did their homework.

Suppose the class has twenty-one student members. Then if (58a) is true, given the meaning of *majority* as 'more than half', at least eleven of the students did their homework, and correspondingly ten or fewer didn't. Similarly, in (58b), at least eleven students didn't do their homework, and ten or fewer did. But if ten or fewer did do their homework, then (58b) is equivalent to (58c).

Return to (57a) on structure (57b), supposing again that there are twenty-one students in the class. Then (57b) entails that eleven or more of the students didn't believe that the official didn't lie, which in turn entails that ten or fewer believed that the official didn't lie. That expresses what (57c) does. So the equivalence between (57a) and (57c) is predicted by our structure in (57b).

Consider next:

(59) a. Scarcely anybody expected him to get there until after 5:00.
     b. Scarcely anybody [<NEG_2> expected] him [to [<[<NEG_1> until after 5:00]$_5$> [get there PP$_5$]]]
     c. Almost everybody expected him not to get there until after 5:00.
     d. Almost everybody expected him [NEG_1 to [<[<NEG_1> until after 5:00]$_5$> [get there PP$_5$]]]

These examples represent a more complicated situation than earlier ones in this section for two reasons. First, the quantifier DPs are more complex than previous ones and involve the "approximative" modifiers *scarcely* and *almost*.[9] Second, the complement contains a strict NPI. However, neither of these points obscures the fact that our Classical NR analysis of (59a) represented in (59b) determines that the complement clauses in (59a) and (59c) are originally syntactically identical, hence semantically identical. They differ only in the semantically irrelevant properties that in the representation of (59a) in (59b), NEG_1 raises into the main clause via Classical NR and is deleted as part of a NEG deletion chain <[scarcely anybody], NEG_2, NEG_1>, while in (59d), NEG_1

raises from the scope position to a higher position in the infinitival complement.

To demonstrate the equivalence between (59a) and (59c), we observe that *scarcely any X* is equivalent to *almost no X*. Consider then sentences like (60a–c):

(60) a. Almost nobody protested.
    b. Almost nobody didn't protest.
    c. Almost everybody protested.

Suppose for argument's sake that *almost nobody* means at most five percent and that similarly, *almost everybody* means no less than ninety-five percent. Now, consider (60) in the context of a student protest, where there are a total of one hundred students. Under these assumptions, in (60a), a maximum of five students protested. In (60b), a maximum of five students didn't protest, which means that ninety-five or more students did protest. But then (60b) is equivalent to (60c).

Now consider (59a) with structure (59b), assuming the same set of one hundred people. We assume [NEG until X] phrases to mean 'not before time point t denoted by X' (with a presupposition that the event at issue did occur at t). If X denotes an interval, then [NEG until X] means 'not before the beginning of the interval denoted by X' (with a presupposition that the event in question occurred during the internal denoted by X). It follows that (59b) claims that five or fewer people didn't expect him not to get there before 5:00. That is equivalent to saying that at least ninety-five people did expect him not to get there until before 5:00. But under the assumptions in effect, given the semantically relevant structural identities between the complement clauses in (59b,d), that is what (59c) claims as well.

The discussion earlier in this chapter was restricted to the [no X] subtype of quantifier DP. But the logic relevant to showing that earlier pairs like (52a,b) are equivalent has been shown to determine that relevant pairs of sentences like (53a,c), (57a,c), and (59a,c) are equivalent as well given respective "extra negation" structures like (53b), (57b), and (59b). Overall, in this chapter we have now illustrated that the following equivalences hold, where V_x is a CNRP:

(61) a. No NP   NEG V_x NEG P = Every NP V_x NEG P
    b. Not many NP   NEG V_x NEG P = Many NP V_x NEG P
    c. A majority of DP   NEG V_x NEG P = A minority of DP V_x NEG P
    d. Scarcely any NP   NEG V_x NEG P = Almost every NP V_x NEG P

This set of equivalences raises an important question that we can barely touch on here. Out of the multitude of distinct quantifier pairs that might occur in equivalences like those in (61), why do exactly these equivalences hold, since certainly a randomly chosen pair of quantifiers—for example, [more than n] and [most]—determine nothing of the sort? Thus, pairs like (62a,b) manifest no equivalence whatever:

(62) a. More than seven doctors didn't believe that.
     b. Most doctors believed that.

The answer hinges on the notion *dual*, defined as follows:

(63) (Peters and Westerståhl 2006:26)
     "[T]he respective quantifiers are each other's duals, where the dual
     of Q_i is the outer negation of its inner negation (or vice versa):
     $Q^d_i = \neg(Q_i \neg) = \neg(Q_i)\neg = \neg Q_i \neg$."

For example, $\exists$ is the dual of $\forall$ because $\exists x P(x) = \neg \forall x \neg P(x)$, and similarly, $\forall x P(x) = \neg \exists x \neg P(x)$. Note that from these equivalences one derives $\neg \exists x P(x) = \forall x \neg P(x)$ and $\neg \forall x P(x) = \exists x \neg P(x)$.

In light of this definition, consider the following equivalences (summarized from the discussion above):

(64) a. Everybody left   = Nobody didn't leave
     b. Many people left   = Not many people didn't leave
     c. A minority left   = A majority didn't leave
     d. Almost everybody left = Hardly anybody didn't leave

In every case, the quantifier on the left, call it Q_1, is equivalent to the quantifier on the right, call it Q_2, combined with a following negation. Also let Q_d be the dual of Q_1. Then we have:

(65) a. $Q_1 x P(x)$ $= \neg Q_d x(\neg P(x))$ (by definition)
     b. $Q_1 x P(x)$ $= Q_2 x(\neg P(x))$ (by preceding discussion)
     c. Therefore, $\neg Q_d x(\neg P(x))$ $= Q_2 x(\neg P(x))$

Therefore, the relevant relation between Q_1 and Q_2 in all the equivalences above is as follows:

(66) Q_2 is the negation of the dual of Q_1.

So our claim is that whenever Q_2 is the negation of the dual of Q_1, it will be possible to set up equivalences of the type discussed in this section.

Finally, given our syntactic analysis of the composed quantifier cases, there are often two semantically equivalent syntactic analyses for a single sentence. Consider, for instance:

(67) a. Nobody thinks that Doris left.
     b. Everybody thinks that Doris didn't leave.
     c. Nobody [NEG$_2$ thinks] that Doris [NEG$_1$ left]

Given the excluded middle property, even without covert NEGs, (67a) has interpretation (67b), as demonstrated in (68):

(68) a. Nobody thinks that Doris left.
   b. Everybody does not think that Doris left. (on reading *every* > *not*)
      (from the logical equivalence $\neg\exists xP(x) = \forall x\ (\neg P(x))$)
   c. In particular, for A an arbitrary individual:
      A does not think that Doris left.
   d. Therefore, by the excluded middle property:
      A thinks that Doris didn't leave.
   e. Since A was arbitrarily chosen:
      Everybody thinks that Doris didn't leave.

(68e) is the same interpretation given by our representation (67c). But as argued in earlier chapters, only a representation like (67c) yields an explanation of the distribution of strict NPIs in the composed quantifier cases, an analysis of Horn clauses, and an account of the sensitivity of strict NPIs to islands. Furthermore, representations like (67c) are independently supported by the analysis of parentheticals in chapter 17. Therefore, as concluded earlier, even if there is an excluded middle property, it is not sufficient to account for the facts we have discussed.

16.8   The Apparently Decisive Argument: Conclusions

We have thus shown how in a system recognizing NEG raising and NEG deletion, both subject to the various conditions we have proposed, one can provide a syntactic analysis of putative composed quantifier cases that involves no quantifier composition at all. This analysis yields a clear and intuitive account of the difference between pairs like (52b,c), a difference that reduces, as desired, to the difference between main verbs that allow Classical NR and those that don't. Our excursus has shown that there is a syntactic treatment invoking Classical NR that requires neither lexicalization operating on the output of Classical NR nor any complex building of one set of quantifier expressions from combinations of raised NEGs with others.

A specific conclusion is that criticisms made by both Gajewski (2007) and Homer (2010) (see (4a,b)) do not hold. Their key point is the assumption that the syntactic view of Classical NR requires not only composition of quantifiers with raised NEGs, but in particular compositions such that *no* must be composed of *every* + NEG. This is undesirable since, as they observe, it is conventional wisdom that in general *no* is a composition of NEG + *some* (an assumption we share, as outlined in chapter 3). But this consideration is rendered irrelevant by the fact that the analysis we have sketched involves no quantifier phrase composition of raised NEGs at all.

A further important conclusion is that we have gone significantly beyond showing that no aspect of the composed quantifier argument has any force against our particular syntactic position. Specifically, in sections 16.3 and 16.4 dealing with the relations between Classical NR and island constraints and between Classical NR and Horn clauses, respectively, we have provided evidence that the present syntactic approach has positive consequences that nothing in past nonsyntactic views matches. Thus, beyond having shown that the composed quantifier argument has no force against the specific syntactic account of Classical NR we have developed, we have shown that our account is superior to known nonsyntactic views of Classical NR on factual grounds.

Despite the conclusion just stated, one might of course adopt and furthermore justify any one of the following syntactic views. Either the structures we have proposed for the supposed composed quantifier cases (e.g., those in (57b) and (59b)), the NEG raisings and NEG deletions such analyses require, or all of these, are impossible. And even internal to a framework in which all can be recognized, there might be arguments against the specific proposed analyses.

But the relevant argumentation in works like Jackendoff 1971, Horn 1978, 1989 [2001], Gajewski 2007, Homer 2010, and others we are familiar with that advocate semantic views of Classical NR doesn't begin to address such issues. The type of facts they lean on could only bear on the general viability of a syntactic view of Classical NR if, minimally, they led to arguments that the kind of syntactic analyses we have sketched and the various principles governing NEG raising and NEG deletion are untenable. However, such arguments are not found in the works just cited, and we strongly suspect that nothing like what would be needed has been presented anywhere.

Rather, we believe the driving force behind the composed quantifier argument has simply been a failure to contemplate a Classical NR analysis that appeals to NEG deletion as well as NEG raising. Thus, discussing examples including (66a), Jackendoff (1971:292) made the flat claim in (69b):

(69) a. Scarcely anybody expected him to get there until after 5:00.

    b. "For these sentences *there is no way to have an underlying negative in the complement sentence* that will condition the use of *until*." (emphasis ours)

But, as we have shown, there *is* a way, provided by our structure for (66a) previously given in (59b) and repeated in (70a):

(70) a. Scarcely anybody [<NEG$_2$> expected] him [to [<[<NEG$_1$> until after 5:00]$_5$> [get there PP$_5$]]]
      b. Almost everybody expected him not to get there until after 5:00.

Since, as noted, *scarcely anybody* means 'almost nobody', the equivalences discussed in the previous section were shown to determine that (70a) is equivalent to (70b), which is correct.

So despite having apparently been taken to be *decisive*, the composed quantifier argument itself has so far never been shown to even bear on the issue of whether or not Classical NR is a syntactic phenomenon. On the contrary, in particular via documentation of the island facts in section 16.3 and the Horn clause facts in section 16.4, we have argued that data relevant to the composed quantifier argument actually provide very strong support for a syntactic view of Classical NR.

17 Parentheticals

17.1 Background

A further argument for a syntactic view of Classical NR can be based on *parenthetical clauses*, that is, those like the expressions italicized in (1). In particular, the argument will be based on the principles determining under what conditions *negative* parenthetical clauses can exist.[1] ((1a,b) are from Ross 1973:133.)

(1) a. Max is a Martian, *we realized.*
    b. Frogs have souls, *I realize that Osbert feels.*
    c. Carmen will, *Ted thinks*, certainly marry Fred.
    d. Carmen will certainly, *Ted thinks*, marry Fred.
    e. Carmen will certainly marry Fred, *Ted thinks.*

We restrict attention throughout to declarative parentheticals like those in (1).

As (1c–e) show, parentheticals can appear in various positions with respect to the independent clause they modify. This possibility need not concern us. Nor will the fact that parentheticals can only modify main clauses, as illustrated in (2):

(2) a. Eugene assumed, I think, that Virginia would marry him.
    b. *Eugene assumed that Virginia would, I think, marry him.

A fundamental question about the nature of parentheticals is the relation between the modified clause and the parenthetical. We will assume that the parenthetical is a reduction of a full clausal structure involving a complement clause that is covert in the parenthetical itself (see Dowty [2008] on parentheticals). So a parenthetical like (3a) is taken to realize an underlying structure of the form (3b):

(3) a. Sally will, Eugene assumes, take a morning flight.
    b. [Sally will take a morning flight] *[LINK [Eugene assumes that Sally will take a morning flight]]*

Hereafter, we refer to the italicized structure as an *afterthought*. Parenthetical constructions are then taken to have the general underlying form in (4):

(4) [$_A$ X] + Afterthought (= [LINK [$_B$ Y [$_C$ Z]]])

We will refer to clause A, that is, the clause modified by the parenthetical, as the *prime* (this is equivalent to Dowty's (2008) *core clause*); to clause B as the *secondary*; and to clause C as the *tertiary*.[2] The idea of the LINK constituent is that it expresses whatever the precise relation between the prime and the afterthought is. Its actual content is unclear. At one point, Dowty (2008) considers that in at least some cases it might be represented by *at any rate*. Another possibility is *at least*. Perhaps there is no overt English representative. Fortunately, the issue of the relation between the prime and the afterthought does not matter for the present argument.

Ross (1973:137) observed that every verb that allows the formation of a parenthetical independently takes *that* clause complements. This generalization would show up in the present account as a restriction of tertiaries to *that* clauses. In a case like (3a), while [Eugene assumes] corresponds to the secondary in (4), [Sally will take a morning flight] corresponds both to X, the prime, and to Z, the elided tertiary. That is, a fundamental aspect of parenthetical formation is (5):

(5) *The Parenthetical Identity Condition*
     The prime modified by a parenthetical clause Q is identical to the
     tertiary of Q.

By stating the relevant identity condition in terms of the prime + afterthought structure, where the relevant components are continuous, we straightforwardly define the identity needed for well-formed parentheticals even for cases like (1c,d), where, in the actual word sequence, the parenthetical is surrounded by parts of the prime.

Evidently, the assumptions so far require that we take the afterthought's tertiary, represented by clause C in (4), to be elided as a function of some kind of clausal ellipsis grounded on the identity with the prime. In section 17.3, we indicate that constructions independent of parentheticals motivate the recognition of such a clausal ellipsis phenomenon. It is also necessary that both the LINK and the *that* complementizer be deleted (or simply fail to appear) under parenthetical formation.

17.2 Negative Parentheticals

We turn to the question of what conditions permit what we can call *negative parentheticals*, of which we distinguish two basic types: those with an overt post-Aux occurrence of NEG, and those lacking that NEG but having a negative subject DP or negative adverbial.

Consider first the overt post-Aux NEG case. As Ross (1973:136–137) observed, such parentheticals are *in general* impossible, a fact only briefly illustrated in (6) ((6a) is from Ross 1973:157):

(6) a. Manny has no Adam's apple, I (*don't) fear.
    b. Cathy was (not), she asserted/proved/reported/said/wrote, divorced from Frank.
    c. Cathy was (not), she *didn't assert/prove/report/say/write, divorced from Frank.

The same pattern holds for a multitude of verbs taking *that* complements.[3]

But, despite (6), what appears to be a negative parenthetical pattern is nonetheless grammatical with a small class of verbs including *anticipate*, *appear*, *believe*, *expect*, *guess*, *imagine*, *seem*, and *think* if the prime is also negative, as illustrated briefly in (7) ((7a) is from Ross 1973:155):

(7) a. There are no more bowling balls, I don't think.
    b. Cathy would *(not), he didn't anticipate/believe/expect/guess/imagine/think, divorce Frank.
    c. Cathy will *(not), it doesn't appear/seem, divorce Frank.

This is not a random class, as Ross noted:

(8) (Ross 1973:157)
"What is significant about the class of verbs which can appear in negative parentheticals is that it is precisely the class of verbs which undergo *Not-Hopping*."

Since *Not-Hopping* was Ross's term for Classical NR, he had discovered that those verbs that exceptionally form *negative* parenthetical clauses of the above type are all CNRPs.

Ross then summarized key issues relating Classical NR and negative parentheticals in the following statements:

(9) (Ross 1973:158)
    a. "The verb of a negative parenthetical must be a verb which allows Not-Hopping."
    b. "Negative parentheticals can only follow a negative clause."
    c. "Normally, negative parentheticals are impossible."

Statement (9b) references facts like the stars on the cases in (7b,c), where the main clause lacks a NEG. We will suggest below that (9b) requires no special stipulations. The stars on the forms without main clause NEGs in (7b,c) will be argued to follow essentially from the identity condition on the clausal ellipsis rendering the tertiary covert. The extensive (but not complete) truth of statements (9a,c) will be argued to follow from a general condition holding for the secondaries of all parentheticals, called the Parenthetical Nondecreasingness Condition, given in (19). In section 17.4, we show how everything that is correct in statements (9a–c) follows from present assumptions.

Given the mass of ungrammatical cases like (6c), one might suggest the following as a simple principle governing English parenthetical formation:

(10) A NEG cannot originate in that part of a parenthetical P corresponding to the secondary of the afterthought structure (see (4)).

While (10) would rightly block all the ungrammatical cases in (6a,c), it would then be necessary to show how it can remain consistent with the grammatical cases in (7b), that is, those where the negative parentheticals are based on CNRPs.

This could be possible under the assumption that the afterthought structure of the grammatical variant of (7b) is (11):

(11) [Cathy would not divorce Frank] LINK [he did not (= NEG_1)
      anticipate/believe/imagine <[Cathy would [<NEG_1> divorce] Frank]>]

Structure (11) is consistent with condition (10) because NEG_1 does not originate in the secondary of the afterthought structure but rather in the tertiary. Such a structure for (7b) is evidently only possible internal to a syntactic view of Classical NR when combined with the fact that the possible main verbs of the secondary of (11) (corresponding to Y in (4)) are all CNRPs. Only CNRPs permit the needed raising of NEG_1 from the tertiary into the dominating secondary. The implication is that condition (10) shows how a syntactic view of Classical NR is the critical factor in explaining Ross's generalization (9a).

However, condition (10) turns out to be independently untenable, and we will show how the cases it gets right follow in distinct ways and how the contrast between the ungrammatical non-CNRP cases in (6) and the grammatical CNRP cases in (7) is to be accounted for. Specifically, we will show that the correct consequences of (10) are special cases of a principle we call the Parenthetical Nondecreasingness Condition; see (19).

A key property of the afterthought structure in (11) for cases like (7b) relates to the identity between the prime and the tertiary of the afterthought needed to define the ellipsis relevant to parentheticals. For that to be subsumed under general assumptions about the identity requirements for clausal ellipsis, ellipsis in parentheticals must be taken to hold on the structure of the tertiary containing a NEG like NEG_1 in (11). Specifically, that must be the case even though NEG_1 has raised out of the tertiary under Classical NR. This could be possible in various ways, either by defining the identity for ellipsis on a pre–Classical NR structure or by appealing to something like the copy theory of movement, in which case Classical NR would leave an exact replica of the raised NEG in its preraised position.

In contrast, an analysis otherwise analogous to (11) but with the CNRP replaced by a non-CNRP cannot, given condition (10), yield a well-formed parenthetical because the analog of NEG_1 could then not raise from the tertiary into the secondary. Therefore, the only way to get a negative parenthetical for a non-CNRP would involve a NEG origin in the secondary, violating condition (10) and, more importantly, violating what we take to be its tenable replacement in (19), the Parenthetical Nondecreasingness Condition.

17.3 Brief Remarks on Clausal Ellipsis

Our idea that clausal ellipsis can be based on structures ultimately formed by Classical NR in such a way that NEG raises out of a constituent that undergoes ellipsis might seem extravagant. But the idea can be supported by constructions independent of parentheticals.

Consider this discourse:

(12) A: Karen is pregnant.
    B: I don't think so.

Clearly, B's response expresses the thought 'Karen is not pregnant' rather than a view about B's thoughts. That is, B's reply appears to be a Classical NR case in which the underlying complement clause is elided in a fashion yielding the anaphoric form *so*.

The same argument can be based on (13):

(13) A: Karen is pregnant.
    B: No, I think not.

In this case also, the response expresses the thought 'Karen is not pregnant' and clearly a 'no opinion' reading is out of the question. Here too, then, there is justification for an elided complement clause of *think*, with its originally contained NEG appearing outside of the ellipsis site, although the exact position that the putatively raised NEG ends up in is not clear to us.

Cases like (12) and (13) may relate to an important discovery made by Ross (1973:151), namely, that parentheticals appear to manifest island constraints. He showed with data like (14a,b) that both the Complex NP Constraint and the Coordinate Structure Constraint appear to constrain grammatical parenthetical formation. (We have irrelevantly changed the locus of the parentheticals and made the objects of *has* heavier to increase their naturalness.)

(14) a. Max has, I believe (*your claim) that Pete pointed out, a wonderful new tuba.
   b. *Max has, Ted is reading a book and will find out, a wonderful new tuba.
   c. Max has, Ted will find out, a wonderful new tuba.

That discovery raises the question of what exactly has been extracted to invoke the relevance of island constraints. Cases like (12) may suggest that the relevant element is a null version of the anaphoric *so*. That form can be overtly present in an extraction position in cases like (15):[4]

(15) Karen is pregnant or so Miranda says.

Cases like (12), (13), and (15) support the view that the clausal ellipsis needed in the analysis of parentheticals as reduced afterthoughts exists independently.

Besides the ellipsis just discussed, the analysis would have to guarantee a covert LINK and the absence of the complementizer *that*. The latter at least is arguably also needed, though, in cases such as (12), (13), and (15).

17.4 More on Negative Parentheticals

We observe next that the same non-CNRP/CNRP-based division of negative parentheticals seen in (6) and (7) is found when such expressions have negative subject phrases yielding clauses resembling those considered in our analysis of the composed quantifier argument in chapter 16.

(16) a. *Cathy will not, nobody asserted/proved/reported said/wrote, divorce Frank.
   b. Cathy will not, nobody anticipates/believes/expects/imagines/ thinks, divorce Frank.

That is, like cases where an overt post-Aux NEG occurs in the parenthetical, cases where a parenthetical instead contains a negative subject are also grammatical when the main verb is a CNRP but ungrammatical when it isn't.

The first conclusion from (16) is that, as claimed earlier, condition (10) cannot be right. Clearly, in grammatical cases like (16b) a NEG has originated in the subject DP of the parenthetical, hence in the secondary of the underlying afterthought. One might try to correct condition (10) by talking about verbal negation, but that would be a mistake, as shown in (17):

(17) a. Cathy was (not), *I deny, divorced from Fred.
     b. Cathy was (not), I don't deny, divorced from Fred.
     c. Cathy was (not), *I doubt, divorced from Fred.
     d. Cathy was (not), I don't doubt, divorced from Fred.

That is, as also noted in Ross 1973:136, with non-CNRP verbs with negative force like *deny*, *doubt*, and *forget*, parenthetical clauses with overt Aux NEGs are possible, just as those with CNRP-based parentheticals are. Ross's claim (9a) limiting all negative parenthetical verbs to CNRPs was, then, partially wrong. The grammatical cases in (17b,d) also violate condition (10), again showing its untenability. Moreover, parentheticals based on the negative force verbs where the verb is not negated are impossible, as shown in (17a,c).

Parallel facts for negative force verbs are seen when parentheticals involve negative quantifier DP subjects instead of Aux-located NEGs. That is, again, negative parentheticals with these negative verbs are possible and, moreover, are possible as modifiers of either positive or negative main clauses:

(18) a. Cathy was (not), no one denies, divorced from Fred.
     b. Cathy was (not), no one doubts, divorced from Fred.

Since condition (10) is untenable, the question arises what principle of the grammar can maintain its correct predictions while remaining consistent with facts like (16b), (17b,d), and (18). We suggest that a constraint along the following lines is needed, one stated in terms of the semantic property of nondecreasingness:

(19) *The Parenthetical Nondecreasingness Condition*
     In an afterthought structure $[_A X]$ + Afterthought$_\Psi$ (= [LINK $[_B Y$
     $[_C Z]]]$), the composition of the meanings of all the elements (e.g.,
     subject, verb, negation, adverb) in the secondary (i.e., clause B) is not
     a decreasing function with respect to the tertiary (i.e., clause C).

This condition allows afterthought secondaries to compose to either increasing or nonmonotonic functions, but not to decreasing ones.

The power of this proposal is seen in examples like (20a–c):

(20) a. *The project is, zero (or more) voters/no politician/few people/
          neither commentator/less than a third of the population is/are
          willing to say, seriously underfunded.

    b.   The project is, some politician/many people/both commentators/ more than a third of the population is/are willing to say, seriously underfunded.

    c.   The project is, exactly two politicians/only Bob/no one but Bob/ seven or more senators/many men but few women is/are willing to say, seriously underfunded.

All of the subject phrases in the parentheticals in (20a) are decreasing phrases, all of those in the parentheticals in (20b) are increasing phrases, and each of those in (20c) defines a nonmonotonic function. And as condition (19) determines, only the cases with decreasing operators are ungrammatical.[5]

One can see that condition (19) correctly blocks cases that the untenable condition (10) got right, such as (21):

(21) *Terry is (not), they didn't say, going to retire.

In such cases, the combination [NEG say] occurring in the secondary of the afterthought in the structure underlying the parenthetical in (21) forms a decreasing function, and nothing else in the secondary combines with that to yield a nondecreasing function. So condition (19) is violated.

This reasoning also reveals why examples like those in (16a) are ill-formed. The secondary in such cases contains a decreasing subject DP and nothing else for it to combine with to render the whole nondecreasing; so again condition (19) is not satisfied. These results represent entailments of Ross's claim in (9a) that are correct. But whereas Ross's (9a) falsely claims that (17b) is ungrammatical, constraint (19) correctly distinguishes between pairs like (17a,b), repeated here:

(22) a.   Cathy was (not), *I deny, divorced from Fred.
      b.   Cathy was (not), I don't deny, divorced from Fred.

The verb *deny* alone in the secondary underlying the parenthetical of (22a) defines a decreasing function, rightly blocking (22a). But, given the nature of the meaning of NEG, [NEG deny] in the secondary of (22b) yields a nondecreasing function, so that (22b) satisfies condition (19).

The same reasoning accounts for the contrast between examples like (23a–c):

(23) a.   *Cathy was (not), every lawyer denied, divorced from Fred.
      b.   Cathy was (not), not a single lawyer denied, divorced from Fred.
      c.   *Cathy was (not), not a single lawyer didn't deny, divorced from Fred.

That is, the composition of the increasing subject DP *every lawyer* with the decreasing verb *deny* yields a decreasing secondary in (23a), violating condition (19), while the composition of the decreasing subject DP *not a single lawyer* with *deny* in (23b) yields a nondecreasing function. Thus, the latter example satisfies condition (19) and can be well-formed.[6] But the addition of a further negation, as in (23c), again yields a decreasing function and hence a violation of (19).

We have argued, then, that a wide variety of negative parentheticals based on non-CNRPs are ungrammatical because the secondaries of their underlying afterthoughts represent one of the situations in (24):

(24) a. The non-CNRP in the secondary is a semantically increasing verb that is negated but combines with no other form in the secondary to yield a nondecreasing expression (e.g., (21)).

    b. The non-CNRP in the secondary is semantically decreasing (e.g., *deny*) and not combined with any decreasing element of the secondary and so yields a nonincreasing expression (e.g., (22a)).

    c. The non-CNRP in the secondary is a semantically increasing verb that composes with a decreasing phrase in the secondary to result in a semantically decreasing expression (e.g., (16a)).

    d. The non-CNRP in the secondary is a decreasing form that is negated and combined with a third decreasing element (e.g., (23c)).

All of these situations violate condition (19). But as we have shown, contrary to Ross's (9a), some of the negative force verbs (e.g., *deny*) can form acceptable negative parentheticals if they are directly negated or have negative quantifier subjects (but not both), since those combinations compose to yield nondecreasing functions, satisfying condition (19).[7]

We also take condition (19) to be the basis for Ross's (9c) claim that negative parentheticals are normally impossible. The claim is true because (i) the class of non-CNRP verbs like *deny* that can permit negative parentheticals is tiny and (ii) the class of CNRPs that at first glance seem to permit negative parentheticals is also relatively small. Moreover, condition (19) guarantees that only a subset of structures formed with verbs like *deny* can be grammatical, and it blocks other non-CNRP-based negative parentheticals under almost all conditions.

The key question needing analysis, though, is why apparent negative parentheticals based on CNRPs can be grammatical despite condition (19) given that their secondaries contain overt instances of NEG. To understand this, consider first one of the variants of a case like (7b), repeated as (25a), with its afterthought structure previously given in (11), repeated as (25b):

(25) a. Cathy would *(not), he didn't expect, divorce Frank.

b. [Cathy would not divorce Frank] LINK [$_A$ he didn't (= NEG$_1$) expect [$_B$ Cathy would [<NEG$_1$> divorce] Frank]]

Given (25b), the reason why negative parentheticals like that in (25a) are grammatical despite condition (19) is straightforward. Structure (25b) satisfies condition (19) since NEG$_1$, which appears *overtly* in the secondary of the afterthought (hence in the parenthetical), originates in the tertiary of the afterthought and has no semantic role at all in the afterthought's secondary. Hence, despite the superficial NEG occurrence in the secondary, the secondary forms an increasing function with respect to the tertiary.

Critically, though, this reasoning holds only under our syntactic view of Classical NR, because that alone permits the NEG of the parenthetical in (25a) to arise in the tertiary rather than in the secondary. Structure (25b) cannot be grammatically replicated when its CNRP is replaced by a non-CNRP. In that case, the analog of NEG$_1$ could not, because of (4) of chapter 1, raise into the secondary clause and so would have to originate in it.

Our account would predict that Classical NR in parentheticals should be blocked by islands. This prediction is difficult to test because of the nature of parentheticals. But one case that shows the island sensitivity of Classical NR in parentheticals can be described as follows. If the parenthetical in (25a) is replaced by *it's true*, the result is acceptable. However, if it is replaced by *it isn't true* or *it is not true*, the result is horrible. That consequence follows from the discovery noted in chapter 12 that the complement of a truth predicate is an island. Therefore, an analysis parallel to that in (25b) is impossible, since the raising of NEG$_1$ would be blocked by the island.

We turn now to more complicated CNRP cases like a variant of (16b), repeated as (26a), which would be represented in present terms with the afterthought structure in (26b):[8]

(26) a. Cathy will not, nobody thinks, divorce Frank.

b. [Cathy will not divorce Frank] LINK [$_A$ nobody [<NEG$_2$> thinks] [$_B$ Cathy will [NEG$_1$ divorce] Frank]]

We observe, first, that the form of the secondary, clause A, represents the same structure type proposed for putative composed quantifier argument cases in chapter 16. That is, critically, the main verb *think*, a CNRP, originates with its own NEG, NEG$_2$, the novel "extra" NEG characteristic of our treatment of the structures relevant to the composed quantifier argument. That (and only that) permits the negative quantifier subject to combine with it to yield an increasing function, satisfying condition (19). This is why we were able in chapter 16 to show the equivalence of structures such as (27a,b):

(27) a. Nobody thinks Cathy will divorce Fred.
    b. Everybody thinks Cathy will not divorce Fred.

In this chapter, we have provided independent support for the "extra" NEG analysis of the composed quantifier cases of chapter 16. Any rejection of our chapter 16 analysis of those cases would also have to offer an alternative to condition (19) to capture cases like (26a). That conclusion raises an additional hurdle for any nonsyntactic account not recognizing the "extra" NEG we have posited in that subset of Classical NR cases, because it is only the "extra" main clause NEG that renders the secondary clause in cases like (26b) nondecreasing.

Next, note that in (26b) NEG_2 can delete NEG_1 when NEG_2 raises from clause B into the secondary clause A, permitted just because *think* is a CNRP. And then *nobody* can delete NEG_2. These deletions satisfy all the conditions on general NEG deletion in chapter 8, in particular, the NEG Deletion Evenness Condition. But again, the account we have given of (26a) in (26b) is only possible under a syntactic view of Classical NR. That in turn requires a general framework countenancing extensive instances of NEG deletion subject to conditions such as those in chapter 8.

Significantly, the considerations just appealed to do not allow analogs of structure (26b) where the main verb is not a CNRP. First, consider an example entirely parallel to (26b) except that *asserts* replaces *thinks*:

(28)   [Cathy will not divorce Frank] LINK
      [nobody [<NEG_2> asserts] [$_A$ Cathy will [$_B$ <NEG_1> divorce] Frank]]

Structure (28) yields not a grammatical output parallel to (26a) but only the ungrammatical (29):

(29)   *Cathy will not, nobody asserts, divorce Fred.

The reason is that there is no appropriate general NEG deleter in the tertiary, clause B of (28), to delete NEG_1. Moreover, NEG_1 cannot find a NEG deleter in the dominating secondary represented by clause A without raising into A because of the NDEL Clausemate Condition, (8) of chapter 8. But NEG_1 cannot raise into the secondary clause A because its main verb, *assert*, is not a CNRP. So a direct analog of (26b) for (29) is impossible.

Suppose, though, that the structure was identical to (28) except that NEG_1 was never present, eliminating the need for it to be deleted, as in (30):

(30)   [Cathy will not divorce Frank] LINK [nobody [<NEG_2> asserts]
      [$_A$ Cathy will [$_B$ divorce Frank]]]

The structure in (30) satisfies condition (19). However, it is still ungrammatical. First, this example violates the identity condition on deletion of the tertiary, the Parenthetical Identity Condition (5). Second, even without NEG_1 the structure would still contain the *covert* NEG_2, so that must be deleted. But without the additional deletion of NEG_1, the resulting NEG deletion chain, <nobody, NEG_2>, would violate the NEG Deletion Evenness Condition. Third, if one suppressed NEG_2 from (30) with or without the suppression of NEG_1, condition (19) would be violated, since the suppression of NEG_2 would render the secondary decreasing. There is thus no path to grammaticality for a negative subject parenthetical based on a non-CNRP like that in (29). Again, this result stands on our view of Classical NR as a syntactic phenomenon and on our posit of NEG deletions subject to the various conditions just cited.

We can now also explicate the fact represented in Ross's statement (9b) that negative CNRP-based parentheticals can only modify negative clauses. That statement need not be stipulated since it follows from the general analysis we have proposed. To see that, consider the afterthought structure of the wrong form of (7c), repeated in (31a), which would be (31b):

(31) a. *Cathy will, it doesn't appear/seem, divorce Frank.
      b.   [Cathy will divorce Frank] LINK [$_A$ it doesn't (= NEG_1) appear
           [$_B$ Cathy will [<NEG_1> divorce] Frank]]

First, this analysis, with NEG_1 originating in the tertiary clause, is the only one that condition (19) permits. If NEG_1 originated in the secondary clause A of the afterthought, the composition of the meanings in the secondary would yield a decreasing function. Second, structure (31b) cannot yield a viable output since there is no identity between the prime, *Cathy will divorce Frank*, and the tertiary, which is the complement of *appear*. Hence, the ellipsis required does not exist and cases like (31a) are blocked with no special stipulations.

The same reasoning shows that more complex cases like (32a) with afterthought structure (32b) are blocked:

(32) a. *Ted will, none of them believe, resign.
      b.   [Ted will resign] LINK [$_A$ none of them [<NEG_2> believe] [$_B$ Ted
           will [<NEG_1> resign]]]

Here, the representation matches the type we justified in the discussion of the composed quantifier argument in chapter 16. But in this parenthetical case, the structure is illegitimate because the prime and the tertiary (clause B) are not identical, the former lacking a NEG, rendering the necessary ellipsis of the latter impossible. On the contrary, if the prime contains a NEG, as in (33a), clausal identity holds, no violation ensues, and, correspondingly, (33b) is perfectly grammatical:

(33) a. [Ted will not resign] LINK [$_A$ none of them [$<$NEG$_2>$ believe]
     [$_B$ Ted will [$<$NEG$_1>$ resign]]]
   b. Ted will not, none of them believe, resign.

So the correctness of Ross's (9b) for this class of cases is also a consequence of our assumptions. And we have in fact shown that everything that was correct in Ross's (9a–c) follows from present proposals.

17.5 Further Implications

Our analysis of parentheticals also has implications for claims we have made in other parts of this monograph. Consider the following example with a negative quantifier in the primary. In order to satisfy the conditions on parenthetical formation we have established, the structure of (34a) has to be (34b):

(34) a. Nobody, I don't think, will resign.
   b. [$<$[$<$[NEG$_1>$ SOME] body]$_3>$ [DP$_3$ will resign]] LINK [$_A$ I do NEG$_4$
      think $<$[$<$[NEG$_4>$ SOME] body]$_5>$ [DP$_5$ will resign]]$>$

One sees that in order for the identity condition between the primary and the tertiary to be met, NEG$_4$ must have raised from the negative quantifier DP. That conclusion confirms our fundamental assumption that NEG raising from negative quantifier DPs is possible. Therefore, the conclusion strongly supports our analysis of unary-NEG NPIs as involving NEG raising. If, instead, the tertiary underlyingly involved an NPI never directly associated with a NEG (as in standard approaches), then there could be no identity between the matrix clause and the tertiary.

An argument parallel to that just based on (34) can be given outside of the domain of parenthetical formation. Consider:

(35) a. I interviewed no students yesterday and Greta didn't either.
   b. I interviewed no students yesterday and Greta didn't interview any
      students yesterday either.
   c. [I [$<$[[NEG$_1$ SOME] students]$_3>$ [interview DP$_3$ yesterday]]] and
      [Greta didn't (= NEG$_2$) [$<$[[$<$NEG$_2>$ SOME] students]$_5>$
      [$<$[interview DP$_5$ yesterday]$>$]]]

A structure like (35c) is the only possibility if the ellipsis in the second clause of cases like (35a) is taken to be subject to syntactic identity. However, if the elided constituent in (35a) contained an NPI with no associated NEG, as on standard analyses of nominal NPIs, then the antecedent and elided DPs in (35a) would not be close to being identical syntactically. That is, only our view that NPIs like *any students* in (35b) are unary-NEG structures whose NEGs have raised out of their originally containing Ds and DPs provides the structure needed for the identity underlying the ellipsis in cases like (35c).

Consider too the following example, illustrating how our analysis of parentheticals interacts with our analysis of Horn clauses. In this case, there is a negative quantifier in the NI focus position of the primary:

(36) a. No suspect, I don't think, have they talked to about this.

   b. <[[NEG$_1$ SOME] suspect]$_3$> [DP$_3$ [have they talked to <DP$_3$> about this]] LINK [I don't (= NEG$_2$) think [<[[<NEG$_2$> SOME] suspect]$_5$> [DP$_5$ [have they talked to <DP$_5$> about this]]]]]

Since the matrix clause in (36a) is a Negative Inversion construction, the only way the identity condition on clausal ellipsis central to parenthetical formation can be met in our framework is if the tertiary of the parenthetical construction in (36b) also manifests (of course covert) Negative Inversion. But since Classical NR occurs in the parenthetical, the tertiary must be a Horn clause. The identity condition between the primary and the tertiary can then only be met via our analysis of the fronted NPI DPs in Horn clauses as negative quantifier DPs. So cases like (36a) provide new and unexpected support for our negative quantifier analysis of Horn clauses.

17.6 Summary

Overall, then, the parenthetical facts in this chapter strongly support our syntactic view of Classical NR because the assumptions we have made previously combine with a variant of Dowty's (2008) afterthought proposal about parenthetical formation and condition (19) to account for the parenthetical facts cited here. We do not see how semantic/pragmatic views of Classical NR can achieve these results, and we are fairly certain that no nonsyntactic account of Classical NR has had anything to say about the CNRP/non-CNRP parenthetical contrasts. (Ross (1973) did offer an account, but it was syntactic.) Finally, our analysis of parentheticals provides powerful independent support for the "extra" NEG approach to the composed quantifier cases of chapter 16.

18 *Never* Raising

In this chapter, we focus on a phenomenon referred to as *Never* Raising. We highlight problems in a potential nonsyntactic account of *Never* Raising akin to the nonsyntactic account that we have given of Classical NR.

The earliest recognition of *Never* Raising we are aware of is found in the following remark:

(1) (Fillmore 1963:220)
"Transposition of NOT(EVER) to Main Verb (Partly Obligatory)
Under certain conditions (e.g. after verbs like WANT or THINK which are themselves not negated) a NOT in the embedded sentence may be moved in front of the main verb. If NOT has been shifted, then an EVER in the embedded sentence may also be moved forward."

Fillmore cited the following example:

(2) I never expect you to do that again.

The point was that in such examples, the main clause *never* can be understood to modify the complement clause.

A subsequent description of *Never* Raising is found in (3):

(3) (Horn 1971:125–126).
"It will be recalled that *hope*, although in the class of intention verbs, does not permit NEG-raising. But consider the following examples:
(20) a. I don't hope to see a brown cow.
    a′.   never
    b. I hope to not see a brown cow.
    b′.   never
    c. I never hope that I see a brown cow.
    d. I never want to see a brown cow.
                wish
                ?care

> While (20a) shares no readings with (20b)—i.e. its negation must originate in the upper sentence—(20a′) does have a reading synonymous with, and presumably derived from, (20b′). (20a′) on this reading expresses a hope, rather than the absence of a hope. . . . There is then, alongside NEG-raising, an optional rule of *never*-raising. . . . *Never*-raising seems to be restricted, unlike NEG-raising, to cases where the lower sentence manifests a *for-to* complementizer (hence the absence of a lower sentence reading for *never* in (20c))."

We agree with Horn (1971) that *Never* Raising represents a syntactic raising phenomenon. Moreover, we believe that that fact strengthens the case that Classical NR does as well.

Here are a few more examples involving main clause predicates distinct from those Horn cited:

(4) a.   You seem to never be happy nowadays.
   b.   You never seem to be happy nowadays.

(5) a.   Kate Middleton is likely to never appear on *Oprah* for money.
   b.   Kate Middleton is never likely to appear on *Oprah* for money.
        (www.huffingtonpost.com/social/jeanrenoir/sarah-ferguson-royal-wedding-oprah_n_860224_87789465.html)

(6) a.   I expect to never see Minnesota again.
   b.   I never expect to see Minnesota again.

(7) Although he is never supposed to use his magic . . .
    (www.bookrags.com/notes/hp/TOP4.html)

Besides the paraphrase relations between putative *Never* Raising cases and otherwise parallel clauses in which the *never* is in the complement, there is evidence for the syntactic character of the phenomenon from adverbial modification:

(8) a.   I never watch foreign movies.
   b.   *Sometimes, I never watch foreign movies.
   c.   I never want you to leave again.
   d.   Sometimes, I never want you to leave again.
   e.   Sometimes, I want you never to leave again.

We find that (8b) is semantically ill-formed in a way that (8d) is not. Modification of a clause C by *sometimes* yields a contradiction if C expresses a negative universal quantifying over time. But example (8d) can express the perfectly coherent claim that sometimes the speaker has the wish that the addressee never leave again, equivalent to the reading of (8e).

A stronger argument for the syntactic character of *Never* Raising is that it obeys island constraints, just like Classical NR:

(9)   a. I plan never to return.
      b. I never plan to return.

(10) a. I plan what to never eat on a long trip.
      b. I never plan what to eat on a long trip.

Examples (10a,b) have sharply different interpretations. The former involves planning about what people should never eat on a long trip, while the latter merely affirms the absence of planning with regard to trip food consumption. So (10a,b) lack the kind of semantic equivalence characteristic of *Never* Raising cases like (9a,b). We attribute this to the fact that *never* would have to have raised out of a *wh*-island to yield a reading of (10b) equivalent to that of (10a).

It is also possible to show that *Never* Raising obeys the Complex NP Constraint. Consider:

(11) a. I wish to never see her again.
      b. I never wish to see her again.

(12) a. I have a wish to never see her again.
      b. I never have a wish to see her again.

Here, while (11a) has a reading equivalent to (11b), not so with (12a,b). So the data in (11)–(12) show that the semantic equivalences characteristic of *Never* Raising are not found in cases where the raised adverbial would have to exit a complex NP island.

Finally, the conclusion that cases like (10b) and (12b) do not involve *Never* Raising is supported by the distribution of strict NPIs, as in (13):

(13) a. I never plan (*when) to tell a living soul about that.
       b. You never (*have a) wish to help a living soul solve problems.

Since *Never* Raising is restricted to nonfinite complements, it is not possible to test the full range of island constructions examined in chapter 12. For example, nonfinite clauses do not permit *it* clefts or clause-internal topics, and hence it is impossible to test those island types.

On the syntactic view elaborated in this monograph, cases like (9b) and (11b) result from the raising of *never* from the embedded to the matrix clause. This raising can be formulated informally as follows:

(14) Never *Raising*

    For a member V of a specific class of verbs with nonfinite
    complements, *never* optionally raises from the clausal complement of
    V into the next higher clause.

Rule (14) is nonspecific about exactly where in the clause the raised adverbial ends up. As far as we can tell, the relevant position is that where *never* occurs when it is not raised from an embedded clause.

Although (14) only mentions *never*, it appears that the little-studied, reduplicated version of *never/ever* also undergoes the relevant raising. In this construction, a sequence of one or more *never*s precedes a sequence of zero or more *ever*s.

(15) a.   Harriet wants to never (never) (ever) see you again.
    b.   Harriet never (never) (ever) wants to see you again.

We will not attempt to extend (14) to account for this case.

Finally, consider the nonfinite complement restriction in (14). Although *Never* Raising appears not to be possible out of finite complements (see (16b)), we find the cases in (16c) and (17) to be fine:

(16) a.   I think I will never be happy again.
    b.   I never think I will be happy again. (not equivalent to (16a))
    c.   I don't ever think I will be happy again. (equivalent to (16a))

(17) a.   I don't ever think I've seen rain come down this hard.
       (twitter.com/KeishaNicole/status/72076919805444096)
    b.   I don't ever think that I laughed so much while reading a book.
       (www.myspace.com/manamina22)

These appear to involve the raising of both NEG and *ever*. One might interpret such cases as involving *Never* Raising with obligatory further raising of the NEG out of the adverb. We dub this *Split Never Raising*.

As expected, Split *Never* Raising shows sensitivity to the same island constraints as Classical NEG Raising and *Never* Raising. Consider:

(18) a.   It is true that Carolyn never feels all that well.
    b.   *It is not ever true that Carolyn feels all that well.

(19) a.   I don't ever think I have been that happy at school.
    b.   *I don't ever think that it is at school that I have been that happy.

(20) a.   I don't ever think that I have been all that interested in physics.
    b.   *What I don't ever think is that I have been all that interested in
       physics.

Sentences (18b), (19b), and (20b) illustrate *Never* Raising from the complement of a truth predicate, from a clause with a cleft construction, and from a pseudocleft construction, respectively.

The topic of Split *Never* Raising merits much further investigation, which we will not be able to pursue here.

Now, what is the relation between *Never* Raising and Classical NR? That there *is* a relation between the phenomena is shown first by the fact that cases like (4b), (5b), (6b), and (7) manifest main clause negations whose scope is understood to be in the complement clause, arguably the defining property of Classical NR. We have indicated how a syntactic approach to *Never* Raising already proposed by Fillmore (1963) and Horn (1971) handles this fact unproblematically.

But how do semantic views of Classical NR like that described in chapter 1 fare? Simply, we see no way such an approach can account for the facts. Assume that *never* means something like 'at no point in time' and further that the excluded middle property holds for *hope* (contrary to what the facts of Classical NR indicate). Then the inferences from (21a) in (21b–d) are justified:

(21) a. I never hope to see a brown cow.
      b. At no point in time do I hope to see a brown cow.
         (from the meaning of *never* equivalent to 'at no point in time')
      c. At every point in time, I do not hope to see a brown cow.
         (from the meaning of *no point in time* and the equivalence
         at no point in time (p) = at every point in time (not(p)))
      d. At every point in time, I hope to not see a brown cow.
         (from the excluded middle property)
      e. I hope to never see a brown cow.

The problem, though, is the hypothetical step from (21d) to (21e), which nothing sanctions. For example, (21d) entails that at the present point in time, I hope to not see a brown cow. However, even if I have such a hope, maybe at the present point in time I have no objection to seeing a brown cow in the future, which is inconsistent with (21e). Perhaps some additional implicature or presupposition can be added to make this inference go through, but we know of no development of such a view.

In conclusion, although we have not studied *Never* Raising extensively, we have shown that there are parallels between *Never* Raising and Classical NR. It can be speculated as well that the two are different instances of a single phenomenon. Furthermore, as we have argued, it is unclear that *Never* Raising can be stated in nonsyntactic terms. If it is true that *Never* Raising and Classical NR are two instances of a single phenomenon, then Classical NR must on these further grounds be analyzed syntactically as well.

19 Nonfinite Clauses

19.1 A Literature Bias toward Finite Hosts

In standard Classical NR cases like (1) and (2), the host is finite:

(1) He doesn't seem to be happy.

(2) Ryan does not think he can leave until Friday.

And, impressionistically, the database found in the decades-old literature on Classical NR as a whole consists overwhelmingly of finite host cases. For instance, we make out that in Horn's (1978) extensive and widely cited study of Classical NR, none of the more than fifty simple negative sentences taken to illustrate English Classical NR (i.e., those not involving main clause negative quantifier DPs) has a nonfinite host. Similarly, all the Classical NR cases in Gajewski 2007 and Homer 2010 have finite hosts. That fact coexists with the proposals in nonsyntactic approaches that the Classical NR phenomenon is purely a function of the interaction of the meanings of the CNRPs with independent semantic or pragmatic principles. Since it is obscure how the semantic properties of CNRPs could be systematically different in their finite and nonfinite instances, on semantic/pragmatic treatments one expects that the same relations should *systematically* hold when the NEG sits in a nonfinite host.[1]

19.2 Basics of Finite/Nonfinite Contrasts

But it was long ago briefly observed that the expectation at the end of the previous paragraph does not hold:

(3) (Seuren 1985:168)
   "A further problem is that NR does not seem to operate freely
   whenever an NR-predicate occurs and *not* is the highest embedded

predicate. NR seems somehow connected with the top of the tree, where it 'hooks' on to speech act properties. . . . In some kinds of embedding NR seems altogether out of place. A sentence like (130c) means what it says, not 'I expect that the minister will think that the plan won't succeed':

   (130) c. I expect the minister not to think that the plan will succeed."

And Seuren merely touched on the tip of an iceberg.[2]

Classical NR seems to us not to be available in a wide variety of cases where a potential host is nonfinite. In all the following sentences *not* precedes *to*, but the contrasts persist as well if *not* follows *to*. Each set involves a strict NPI that is ungrammatical when its associated NEG would have raised to a position in a nonfinite host:

(4) a. She does not believe that Rodney will leave until 10:00.
    b. It is possible for her not to believe that Rodney will leave (*until 10:00).
    c. It is possible for her to believe that Rodney will not leave until 10:00.

(5) a. Curtis does not think that they have visited her in ages.
    b. *For Curtis not to think that they have visited her in ages is strange.
    c. For Curtis to think that they have not visited her in ages is strange.

(6) a. I didn't think that the play was half bad.
    b. *They expect me not to think that the play was half bad.
    c. They expect me to think that the play was not half bad.

(7) a. Terry didn't figure that Rodney would do jackshit$_A$.
    b. *It was wise for Terry not to figure that Rodney would do jackshit$_A$.
    c. It was wise for Terry to figure that Rodney would not do jackshit$_A$.

(8) a. They don't expect that she will feel so hot after the operation.
    b. *It is shocking for them not to expect that she will feel so hot after the operation.
    c. It is shocking for them to expect that she will not feel so hot after the operation.

(9) a. They don't think that she can help cheating.
    b. *They are certain not to think that she can help cheating.
    c. They are certain to think that she cannot help cheating.

While (4a) has a Classical NR reading, in (4b) only the short version is grammatical, and it does not intuitively have the Classical NR interpretation. Just so, while all of the (a) examples in (4)–(9) seem fine, we find the (b) examples ungrammatical.

Further examples seem to reveal the same pattern seen in (4)–(9): lack of a Classical NR reading for a NEG raised into a nonfinite clause and the impossibility of a strict NPI in the relevant complement clause:

(10) a.   That film doesn't sound like it was half bad.
     b.   *For that film not to sound like it was half bad is amazing.
     c.   For that film to sound like it was not half bad is amazing.

(11) a.   It does not appear that Jane will resign until next month.
     b.   *It is likely not to appear that Jane will resign until next month.
     c.   It is likely to appear that Jane will not resign until next month.

(12) a.   It wasn't believed they saved jackshit$_A$ from the wrecked cruise ship.
     b.   *For it not to have been believed that they saved jackshit$_A$ from the wrecked cruise ship would have been shocking.
     c.   For it to have been believed that they didn't save jackshit$_A$ from the wrecked cruise ship would have been shocking.

(13) a.   Karla didn't figure that they would touch that topic with a ten-foot pole.
     b.   *For Karla not to figure that they would touch that topic with a ten-foot pole would be mistaken.
     c.   For Karla to figure that they would not touch that topic with a ten-foot pole would be mistaken.

(14) a.   Jean didn't figure that the movie would be all that bad.
     b.   *Jean appears not to have figured that the movie would be all that bad.
     c.   Jean appears to have figured that the movie would not be all that bad.

(15) a.   I don't imagine that she will stop at anything.
     b.   *For me not to imagine that she will stop at anything would be unwarranted.
     c.   For me to imagine that she won't stop at anything would be unwarranted.

The failure of many nonfinite clauses to participate in the Classical NR phenomenon, illustrated so far only with infinitives, also holds for gerundives:

(16) a.   *I can't advocate not believing that Virginia will resign until January.

    b.   I can't advocate believing that Virginia will not resign until January.

(17) a. *John contemplated not believing that Sally would resign until January.

       b. John contemplated believing that Sally would not resign until January.

(18) a. *Their not believing that she was feeling so hot is worrisome.

       b. Their believing that she was not feeling so hot is worrisome.

(19) a. *They continued not believing that she was feeling so hot.

       b. They continued believing that she was not feeling so hot.

It appears that all the ungrammatical cases embody generalization (20):

(20) *The Classical NR Nonfiniteness Condition*

If NEG_1 originates in a finite clause C_1 immediately contained in a nonfinite clause C_2, NEG_1 cannot raise into C_2.

19.3 Composed Quantifier Cases

Condition (20) combines with our analysis of the composed quantifier cases in chapter 16 to make further predictions beyond those in post-Aux NEG cases like the (b) examples in (5)–(15). In particular, examples where a complement clause NEG is not only raised by Classical NR but deleted in the main clause should also be ungrammatical if the Classical NR host is nonfinite while the origin is a finite clause. Consider the following data:

(21) a. Nobody thinks that Steve has visited her in ages.

       b. *For nobody to think that Steve has visited her in ages is strange.

       c. For everybody to think that Steve has not visited her in ages is strange.

(22) a. Nobody expects that she will feel so hot after the operation.

       b. *It is shocking for nobody to expect that she will feel so hot after the operation.

       c. It is shocking for everybody to expect that she will not feel so hot after the operation.

While the judgments above are subtle, we find (21b) and (22b) to be ungrammatical. The structure for the relevant portion of (21b) would be (23):

(23) For nobody to <NEG_2> think that John has visited her [<NEG_1> in ages]

In this structure, there is a covert NEG$_2$ modifying the infinitival verb *think*, and a covert NEG$_1$ associated with the strict NPI. The intended NEG deletion chain is shown in (24):

(24) <Nobody, NEG$_2$, NEG$_1$>

However, since NEG$_1$ is prohibited from raising to the nonfinite clause by condition (20), NEG$_2$ is blocked from deleting NEG$_1$ by the NDEL Clausemate Condition, (8) of chapter 8. That is why (21b) is ungrammatical.

It seems clear that the finite/nonfinite distinction is relevant. But that is a syntactic distinction. And, of course, nothing in the known nonsyntactic views of Classical NR we have discussed, those involving the excluded middle property, provides any basis for the fact that a syntactic distinction like finite/nonfinite plays what appears to be a major a role in the distribution of this negation phenomenon. On the contrary, though, the finite/nonfinite contrast is unsurprising on our basic assumptions, which take Classical NR to be an instance of syntactic raising.

20 Conclusion

We summarize a few of the consequences of general importance that we believe follow from the arguments in the previous nineteen chapters. We need not linger over the fact that we have provided considerable new evidence for the syntactic nature of Classical NR, especially the evidence based on island facts, Horn clauses, and parenthetical clauses. Nor will we recapitulate our demonstration that the composed quantifier argument has no force against our syntactic view of Classical NR and that some of the data from that domain (islands, Horn clauses, and parentheticals) actually strongly support our syntactic view. Instead, we highlight some of the more general theoretical implications of our work.

First, following Postal 2005, we have argued that there are two types of NPIs: unary-NEG structures and binary-NEG structures (reversals). These are illustrated in (1):

(1) a. I didn't see any pyramid.   (unary-NEG structure)
    b. Everybody who knows any physics . . .   (binary-NEG structure)

In (1a), the underlying structure of *any pyramid* is [[NEG SOME] pyramid]. NEG raises away from *any pyramid* to a position right-adjacent to the finite Aux. In (1b), the underlying structure of *any physics* is [[NEG$_2$ [NEG$_1$ SOME]] physics]. The two NEGs are deleted in a NEG deletion chain initiated by *every*.

In chapter 4, we gave various diagnostics supporting this distinction (several of which expand the set found in Postal 2005). In addition, the distinction between unary- and binary-NEG NPIs played a crucial role in analyzing the scope of NPIs (see chapter 9), the distribution of NPIs in islands (see chapter 12), and the interaction of NPIs with the excluded middle property (see chapter 16).

As we showed in chapter 14, the distinction between unary- and binary-NEG NPIs receives striking support from the analysis of Horn clauses: specifically, only unary-NEG NPIs trigger Negative Inversion in Horn clauses.

Consider this result from the point of view of current theories of NPIs. One common approach analyzes them as existential quantifiers:

(2) a. (G. Carlson 1980:800)

"*Any* is an existential quantifier which must appear within the scope of negation." (". . . for those instances where *not* is the triggering element.")

b. (Linebarger 1980:217)

"The three arguments presented here in support of the E-theory (in which polarity *any* is represented as an existential quantifier in the scope of NOT) . . ."

A second approach analyzes them as indefinites introducing a variable:

(3) (Ladusaw 1996a:211)

"Since Klima 1964, these NPIs have been termed as 'indefinites', and it is best to interpret this term in the sense of Heim 1982."

Under either approach, the NPI is analyzed as an indefinite, a point highlighted in the following passage:

(4) (Kadmon and Landman 1993:357)

"The NP with *any* has the usual semantic properties of an indefinite. We won't make a choice here concerning the proper way of treating indefinite NPs. If indefinite NPs are best regarded as existential quantifiers, then so is the *any* NP; if indefinite NPs are best treated as new variables (Heim 1982), then the *any* NP too is a new variable. From either assumption the existential behavior of PS [polarity sensitive] *any* follows without problems."

Under either approach, the behavior of Negative Inversion in Horn clauses is a mystery, for the simple reason that indefinites never trigger Negative Inversion (see chapter 14):

(5) a. I lent some money to a/some man I know.
b. *To a/some man I know did I lend some money.

Second, while it is widely assumed that natural language negation is a clausal modifier (negating the proposition denoted by the clause), as in Klima's (1964) influential work and many others, we have described a broad range of English negation facts with no appeal to clausal negation at all. Under our analysis, the standard cases usually taken to motivate English clausal negation actually represent NEGs raised from verbal/adjectival phrases to a position right-adjacent to Aux. And we have assumed a rich system in which NEGs also originate on other categories, most notably D (SOME). We argued in chapter 14 that the correct analysis of Horn clauses in particular is inconsistent with analyzing the NEG right-adjacent to Aux as clausal negation.

We take the success of our accounts to support the view that clausal negation—with its semantic correlate, propositional negation—does not have the primary role in natural language negation that is often assumed.

Third, throughout this monograph we have relied heavily on the idea of quantificational DP scope positions. The scope position of a quantificational DP is distinct from its overt position. That is, the same DP is taken to occur in (at least two) distinct positions. Furthermore, the scope position is the position that determines the element that the quantifier takes as an argument semantically. In chapter 5, we argued that if NEG raises out of a scope-bearing DP, it must raise out of the DP occurrence in scope position. Furthermore, the idea that NPIs can occupy scope positions distinct from their surface positions played a key role in understanding the distribution of strict NPIs and quasi–Horn clauses. These arguments support the general claims of G. Lakoff (1971:238–243), McCawley (1971:228–230, 1973:150, 294–295), Seuren (1974a:192–195, 1974b:106, 118–120, 1996:301, 318–319, 1998:522–524), May (1985), and Heim and Kratzer (1998) that quantificational DPs must appear in scope positions different from the positions in which they appear overtly.

Fourth, the analyses in this monograph rely crucially on the assumption that syntactic structures involving negation typically contain many unpronounced (deleted) syntactic elements. In particular, we argued in chapters 7, 8, and 16 that many instances of NEG are deleted (and so do not appear overtly). These NEGs nevertheless play a critical role in the syntax and semantics of the sentences in which they have covert occurrences. Such an assumption played a particularly important role in our discussion of the composed quantifier argument against Classical NR in chapter 16.

In this regard, our analyses point in the same direction as those in Collins and Postal 2012. There, we argued that understanding the syntax and semantics of imposters (third person DPs such as *yours truly* that refer to the speaker) requires postulating null pronouns internal to the structure of imposters and null indexical DPs at the left periphery of the clause. These null elements were crucial in accounting for a wide range of complicated pronominal agreement facts. In this way, we made a case for the syntactic representation of unpronounced elements that play a role in interpretation.[1]

Finally, we reiterate a point also made in Collins and Postal 2012:257n1: namely, even in well-studied domains like negation and even in a heavily studied language like English, there are vast unexplored factual areas whose investigation is required for a deep understanding of the nature of natural language syntax.[2]

Notes

Chapter 1

1. Among the possible syntactic views of Classical NR that are not transformational are those that involve no generative rule at all. This would be the case in any framework assuming a grammar to be a model-theoretic system; see Johnson and Postal 1980, Pullum and Scholz 2001, 2005, Pullum 2007, and Postal 2010. In the framework of Postal 2010, a syntactic version of Classical NR would involve a Type I foreign successor of an arc in the complement whose head node is NEG. This formulation guarantees that the complement arc A headed by the raised NEG, NEG_1, is erased and that only the foreign successor arc B of A headed by NEG_1 remains unerased. This guarantees that NEG_1 appears superficially only in the main clause.

2. Seuren 1985:166–172 represents a rare later defense of syntactic views against nonsyntactic alternatives. McCawley 1998:595–604 is the most recent instance we can cite of support for a syntactic view.

3. See Horn 1971:120, 1975:282, 1978:136–150, Jackendoff 1971:293, Seuren 1974a:184–185, 1974b:121, Smith 1975:68–74, and Prince 1976:405 for various instantiations of this line of argument. Horn (1978:143–150) elaborates many difficulties facing this argument type.

4. The term *strict NPI* has been used in various senses in the literature; see Horn 1978:136–140, Linebarger 1987:47, Progovac 1994:81, 145 (citing Linebarger 1980), van der Wouden 1997:76, Giannakidou 2011:1680. Our usage (an NPI requiring a local licenser) essentially follows that of Linebarger, Progovac, and Horn.

5. Contrasts like the one in (7) must be segregated from cases of so-called *secondary triggering*, in which a strict NPI cooccurs in a local domain with a nonstrict NPI; see, for example, Horn 1989 [2001:181]. Such cases are grammatical for some speakers even in NEG-free complement clauses with non-CNRPs; compare (7a) and (i).

(i) Calvin did not claim that he had taken any drugs until his 18th birthday.

We cannot consider why examples like (i) are well-formed for some speakers. But we suspect that the key aspect is that the nonstrict NPI phrase, here *any drugs*, and the strict NPI, here *until his 18th birthday*, form a polyadic quantifier with main clause scope. The issue of polyadic quantification and NPIs is described in detail in chapter

6. The more general confounding factor of high scope is addressed in chapter 9 and later chapters. In terms of those discussions, *any drugs* and *until his 18th birthday* take matrix clause scope and are interpreted as a polyadic quantifier with a shared D containing a NEG. Hence, the strict NPI *until* phrase is locally related to a NEG, but that relation holds in the main clause. We suspect that it is polyadic quantifier formation that allows *until* to take wide scope in (i).

6. We provide here a list of other strict NPIs that, as far as Classical NR is concerned, we believe function in essentially the same way as those we do cite. Readers may wish to substitute some of these in examples should they find that certain NPIs that we consider strict lack that property in their dialects. We cite them with a preceding *not* to bring out the often idiomatic meaning: *not believe one's eyes, not for anything in the world, not give it another thought, not be half bad, not long for this world, not miss much, not move a muscle, not be much of (something), not one iota, not be one's place, not sleep a wink, not feel so hot, not take no for an answer, not touch (something) with a ten-foot pole, not worth a dime.*

We should stress that the categorization of NPIs as strict in no way precludes considerable diversity among them. To see the possible variety and poorly understood complexity of the matter, it suffices to consider the following paradigm kindly provided to us by Larry Horn (personal communication). The arguably strict NPIs are italicized:

(i) a. *Like he'd do that for *anything in the world*.
    b. *Like that paper was *half-bad*.
    c. *Like she misses *much*.
    d. Like he'd do *one iota of work/move a muscle* for us.
    e. Like I could *sleep a wink* with this racket.
    f. Like I'd touch that with *a ten-foot pole*.

7. Pullum and Huddleston (2002:825) deny that *stop at nothing* has a *stop at anything* variant. But that claim is just wrong for us, and the Web provides multiple examples of the supposedly impossible variant:

(i) a. He won't stop at anything to get her.
      (www.fanfiction.net/s/8378383/1/The-Prodigal-Daughter)
    b. And tonight I learned that she won't stop at anything to get it.
      (piratebootyahoy.tumblr.com/post/303i748271)
    c. When the dolphin's tail is removed to save her, the boy won't stop at anything to get a prosthetic tail for his beloved friend.
      (www.sandiegoreader.com/events/2012/sep/07/46804/)

8. As discussed in Postal 2004b:chap. 5, members of the JACK class in general have both NPI uses, equivalent to 'anything', and non-NPI uses, equivalent to 'nothing'. Only the former is relevant here, and throughout this monograph all stars on sentences containing such forms refer only to that use, which is (thus redundantly) indicated by inscriptions like *jackshit*$_A$, *squat*$_A$ (where A picks out the 'anything' reading).

9. Examples like (ia–d) with strict NPIs in restrictive relative clauses parallel cases in (6)–(14):

(i) a. No one who left early/*until 10:00 was arrested.
    b. *No one who would stop at anything was hired.

c. No one who said anything/*breathed a word about it was promoted.

d. No one who criticized anyone/*a living soul got interviewed.

e. No one who learned anything/*a fucking thing about that organization survived.

f. No one who worked/*lifted a finger to help Louise regretted it.

g. No one who knows anything/*squat$_A$ about lasers believes that.

h. No one who has been to Bulgaria recently/*in years would agree with that.

Such facts reveal that the possibility of a strict NPI occurring in the complement clause of a CNRP without a local licenser is the special case that needs explication. The contrast between nonstrict NPIs and strict NPIs in this relative clause context can be explained in the same way as the contrasts between these two types of NPIs in the complement clause contexts discussed in section 12.10.

10. Relevantly, Pullum and Huddleston (2002:839–842) discuss the Classical NR phenomenon in some detail without even raising the possibility that it might be syntactic. And Sailer (2005) states:

(i) "Syntactic analyses of NR have been refuted by argumentation as those referred by Horn or, most recently Klooster (to appear)."

11. While this claim about *hope* is standard in the Classical NR literature and certainly represents our dialects as well, the Web provides examples suggesting that for some English speakers, *hope* is a CNRP:

(i) I really don't hope I have to wait until June 2011. It's bad enough they've put back The Last Guardian until ...
(www.gamespot.com/news/3d-hd-team-ico-collection-official-6276184)

(ii) Although I don't hope to let this happen again (until it is wanted and planned of course), I feel very good about my experience and am very thankful for every ...
(http://www.fwhc.org/stories/alycia.htm)

These examples provide some support for Horn's view that there is a universal semantic characterization of possible CNRPs, with lexical specifications restricting the maximum class in particular languages.

Chapter 2

1. The presence of syntactic negation in the initial clause of a coordination is not sufficient to sanction a following *neither* expression:

(i)   a. Carl is not a doctor and neither is Helen.
      b. Carl is a nondoctor and *neither is Helen.
(ii) a. Helen can't levitate and neither can Valerie.
      b. Helen can (simply) not levitate and *neither can Valerie.

For the purposes of this monograph, we need not attempt to provide a sufficiency condition for phenomena like *neither* expressions, but our best guess is that such forms require that the initial licensing clause have a NEG associated with its Aux—sometimes, though, a covert NEG.

Chapter 3

1. Robin Lakoff (1969a) offered arguments against a SOME→*any* rule based on semantic differences between sentences that differ only with respect to the presence of *some* versus *any*. Her cases all involve what we consider reversals (see chapter 4). We do not see her results as inconsistent with our structures or with the viability of our rule (7).

Chapter 4

1. Giannakidou (2011:1700) remarks as follows, criticizing proposals in Szabolcsi 2004, based on ideas formulated rather differently in Postal 2005 and in the present monograph:

(i)   "However, Szabolcsi treats *some* as ¬¬∃, with the two negations canceling each other out, and it is difficult to see this as more than mere stipulation. What is the evidence for the two negations? And why do we never see overt realizations of them in *some* crosslinguistically? This is typologically quite surprising, because negation in languages is never 'forgotten' to be marked, if there (Horn 1989 [2001]). Ultimately, why would a language bother to implement two negations on an expression just to cancel them out?"

While aimed specifically only at a single analysis proposed by Szabolcsi, one not identical to that advocated here, to the extent that they were valid these remarks would, not surprisingly, apply to all present reversal structure analyses.

The remarks in effect offer four criticisms. The first is that the proposal is a mere stipulation. Even if the criticism that the proposal is a mere stipulation were true of Szabolcsi's article (it isn't), here we support the proposal. The second merely asks for evidence, which we provide in section 4.9. The third asks why such negatives are never overtly realized in forms meaning *some* crosslinguistically. However, Szabolcsi (2004:431) presents a plausible case of an overt reversal NEG pattern (i.e., *non nemo*) for Latin. The fourth asserts that "negation in languages is never 'forgotten' to be marked, if there." We read this formulation as saying that negations are never deleted. That is an enormously broad, crosslinguistic generalization backed by no supporting evidence or argument. And it is arguably false for English and other languages. In chapter 7, we argue for NEG deletion on the basis of data from French, German, and English. In fact, the entire substance of the present monograph is an extended argument that the claim is false for English.

We thus find that overall, Giannakidou's criticisms of an early version of our proposed reversal structures have no real force.

2. The remarks here about (15a) are, however, inconsistent with our speculative claim at the beginning of chapter 6 that structures like (15a) are ambiguous between unary- and binary-NEG analyses. We expect that a deeper understanding of the conditions under which examples like (15a) permit a reversal analysis will resolve this issue. But we cannot pursue that here.

3. Our account of the asymmetry between strict and nonstrict NPIs in VP ellipsis might shed light on the fact that, for us, *only* licenses nonstrict NPIs but not strict ones:

(i)   a.   Only Wanda has ever been to France.
        b.   Only Wanda knows any physics.

However, *only* does not license strict NPIs (see Gajewski 2011:120):

(ii)   a.   *Only Wanda is feeling so hot.
        b.   *Only Wanda told a living soul.
        c.   *Only Wanda got here until 6:00.
        d.   *Only Wanda has seen Mary in ages.

We suggest that the difference between weak and strong NPIs in the scope of *only* is the result of factoring in the presupposition. Consider first (iia). The assertion and presupposition are given in (iii):

(iii)   a.   Presupposition: Wanda is feeling so hot.
        b.   Assertion: Nobody else is feeling so hot.

The problem here is that the NPI *so hot* is not licensed in the presupposition, since there is no NEG in the presupposition that could have moved away from it. Since we assume that (iiia) is syntactically ungrammatical (the NPI *so hot* needs a syntactic NEG), the above account assumes that presuppositions are grammatical objects (not merely semantic representations). We cannot develop here how such issues as presupposition projection would be treated in a theory that considers presuppositions to be actual syntactic structures.

In this light, consider (ib), whose assertion and presupposition are given in (iv):

(iv)   a.   Presupposition: Wanda knows some physics.
        b.   Assertion: Nobody else knows any physics.

The difference between this case and (iii) is that there is an indefinite *some physics* that is equivalent semantically to the NPI *any physics* in (ib). Furthermore, *some physics* is not an NPI and so the problem encountered in (iiia) is not present in (iva).

Under this approach, the difference between strict NPIs and nonstrict NPIs is that the latter (reversal NEG structures) are always semantically equivalent to indefinites, and hence the relevant presuppositions can contain an indefinite instead of the NPI.

4. Condition (47) does not capture the fact that possessive cases like (i) are grammatical:

(i)   We found nobody's dog at all.

We believe the solution involves reference to the scope occurrence of genitive DPs like *nobody* in (i). But we will not elaborate.

5. Our analysis of a form like *few* as involving a covert NEG faces the issue of this type of contrast:

(i)   a.   Very few cats are vegetarians.
        b.   *Very not many cats are vegetarians.

Arguably, the ungrammaticality of (ib) is a special case of a general fact about English, namely, that *very* cannot modify a phrase of the form [overt NEG +X]. This is justified independently of any assumptions about *few/little* by facts like (iia,b):

(ii)   a. She is very (*not) smart.
       b. Victor is very (*not) worried about that.

We assume that cases like (ia) escape this ban simply because the NEG they contain is covert.

Chapter 6

1. The idea that an NPI in the scope of antiadditive quantifiers can be analyzed in terms of polyadic quantification is also discussed in Szabolcsi 2004:435, and n. 26. Szabolcsi cites precedents including Moltmann 1995:sec. 4.

2. The polyadic quantificational account given here of cases like (23) can be taken to represent inter alia a response to the entirely correct criticism in Gajewski 2008:84 of the proposals made in Postal 2000, 2005 to handle parallel cases. Gajewski focuses in particular on this example:

(i)   No student read any book but *Moby-Dick*.

He observes rightly that the attempts of those works to capture the right meaning from combinations of the quantifier DPs [[NEG SOME] student] and [[[NEG SOME] book] but *Moby-Dick*] failed badly. The problem was precisely that those works did not appeal to any notion of polyadic quantification, so that the two quantifier DPs would have interacted with one taking scope over the other, yielding incorrect meanings equivalent to 'every student read some book other than *Moby-Dick*'. The present account maintains the view of those earlier works that each DP of the relevant type has a D of the [NEG SOME] type, but adds the extra structure of their sharing the same D at the level relevant for interpretation, permitting the derivation of the correct polyadic meaning, as described in the text.

Chapter 7

1. In a section on the use of *ne* in clauses expressing negation in the absence of standard overt forms with that function, Martinon (1927:542) remarked on the two expressions *ne dire mot* 'not to say a word' and *ne souffler mot* 'not to breathe a word', giving these examples:

(i)   a. Il ne   dit   mot.
         he PRT says word
         'He doesn't say a word.'
      b. Il ne   souffle mot.
         he PRT blow   word
         'He doesn't breathe a word.'

Exemplifying with (ii), he added that unlike in the situation in (ia), when the indefinite article occurs with *mot*, the standard negative form *pas* is obligatory:

(ii) Il ne dit pas un mot.
      he PRT says not a   word
      'He doesn't say a word.'

He also added that neither *un* nor *pas* is ever possible after *souffler*.
  We take the cases in (i) to also involve NEG deletion, determined by the verbs.

2. We are indebted to Christina Behme and Manfred Sailer for extensive help with the German data.

3. Christina Behme informs us that German speakers by no means uniformly accept (15b). This does not ultimately affect the essential argument here.

4. A constraint we do not understand is seen in (i):

(i)   *Rachel is too nice not to help anyone.

Here, an NPI is not grammatical. But this fact does not threaten our proposal for these cases, since corresponding finite clause cases with no NEG deletion also seem unacceptable:

(ii) *Rachel is so nice that she would not not help anyone.

5. The fact that in the abstract structure (28) the covert NEG_2 precedes the modal it modifies while in the actual string of words (29b) the analog of NEG_2 follows the corresponding modal is unproblematic. The latter word order simply represents the fact that even when a NEG originates as a modifier of a modal M, it must, if overt, appear following M. On one account of this requirement, the modal would obligatorily raise over the negation, giving the order modal > NEG. This English word order constraint thus determines that modal + NEG word order provides as such no information about whether a NEG modifies the modal it follows, as on one reading of (i), or modifies some distinct element, as in the other reading of (i):

(i)   Svetlana can not swim. (= 'It is not possible for Svetlana to swim' or 'It is possible for Svetlana not to swim')

6. Another illustration of NEG deletion is based on the apparently odd usage of *yet* seen in (ia,b), from Mittwoch, Huddleston, and Collins 2002:713:

(i)   a. I have yet to see a better account than the one you proposed ten years ago.
      b. Wilhelmina has yet to turn in a paper.

  These sentences seem synonymous with the following overtly negative sentences:

(ii) a. I have not yet seen a better account than the one you proposed ten years ago.
      b. Wilhelmina has not yet turned in a paper.

  We assume that cases like (ia,b) involve NEG deletion. But we cannot pursue the needed analysis for reasons of space.

7. Example (i) from Pullum and Huddleston 2002:845–846 illustrates the phenomenon of *expletive negation*, that is, cases where a NEG seemingly has no semantic function. This is extremely limited in English but productive in other languages.

(i)   I wouldn't be surprised if it didn't rain.

That is, unexpectedly, (i) has the meaning 'I wouldn't be surprised if it rained' as well as the expected negative reading 'I wouldn't be surprised if there was no rain'. We would analyze the unexpected reading of such cases as in (ii), representing a distinct case of NEG deletion:

(ii)   I wouldn't be surprised if it did [NEG$_2$ [NEG$_1$ rain]]

Here, NEG$_2$, which is deleted, represents what we called a reversal in chapter 4. So only NEG$_1$ is realized overtly in (i).

This analysis is an alternative in present terms to the view in van der Wouden 1994:41. That view recognizes only a single NEG in expletive negation cases, but one manifesting a distinct (null) meaning rather than the standard meaning explicated in section 3.7.

Chapter 8

1. A small class of verbs with negative force including *fail*, *hesitate*, and *refuse* taking infinitival complements admit strict NPIs in their complements, as in (i):

(i)   a. Byron refused to do a damn thing.
       b. Byron refused to take no for an answer.
       c. Byron refused to give her the time of day.

Such NPIs are unary-NEG structures, so the representation of (ia) would include (ii):

(ii)   Byron refused to do [NEG$_1$ SOME damn thing]

NEG$_1$ in (ia) could be deleted here by the negative verb *refuse*, instantiating lexical NEG deletion. However, (ii) yields the same interpretations as the narrow and wide scope interpretations of (iii). Neither of these is the interpretation of (i).

(iii)   Byron refused to do nothing.

Moreover, if *refuse* is not the NEG deleter of NEG$_1$, it is unclear what could be its lexical NEG deleter. If (ia) is an instance of general NEG deletion, there must be another NEG; if there weren't, (ia) would be inconsistent with the NEG Deletion Evenness Condition in (18). Arguably, then, in present terms the correct structure involves an additional NEG somewhere. But we cannot pursue these cases here.

2. We observe that our assumptions determine that NEG deletion chains have what we can call an *anticyclic* property. Thus, for instance, representing NDEL by $\Rightarrow$, NEG deletion chains of the form (i) are impossible:

(i)   NEG$_1$ $\Rightarrow$ NEG$_2$ $\Rightarrow$ NEG$_3$ $\Rightarrow$ NEG$_4$ $\Rightarrow$ NEG$_1$

In (i), NEG$_1$ is ancestrally related to each of NEG$_2$, NEG$_3$, and NEG$_4$ by NDEL, but those NEGs are also ancestrally related to NEG$_1$. Thus, (i) contains no initial element in the set of deleted NEGs, and no NEG that fails to be a NEG deleter, violating condition (23c) in the definition of NEG deletion chain.

As a special case of this reasoning, minimum cyclic chains like (ii) and (iii) are also impossible:

(ii)   NEG$_1$ $\Rightarrow$ NEG$_1$
(iii)   NEG$_1$ $\Rightarrow$ NEG$_2$ $\Rightarrow$ NEG$_1$

This is important because it means NEGs cannot just disappear on their own and that two NEGs cannot alone justify their mutual deletion. NEGs can only be covert if they have a distinct NEG deleter, which, if not NEG, must be either a lexical one and marked in the lexicon as such, or a general one, meeting the narrow conditions on that status. And given condition (23a), any legitimate sequence of NEG deletions must begin with a non-NEG.

Chapter 9

1. A parallel remark could be made about the negative force verb cases like (i) of note 1 of chapter 8.

2. Gajewski (2007:307) presents the following interesting contrast:

(i)   a.   An applicant is not allowed to have left the country in at least two years.
b.   *An applicant is not required to have left the country in at least two years.

On the assumption that *in at least n years* is a strict NPI, (ia,b) provide two challenges for views of strict NPIs. First, why is (ia) grammatical, since the context between the main clause NEG and the NPI contains no CNRP(s)? Second, why does whatever permits (ia) not equally permit (ib)?

The obvious suggestion in current terms is that (ia) represents a high-scope structure with the combination of the NEG and *in at least two years* scoping over everything to the right of the main clause Aux. This would yield a meaning for (ia) representable as something like (ii):

(ii)   'There is no point in time t where t is a point in time less than two years before the present moment such that it is permissible for an applicant to have left the country at t.'

This seems to us like a plausible candidate for the meaning of (ia). If so, the view that (ia) is not a Classical NR case can be justified.

Then the question is why a parallel analysis is not available for (ib). We note first that the strict NPI *until* is possible in both contexts:

(iii)   a.   An applicant is not allowed to have left the country until last year.
b.   An applicant is not required to have left the country until last year.

This suggests that what is wrong with (ib) has specifically to do with the meaning of *in at least n years.*

Support for that view and for the claim that the (ia,b) contrast shows nothing general about the nature of strict NPIs is provided by the grammaticality of both pairs of strict NPI cases like those in (iv):

(iv) a. An applicant is not allowed to have done a fucking thing/jackshit$_A$.
      b. An applicant is not required to have done a fucking thing/jackshit$_A$.

We have nothing further of substance to say about the (ia,b) contrast. Gajewski proposes a semantic account based on the fact that in (ia) the main clause context yields an antiadditive operator while that in (ib) does not. We advance further problems for a pure antiadditivity approach to strict NPIs in chapter 10.

Finally, if the cases cited in this note really involve high-scope analyses, then they do not directly bear on any analysis of Classical NR.

3. Vincent Homer (personal communication) observes contrasts like the following:

(i)   a. It is unlikely that Kyle said a thing.
      b. *It is not unlikely that Kyle said a thing.

The issue he raises is why Classical NR, which is fine with the strict NPI *a thing* in (ia), fails in (ib). Homer suggests (as part of a general view of NPI licensing) that the ungrammaticality is due to the fact that the meaning of the external NEG in (ib) combines with the meaning of the prefixed negation *un-* to create an increasing context. We are unconvinced that (ia) represents Classical NR, but we cannot pursue this issue here.

4. The discussion in the text of the strict NPIs *in ages*, *so hot*, and *all that* raises the question of whether these NPIs fail to occur in scope positions at all and so are scopeless, or whether they do appear in scope positions but those scope positions are limited to the smallest finite clause containing the overt occurrence of the strict NPI. Our belief is that all these NPIs do occur in scope positions.

The only candidates we know of for NPIs not occurring in scope positions are verbal ones such as that involving modal *need*:

(i)   a. He need not apply.
      b. Nobody need apply.

(ia) is a unary-NEG structure of the form [NEG need] (where on one analysis both NEG and *need* undergo various raisings to yield the surface structure in (ia)). However, we believe that (ib) is a binary-NEG structure, for the following reason. If *need* in (ib) were a unary-NEG structure, the mechanisms for polyadic quantifier formation in chapter 6 would be inapplicable, since *need* does not take scope. But under conditions where both *need* was a unary-NEG structure in (ib) and polyadic quantifier formation was impossible, there would be no way for the unary NEG in (ib) to be deleted. Therefore, the only remaining analysis is that *need* in (ib) is a binary-NEG structure.

Even though *need* does not appear in many typical reversal contexts, as shown in (ii), it appears in other contexts unavailable to strict NPIs, as shown in (iii):

(ii) a. *If you need leave, please let me know.
      b. *Everybody who need leave should let me know.
      c. *At most half of the class need leave.

(iii)   a.   I didn't claim that Mary need apply.
        b.   *I didn't claim that Mary got here until 6:00.
        c.   *I didn't claim that Mary had seen her father in ages.

Therefore, to maintain that *need* can appear in a binary-NEG structure (to account for (ib) and (iiia)), further constraints are necessary to rule out (iia–c). We cannot pursue this issue here.

This note highlights the issue of scopeless NPIs, which so far remains uninvestigated. It also highlights the issue of the classification of NPIs based on the various tests given in this monograph. In some cases, as with *need*, the classification of an NPI as either a unary-NEG structure or a binary-NEG structure is not as straightforward as might have been expected given our framework.

Chapter 10

1. We observe that the behavior of *forget* with infinitival complements illustrated in (19) contrasts with that of verbs like *fail*, *hesitate*, and *refuse* mentioned in note 1 of chapter 8. The latter determine antiadditive contexts for their infinitives and allow strict NPIs, while the strict NPIs in the antiadditive infinitives in (19) are ungrammatical. This contrast highlights the insufficiency of antiadditivity for licensing strict NPIs and forms an interesting puzzle for views of NPIs.

2. The more general failure of *zero or more* forms to license NPIs is noted by Krifka (1995:217–218). On similar grounds, Hoeksema and Klein (1995:153) propose that an NPI licenser must define a function that is decreasing but also not increasing.

Chapter 11

1. Pollack (1974:29) cites Clinkenbeard 1969 (which we have not seen) for claims to the effect that (ic) (to which we have added *until tomorrow*) lacks the Classical NR ambiguity found in (ia,b):

(i)   a.   Joel does not believe that Hildy is coming.
        b.   It is not believed by Joel that Hildy is coming.
        c.   That Hildy is coming (*until tomorrow) is not believed by Joel.

And of course the subject clause in (ic) is an island while the clauses in (ia,b) are not. But Pollack does not attribute the nonambiguity of (ic) to the island property, instead invoking hesitantly some semantic ideas of Kiparsky and Kiparsky (1971) about subject positions.

See Bumford 2011 for a more recent discussion of islands and Classical NR.

2. In considering whether Classical NR is constrained by the Coordinate Structure Constraint, one relevant issue is that certain sorts of intervening scopal elements block NPI licensing (see Linebarger 1980). It can be plausibly argued both that conjunctive *and* is a member of that class and that in cases like (1b) it scopes between the main clause NEG and the NPI *yet* (Chierchia 2004).

3. See Postal 2010:chap. 9 for discussion of the constraints dividing English complement clauses with respect to these properties.

4. The situation in the text is complicated by the fact that for some speakers, including one of us, examples like the ungrammatical ones in (4)–(6) are rescued by the secondary triggering effect, mentioned in note 5 of chapter 1. When this is present, the additional presence of a nonstrict NPI in the context where a strict NPI alone is ungrammatical leads to acceptability. Thus, for one of us, whereas (6c) is impossible, (i) is unexceptional:

(i)   That any of them have prayed in years was not believed by Laura.

As indicated in the note cited above, our speculative view of these cases assumes that they are possible because the two NPI structures form a polyadic quantifier. In addition, in cases like (i), that polyadic quantifier has scope higher than the topic or subject clause, so there is no NEG raising out of the relevant islands and, critically, for some speakers, such polyadic structures with their shared Ds apparently have greater ability to scope out of islands than do simple quantifier DPs.

Chapter 12

1. Many examples involving a complex noun phrase island are nonetheless better if *any* is the determiner of the noun phrase:

(i)   a.   I don't have any faith that they will find a living soul in town.
        b.   I don't have any expectations of finding a living soul in town.
        c.   I don't see any likelihood of Jim calling Irene until tomorrow.
        d.   I don't have any intention of lifting a finger yet.
              (narutoforumrp.proboards.com/index.cgi?action=gotopost ...)

Possibly, such cases involve the secondary triggering effects mentioned in note 5 of chapter 1 and note 4 of chapter 11. The possibility of a strict NPI scoping out of an island, which we have previously mentioned, may also be in play in such cases. But we cannot discuss these issues here.

A reviewer suggests that the following two examples are acceptable:

(ii)   I don't have the intention of lifting a finger to help her.

(iii)   I don't have the desire to do anything to help.

We do not find the first acceptable. The second exemplifies a nonstrict NPI. Notably, the string *don't have the intention of lifting a finger* gets zero Google hits, while the string *don't have the desire to do anything* gets tens of thousands.

2. There is a difference in aspect between the occurrences of the verb *plan* in (20) and in (22) that might be relevant. (22) is habitual, but (20) is not. This difference might also account for the lack of Classical NR in examples like (22b).

3. Seuren (1974a:192) takes his highest-operator condition to be the basis of facts like (ia,b):

(i)   a.   I suppose John might not be at home.
        b.   *I don't suppose John might be at home.

In his terms, the NEG itself is not the highest operator in (ia); rather, the modal *might* is. This works because of a well-known constraint forbidding some modals including *might* from occurring under the scope of clausemate negation, accounting for the fact that (ia) has only the *might* > NEG reading. Given this constraint, Classical NR is blocked in (ib) by condition (38).

Chapter 13

1. Andrew Radford (personal communication) reminds us that the subject-Aux inversion characteristic of Negative Inversion only occurs in the clause actually containing the overt NI focus, not in lower clauses that the NI focus either originated in or passed through:

(i) a. None of the proposals would he accept.
   b. None of the proposals could we persuade him that he should/*should he accept.
   c. None of the proposals could we persuade him that he should tell Martha that she should/*should she accept.

There are various ways in different frameworks that this condition could be imposed, a matter we cannot go into here.

2. We neither agree with the markings on *regret* in Horn's example (99a) nor see any principle that would yield the indicated ungrammaticality. The ungrammaticality in his example (99c) is, however, arguably due to conditions on licensing the NPI in the complement. In general, a "negative" verb that licenses NPIs in its complement clause (of which *regret* is one) cannot do so if negated. None of these facts are relevant to the current discussion.

3. The only twenty-first century mention of cases like (3) we are aware of appears in Den Dikken and Giannakidou 2002. These authors state:

(i) (Den Dikken and Giannakidou 2002:53n25)
   "Richard Kayne (personal communication) suggests that (62b) [*I don't think that any linguists, I will invite to the party] becomes better if negative inversion applies in the embedded clause.
   (i)   ?1 don't think that any linguists would I invite to the party.
   However, this judgment seems rather hard to replicate; note that for most speakers negative inversion with past tense remains unacceptable (but see Postal 2000 [2004a]).
   (ii)   *I don't think that any linguists did I invite to the party.
   To the extent that cases like (i) are acceptable, the fact that a nonnegative constituent like *any linguists*, being licensed by a negation in the matrix clause, may trigger negative inversion raises interesting questions orthogonal to our concerns in this article."

Their attribution of their awareness of Horn clauses to a then recent personal communication suggests that Den Dikken and Giannakidou were unaware of Horn's discovery and McCawley's (1998) brief discussion.

4. While McCawley (1998:598) provided a brief discussion of such cases, this in essence merely restated the syntactic sketch given by Horn.

Chapter 14

1. The grammaticality of (ia) alongside (ib) need not be taken as attacking the claim that subject-Aux inversion is obligatory with Negative Inversion:

(i)   a. Those professors, none of whom they granted tenure, . . .
        b. Those professors, none of whom did they grant tenure, . . .
        c. Those professors, some/none of whom he thinks were granted tenure, . . .

The reason is that (ia) can be taken to be a non–Negative Inversion case, with the leftward position of the negative phrase a function of the nonrestrictive relative clause type of pied-piping found in (ic).

2. As far as we know, the properties of increasing expressions like *no fewer than* have never been studied from the point of view of negative polarity licensing. Consider the following Web example, which we also find acceptable:

(i)   Note that *no fewer than three sources should ever* be used in a faux-scholarly piece.
        (www.copypress.com/blog/frank-formatting-how-to-determine-audience
        -perception/)

This is remarkable given the common view that NPI licensers must be at least nonincreasing forms.

However, other NPIs seem much worse, as shown in (ii)–(v). We can, however, not pursue this important issue here.

(ii)   *No fewer than three students sang at all.

(iii)   *No fewer than three students live there anymore.

(iv)   *No fewer than three students have arrived yet.

(v)   *No fewer than three students need sing.

3. George Lakoff (1970a) and Lawler (1971) discussed data like (23a,b). Lakoff suggested that such contrasts relate to distinctions among adverbials, whereby some adverbial types permit only Negative Inversion constructions like (23a), others only those like (23b). But Lawler (1971:164–166, 171–172) showed that the facts are far more complex than Lakoff's proposal suggested. Progovac (2000:103–104) also seems to assume that the relevant condition involves different classes of adverbs, and she invokes the notion of "negativizing a predicate," which seems incompatible with data like (iic) below.

George Lakoff (1991) cited a range of grammatical and ungrammatical instances of Negative Inversion. His examples were partly parallel to those offered by Klima (1964) and Jackendoff (1972). He proposed the following semantic condition to account for the data, presumably intended to represent a necessary condition on Negative Inversion:

(i)   (G. Lakoff 1991:57)
      "Inversion occurs with negative adverbs that entail that the event expressed in
      the main clause does not occur."

But while valid for a range of examples, the claim is much too general and is falsified
by data like these:

(ii)   a. Under not every view of logic are all contradictory propositions false.
       b. With not so many types of rifle can one hit a target like that from a mile
          away.
       c. Only after many attempts was the interception of the rocket successful.
       d. Not less than thirteen times did they repeat the experiment.

In (iia), the domain doesn't even involve an event; in (iib), targets are hit; in (iic), many
attempts are made; and in (iid), the experiment is repeated at least thirteen times.

   Haegeman (2000:47) makes the interesting observation that both types of adverbials
seen in cases like (23a,b) in the text can cooccur:

(iii)   With no job, on no account should you leave London.

   We have not studied phenomena of the sort at issue in (iii) seriously, but we believe
that they do not bear negatively on the claims about Negative Inversion in the present
monograph.

4. Formulation (25) determines correctly that, as long as the scoping requirement is
met, it is irrelevant how deeply embedded an increasing or decreasing negative expression is:

(i)   a. Not many gorillas' trainers' wives did they invite to the party.
      b. No less than thirty gorillas' trainers' wives did they invite to the party.

These are grammatical because the ultimate possessor at the lowest level scopes above
possessed phrases containing it.

   In (25), V is a DP. We leave aside the analysis of examples like the following, where
the scope-bearing element V might not be a DP:

(ii)   Not in a thousand years will we be able to pay that loan back.

(iii)   Not until after April 22 will I be able to participate.

5. Pieter Seuren and Vincent Homer have pointed out to us striking *only* phrase contrasts like (ia,b):

(i)   a. Only last summer he made headlines (and now he is dead).
      b. Only last summer did he make headlines (after much trying).

We find that the *only* of the adverbial-focusing case (ia) paraphrases *as recently as* or
adverbial *just* and appears to be an increasing operator, while that of the Negative
Inversion case (ib) paraphrases *not before* and appears to be a decreasing operator. We
suggest that *only last summer* in (ia) is a reduction of *at a point in time only as far
back as last summer*. Under these assumptions, the fronted phrase in (ia) would not
qualify as an NI focus under condition (25), since it is not SYNNEG and does not
define a decreasing function, while that in (ib) would, either because it is Strawson
decreasing or because it is SYNNEG (under the speculative proposals in the text about

only). And while we have not said anything about the conditions on adverbial preposing, arguably it is subject to a condition similar to that on topicalization discussed in
chapter 15. In that case, the posited increasing phrase would rightly qualify for adverbial preposing in (ia). Compare the clearly decreasing adverbs in (ii), which yield
ungrammatical adverbial-preposing constructions even if there is no overt NEG:

(ii)   a. *During no/not many summers he visited Nice.
        b. *During less than three summers he visited Nice.

6. Another case supporting the unity of NI foci and the fronted phrases in Horn clauses
is provided by the following fact. Larry Horn informs us that a Web example like the
following is acceptable:

(i)   No genius am I, more like someone into insane sounds.

However, for us (i) is extremely bad and the corresponding Horn clauses have the same
character:

(ii)   a. *They don't believe that any genius am I.
        b. *It's not likely that any genius am I.

7. The following examples illustrate other constraints on Classical NR from Horn
clauses:

(i)   a.   I believe that not (even) a red cent did she offer them.
       b.   I don't believe that *(even) a red cent did she offer them.
       c.   I believe that not (even) once did she call her uncle.
       d.   I don't believe that *(even) once did she call her uncle.

Although *a red cent* and *once* are strict NPIs, Horn clauses directly corresponding to
these are ungrammatical. However, placing the word *even* in front of *a red cent* and
once yields grammatical variants of (ib,d) and has no effect on the meaning or grammaticality of (ia,c). This suggests that what is involved in the ungrammatical versions
of (ib,d) is not a further constraint on the feeding of Classical NR by NI foci but a
restriction on the deletion of *even*. *Even* deletion is apparently not permitted in NI foci
from which the associated NEG has raised out.

8. McCawley (1998:598) also gave an example of a different type:

(i)   *I doubt that at any time has he visited Smith.

9. Consider cases like (i) from Lindholm 1969:153–154, cited in Horn 1978:148:

(i)   a.   It isn't clear that he'll leave until next week.
       b.   I didn't claim that I'd finish the paper until Friday.

As Horn noted, while Lindholm accepted these cases of the strict NPI *until* phrase
under non-CNRPs, there is considerable speaker variation about that judgment. Only
one of us finds both (ia,b) acceptable. For us, the critical fact is that the strict NPI *until*
phrase is scope-bearing, roughly meaning 'at some time before'. Thus, there is the
possibility of a high-scope analysis not invoking Classical NR, and that is how we
believe cases like (i) are interpreted by those who accept them (even though *until*
phrases do not usually take scope out of finite clauses).

Compare, though, cases with the strict NPI *half bad*:

(ii)   a. *It isn't clear that the meal was half bad.
       b. *I didn't claim that the meal was half bad.

Even the one of us who accepts (ia,b) finds these entirely impossible.

10. We have observed over a number of years that quasi–Horn clauses tend to be more acceptable if the complement clause contains another NPI besides that in the NI focus position. This condition is met in most of the Web examples of quasi–Horn clauses we have been able to find. We have no account of this fact, nor is it clear that a grammar is required to provide any.

11. Consider the following:

(i)   a. Ted need promote nobody.
       b. Nobody need Ted promote.
       c. I believe that Ted need promote nobody.
       d. I believe that nobody need Ted promote.
       e. I don't believe that Ted need promote anybody.
       f. I don't believe that anybody need Ted promote.

On one reading of (ia), *nobody* takes main clause scope, rendering (ia) equivalent to 'There is nobody that Ted need promote'. On another, "split" reading (see de Swart 2000 and especially Iatridou and Sichel 2011), (ia) is equivalent to 'It is not necessary that Ted promote somebody'. In (ib), condition (25) only allows the NI focus *nobody* to have main clause scope, since an NI focus scope position must be higher than the scope position of anything in the clause it extracted from. Therefore, the split reading is disallowed for (ib).

The ambiguity in (ia) is replicated in (ic), but the Negative Inversion case (id) uniquely manifests the high-scope reading for *nobody*. Critically, the Horn clause case (if) also lacks the ambiguity and has only the high-scope reading, not the split reading. That too follows from condition (25) under our NEG-based analysis of Horn clauses and the syntactic view of Classical NR that treats the *any* phrase in (if) as an NI focus. We see no means for a nonsyntactic approach to Classical NR to determine that the properties of the Horn clause in (if) match those of the uncontroversial NI focus case (id), especially since (ie) can paraphrase the split reading of (ic).

Split readings challenge the present framework. How can our view associate the negation of *nobody* with a position dominating *need*, while placing the existential part under *need*? Consider (ii):

(ii) Ted_1 [<NEG_2> need] [<[[<NEG_3> [NEG_4 SOME]] body]$_5$> [PRO_1 promote DP_5]]

This possible structure for (ia) resolves to the split reading 'It is not necessary that somebody x is such that Ted promotes x'.

Structure (ii) indicates how split readings could be represented syntactically internal to our view and has the further virtue of eliminating an exception (Hoeksema 2000:130–131) to the idea that an NPI, here *need*, must be c-commanded by its licenser. In terms of (ii), utilizing standard terms, *nobody* is not the licenser of the NPI verb *need*, since arguably it is not the NEG deleter of NEG_2, which would violate the nonincreasing condition on general NEG deleters (because [[<NEG$_3$> [NEG$_4$ SOME]] body]$_5$ is increasing).

But while those are positive features of (ii), it raises problems—specifically, the same issues about NEG deleters noted in section 4.10 for our proposed free choice *any* structure. In (ii), both NEG$_2$ and NEG$_3$ are covert and would hence need NEG deleters, leaving NEG$_4$ to be the overt NEG determining the shape *nobody*. There then exists the same range of possible choices for the needed NEG deleter patterns as those sketched in chapter 4. Both possibilities would again involve autocannibalistic NEG deletion, with [NEG$_2$ need] deleting NEG$_2$. As in the discussion of section 4.10, we cannot attempt here to develop a definitive position on the needed NEG deleter pairings.

We observe that in the terms sketched, the grammaticality of the split reading in (ia) and the presence of a negative form like *nobody* are linked. Assuming that [NEG$_2$ need] is the NEG deleter of NEG$_2$, two limitations on the needed NEG deletion chains would be involved. First, NEG$_3$ would have to be a reversal NEG. Second, the initiator can be [<NEG> need], while most other verbal forms—for example, [<NEG> must]—cannot be, as (iii) has no split reading:

(iii)   Ted must promote nobody.

The implication would be that verb-initiated English instances of autocannibalistic negation are extremely limited.

Chapter 15

1. We observe that the formulations of Negative Inversion in (3) and the Topicalization Condition in (5) are both compatible with the existence of examples in which the two phenomena combine, as in (ia,b) from Haegeman 2000:27:

(i)   a. Beans, never in my life will I eat.
        b. Such people, under no conditions will they consider hiring.

We suspect that many speakers will find such sentences marginal, but it is nonetheless important that the pattern in (i) does not threaten the present system.

Take (ia). In current terms, it would be analyzed as (ii):

(ii)   [$_{TopP}$ <[Beans]$_5$> [$_{TopP}$ DP$_5$ [$_{FocP}$ <[[NEG SOME] ever in my life]$_3$> [$_{FocP}$ <PP$_3$> [will I <PP$_3$> eat <DP$_5$>]]]]]

Here, *never in my life* is a legitimate NI focus since the relevant scope occurrence is higher than anything in the FocP and is both SYNNEG and decreasing. Similarly, *beans* is a legitimate topic since its scope position is higher than anything in the TopP and it is neither SYNNEG nor decreasing.

2. Some speakers we have encountered find (7c) acceptable. We don't. We have no account of this variation.

3. Our accounts of Negative Inversion in (3) and the Topicalization Condition in (5) create serious problems when combined with the negative quantifier analysis of free choice *any* (FCA) forms we proposed in section 4.10. Since FCA forms are SYNNEG and decreasing, the chapter 4 analysis combines with the Negative Inversion Condition

to allow FCA forms to undergo Negative Inversion and also combines with the Topicalization Condition to determine that they can't undergo topicalization. But both entailments are false:

(i)   a. *Any adult chimpanzee can they train to tap dance.
       b. Any adult chimpanzee, they can train to tap dance.

We cannot adequately address this evidently serious issue here. But we speculate that a solution could take the following form. First, one would revise the definition of SYNNEG so that forms that are autocannibalistic NEG deleters are not SYNNEG. Hence, under the analysis in chapter 4, FCA phrases would not be SYNNEG. Second, it would be necessary to appeal to the speculative version of the Negative Inversion Condition in (21) of chapter 14, that is, the version that does not mention the decreasing property. Third, it would be necessary to appeal as well to a corresponding version of the Topicalization Condition that only made reference to SYNNEG. In other terms, solving the problem raised by the facts in (i) seems to drive us toward totally nonsemantic accounts of the Negative Inversion and Topicalization Conditions.

4. If one fixes the tense and the time adverbial of (9b) such that the clause can be interpreted generically, sentences otherwise parallel to the complement of (9b) are irrelevantly grammatical on a free choice analysis of *any clothes*:

(i)   (I don't think that) in any clothes, Bill looks attractive.

The long variant of (i) would not have a Classical NR analysis.

5. A multitude of Negative Inversion and topicalization structures not blocked by our Negative Inversion Condition in (3), by our Topicalization Condition in (5), or by any other principle we have invoked are nonetheless sharply ungrammatical. We refer in particular to examples like these:

(i)   a. *Any students didn't I talk to yesterday.
       b. *A single dentist didn't they interview for that story.
       c. *Until Friday won't the books arrive.
       d. *Any students did no professors contact.

Each of (ia–d) corresponds to a related grammatical Negative Inversion case, respectively (iia–d):

(ii)   a. No students did I talk to yesterday.
       b. Not a single dentist did they interview for that story.
       c. Not until Friday will the books arrive.
       d. No students did any professors contact.

The problem is that in present terms, each of the NPI NI foci in (i) could be a unary-NEG phrase, hence would both be SYNNEG and define a decreasing function, satisfying the Negative Inversion Condition in (3).

    We suggest that examples like (ia–d) are blocked by the following condition:

(iii)   *The NEG Deletion Anti-C-Command Condition*
       If A and B are overt occurrences, and A = NEG_1 or heads a NEG deletion
       chain $<A, \ldots, NEG_1>$, and B = $[<NEG_1> X]$, then B does not c-command A.

While space precludes detailed discussion, condition (iii) would, for instance, block (ic) on the analysis (iv):

(iv) $<[<NEG_1>$ until Friday]$_3>$ XP$_3$ [won't (= NEG$_1$) the books arrive XP$_3$]

In (iv), XP$_3$—that is, the overt *until* phrase in the NI focus position—corresponds to variable B in condition (iii), while the clitic *n't* = NEG$_1$ corresponds to variable A. But XP$_3$ c-commands *n't*, violating condition (iii).

The structure in (iv) is independently blocked as a scope conflict. Since NEG$_1$ has raised to a position right-adjacent to the finite Aux, the scope position of [not until Friday] must be lower than the finite Aux. On the other hand, the scope position must be higher than the NI focus position, in order to satisfy (3), the Negative Inversion Condition.

Parallel facts exist with topicalization since, in particular, as noticed by Lasnik and Uriagereka (1988:156), Progovac (1994:41), and especially Hoeksema (2000:123), NPIs never topicalize. We illustrate much more briefly:

(v)   *Any gorillas, at most three researchers could communicate with.

Here, since *any gorillas* is a reversal structure, it is not SYNNEG and does not define a decreasing function, so its topicalization does not violate the Topicalization Condition (5). Its ungrammaticality does, however, follow from condition (iii) in a way parallel to (iv).

While it might be claimed that condition (iii) is an ad hoc stipulation, it also blocks a range of non–Negative Inversion and non-topicalization cases like those in (vi):

(vi)   a. *Any cats like few dogs.
        b. *They have ever helped not a single refugee.
        c. i. *She believes any of those groups not to have helped the refugees.
           ii. She believes not to have helped the refugees any of those groups.

Other approaches to NPIs deal with such cases by proposing various c-command and/ or word order conditions that we claim (iii) renders superfluous.

Chapter 16

1. Arguably, elements of the composed quantifier argument originate in Jackendoff 1971.

2. The lexicalization assumption central to the composed quantifier argument was not a straw man due to Horn. Actual proposals of that sort had been made. So Seuren (1974a:195–197) explicitly claimed the underlying structure of the Classical NR reading of (ia) was (ib), requiring lexicalization of *everybody* + NEG as *nobody*:

(i)   a. Nobody thought that John would get here until tomorrow.
        b. Everybody thought that John wouldn't get here until tomorrow.

3. Nothing changes if NEG$_2$ in (13b) is regarded as originating at the verb phrase level (instead of modifying the verb itself).

4. In connection with our analysis (14b), readers may ask why cases like (ib–d) are ungrammatical given that (ia) shows there is no general ban in our dialects on the combination of a negative quantifier subject with a negated verb:

(i)   a.   Nobody doesn't think that gerbils are telepathic.
      b.   *Nobody doesn't think that gerbils eat any meat.
      c.   *Nobody doesn't think that Eileen knows jackshit$_A$ about gerbils.
      d.   *Nobody doesn't think that at any time had he owned a gerbil.

Given previous discussion, for (ic,d) to be grammatical, the unary NEG associated with *jackshit$_A$* in (ic) and that associated with the NI focus in (id) must raise into the main clause and be deleted. But the resulting NEG deletion chains, unlike those associated with the grammatical examples we have treated like (14b), would involve only a single deleted NEG and thus violate the NEG Deletion Evenness Condition. So far, then, the data in (i) raise no issues for our system of ideas.

But (ib) is problematic since it can have an analysis where the NPI is a reversal structure while the post-Aux NEG in the main clause originates on the V/VP. Both of the binary-structure NEGs can then be deleted either by *nobody* or by [NEG think] (with or without the reversal raising to be their clausemate, depending on the major point about reversals left open in chapter 8). In either case, no violation of the NEG Deletion Evenness Condition ensues and, in fact, no condition we have proposed blocks that analysis.

We cannot pursue this issue in the present monograph.

5. Like our formulation of Classical NR in (4) of chapter 1, assertion (16) in the text makes no distinction between the raising of unary and the raising of binary (reversal) NEGs. But we have cited no case of Classical NR instantiated by the raising of a reversal NEG; in fact, the question of whether Classical NR ever targets reversal NEGs needs much further study.

One issue that we have sidestepped is whether reversal NEGs ever undergo NEG raising, in the general sense. The discussion in chapter 8 of the NDEL relation leaves that open. It is possible that reversal NEGs never undergo any kind of NEG raising, hence not Classical NR in particular.

Putting aside this issue, we cannot currently cite an actual English example where it can be argued that a reversal NEG undergoes Classical NR. One reason for this might be that almost all the English reversal cases we know of involve the deletion of both NEGs of a binary-NEG structure. Therefore, constructing examples illustrating Classical NR is difficult, because neither NEG is visible.

We can, however, cite two plausible exceptions to the generalization that both NEGs of a reversal structure are uniformly deleted. First, the reversal analysis of the specific expletive negation case mentioned in note 7 of chapter 7 recognizes a nondeleted reversal NEG originating on a V/VP in a type of complement clause. But the needed environment precludes any possibility of interaction with Classical NR since the main verb in such cases cannot be a CNRP. So such a case provides no way of testing the possibility of Classical NR with reversals.

Second, the speculative analysis of the split reading of modal *need* cases sketched in note 11 of chapter 14 recognizes an undeleted reversal NEG. But there again, the context is limited to the complement of a non-CNRP and again the interaction of reversal NEGs and Classical NR cannot be tested.

While we thus cannot describe an actual case of a reversal NEG raising under Classical NR, we can characterize the kind of structure/interpretation that would support the existence of the Classical NR of reversals. Such a case would be represented by grammatical sentences with a CNRP main verb like (ia) having structure (ib) and having the interpretation (ic) (which in fact is not a possible interpretation of (ia)). For simplicity, and without materially affecting the discussion, we ignore scope occurrences in these representations.

(i)   a.   I don't believe she understands anything.
       b.   I do NEG_2 believe [she understands [[<NEG_2> [<NEG_1> SOME]] thing]]
       c.   'I believe she understands something.'

Because the Classical NR structure in (ib) yields an impossible interpretation for (ia), such a case seems to support the claim that Classical NR does not in fact function for reversal NEGs. However, this case cannot show anything conclusive about constraints on Classical NR since (ib) independently violates the conditions on NEG deletion in chapter 8. First, while NEG_1 is a deleted NEG, there is no viable NEG deletion chain for it to be part of since there is no non-NEG NEG deleter satisfying the General NEG Deletion Condition. In any event, any NEG deletion chain containing NEG_1 would violate the NEG Deletion Evenness Condition of chapter 8, since NEG_2 has an overt occurrence.

6. Despite its virtues, our account so far wrongly permits cases such as (i) with the structure in (ii):

(i)   *At most half of the class thinks that Felicia arrived until 6:00.

(ii)   At most half of the class NEG_2 thinks that Felicia arrived [NEG_1 until 6:00]

So far, nothing precludes NEG_1 from raising into the matrix clause and being deleted by NEG_2, which can be deleted by *at most of half the class*. That follows given that such an expression defines a nonincreasing function. It then satisfies the conditions for being a general NEG deleter under (11) of chapter 8, the General NEG Deletion Condition. To block this analysis, we propose the following:

(iii)   *The Antiadditive NEG Deletion Condition*
         If NEG_1 originates in B = [NEG_1 Y] (where B is a unary-NEG structure),
         and
         <A, . . . , NEG_1, . . . > is a NEG deletion chain, then A = [NEG X] and
         defines an antiadditive function.

We observe that (iii) is obeyed in the formation of polyadic quantifier structures (see chapter 6). Moreover, (iii) is not an ad hoc stipulation designed to defend our account of the composed quantifier argument cases against facts like (i). Condition (iii) also rightly blocks cases like those in (iv), shown by examples like those in (18)–(20) in chapter 10 to incorrectly be allowed by purely semantic treatments of NPIs restricted in standard terms to antiadditive licensers:

(iv)   a. *Zero (or more) doctors felt all that well.
        b. *Zero (or more) doctors did jackshit$_A$ on Thursday.
        c. *Zero (or more) doctors did a single thing about that.
        d. *Zero (or more) doctors have seen Mary in ages.

The one problematic issue related to (iii) that we are aware of involves cases like (v):

(v)   No one except Georgina thinks that Felicia arrived until 6:00.

Here, the expression *no one except Georgina* is strictly speaking not antiadditive and not even decreasing because of the positive presupposition associated with the exceptive, which renders the whole nonmonotonic. As in earlier discussions, such as that of (6) and (7) in chapter 14, a plausible solution would appeal to Strawson decreasingness and Strawson antiadditivity.

7. The class of quasi–Horn clauses with overt matrix NEG also includes cases involving the same sort of nominalizations, as in (i):

(i)   The States couldn't provide us with evidence that at any time had there been a
       request for road closure.
       (share.pdfonline.com/.../GG%20letter.htm)

8. Suppose the structure of a case like (48a), repeated here as (ia), were not (48b), repeated here as (ib), with the "extra" NEG on the main verb. Suppose it instead had an "extra" NEG as a complement clause clausal NEG, as in (ic):

(i)   a. No one thinks that Alfred knows jackshit$_A$ about physics.
       b. No one [<NEG$_2$> thinks] that [<[[NEG$_1$ SOME] jackshit$_A$]$_3$> [Alfred knows
          DP$_3$ about physics]]
       c. No one thinks that [[<NEG$_2$> [<[<NEG$_1$> SOME] jackshit$_A$]$_3$> [Alfred
          knows DP$_3$ about physics]]]

While a structure like (ic) has many of the virtues of the structures we actually advocate for composed quantifier cases, namely, those like (ib), it is not really adequate. Most importantly in the present context, a structure like (ic) fails to ground the equivalence of (ia) and (ii):

(ii)   Everyone thinks that Alfred doesn't know jackshit$_A$ about physics.

The reason is that (ic) means no one thinks p. That being the case, there is no reason why a structure like (ic) would be incompatible with the 'no opinion' reading, that is, no reason why it imposes the excluded middle property. But as we have shown, that property is crucial to determining the equivalence of (ia) and (ii). This argues that (ic) is not a correct representation of (ia).

The conclusion that (ic) is not the correct structure of (ia) is greatly strengthened in section 17.5. There, strong independent evidence for the matrix NEG$_2$ in (ib) is provided.

The question then arises of what principle precludes the existence of representations like (ic). We have not studied this question seriously. But given that a fundamental feature of structures like (ic) is that the clausal NEG, NEG$_2$, raises and is deleted (by *no one*) in the main clause, one speculation is that either there are no clausal NEGs or, if there are, they have a very restricted distribution.

9. A problem arises from the interaction of structures like (59b) and the Antiadditive NEG Deletion Condition of note 5. The assumption is that (59b) determines a NEG deletion chain of the following form:

(i)   <[Scarcely anybody], NEG$_2$, NEG$_1$>

The condition just mentioned would then require that *scarcely anybody* be of the form [NEG X] and be antiadditive, since NEG_2 is a unary NEG. Yet *scarcely anybody* does not obviously meet either of these requirements.

We speculate that the condition could be met if "approximative" modifiers like *almost* and *scarcely* are really NP modifiers, which specify that the set being quantified over is not precisely the set denoted by the NP without them but rather that set minus a contextually determined very small number of elements.

Moreover, *scarcely*, among others, would have to be regarded as a lexical NEG deleter, accounting for the equivalence of *scarcely anybody* and *almost nobody*, and other similar pairs.

We cannot pursue these speculations here.

Chapter 17

1. See Ross 1973 for an extensive, groundbreaking discussion of parentheticals.

2. If secondaries originate as in schema (4) but can end up inside the primaries they modify by movement, then the end position of such a secondary does not c-command its position of origin, as the C-Command Condition on Movement of chapter 5 requires. This might challenge the view in schema (4) or the assumption that movement is involved, but we will not pursue this issue.

3. Alexander and Kunz 1964, list 1, furnishes a large inventory of English verbs taking *that* clause complements.

4. The discussion here has important similarities with the invocation of fronted anaphoric *so* in connection with quotative inversion in Collins 1997:38–39.

5. A potential problem for condition (19) is represented by cases like (i), based on the decreasing form *at most n*:

(i)   Waldo will, at most three people said, refuse to participate in the discussion.

One of us finds this acceptable, a fact for which we have no explanation.

6. An important issue we have not addressed in this chapter is that the notions *decreasing/increasing* are extensional and when propositional attitudes are involved, they do not strictly apply in relevant cases. To see that, consider:

(i)   a. Stan doubts that Karen eats green vegetables.
        b. Stan doubts that Karen eats spinach.

(ii)   a. Stan thinks that Karen eats green vegetables.
        b. Stan thinks that Karen eats spinach.

We have assumed in the chapter that *doubt* is decreasing and *think* is increasing. But this assumption is not supported by the data in (i) and (ii). Even if (ia) is true, (ib) may be false or without a truth value if Stan has never heard of spinach before. Similarly, even if (iib) is true, if Stan does not realize that spinach is a vegetable, then (iia) may be false.

What appears to be relevant is a weaker notion than entailment tout court, one that depends on "thinkers" of propositional attitude verbs being aware of the inclusion relations relevant to the inferences. For example, in (i), if Stan knows that spinach is a green vegetable, then we find that (ia) plus that assumption does entail (ib). And similarly in (ii). But we cannot develop this line of analysis here.

A related issue involving condition (19) is raised by parentheticals formed with the verb *forget*. These behave just like the cases in (22) and (23) with the negative force verbs *deny* and *doubt*:

(iii) a. Cathy was (not), *I forgot, divorced from Fred.
       b. Cathy was (not), I didn't forget, divorced from Fred.

(iv)   a. *Cathy was (not), everyone forgot, divorced from Fred.
       b. Cathy was (not), no one forgot, divorced from Fred.

The problem is that *forget*, because of the factivity presupposition associated with its complement, is not strictly decreasing. So for instance (vb) does not actually entail (va):

(v)   a. John forgot that Cathy ate spinach.
       b. John forgot that Cathy ate a green vegetable.

That is, Cathy might not in fact have eaten spinach but only some other green vegetable(s). Hence, it is unclear that (iiib), (ivb) satisfy condition (19) or that (iiia), (iva) don't. The issues would seem to fall into the domain of problems often discussed in terms of Strawson decreasingness (e.g., the fact that *forget* licenses NPIs in its complement).

7. We have not considered the case where a secondary is based on a semantically increasing non-CNRP that is negated and that combines with a decreasing phrase in the secondary, that is, cases like (ia):

(i)   a. *Glenda will (not), nobody didn't assert/figure out/learn/state, visit Paris.
       b. Glenda will (not), everybody asserted/figured out/learned/stated, visit Paris.

Since the forms in the secondary in (ia) compose to yield an increasing function, hence the equivalence to (ib), such cases, though sharply ungrammatical, are not blocked by condition (19). This is not a counterexample to (19), only a fact it fails to determine. We have no current account for this situation. We note, though, that in standard English, nonparenthetical forms like (ii) are marginal:

(ii)   ?Nobody didn't assert/figure out/learn/state that Glenda will not visit Paris.

In fact, they only seem good at all with strong stress on *did*. Perhaps, then, there is a conflict between properties of parentheticals we have not discussed and the conditions determining strong stress.

8. Examples like (25a) and (26a) are not consistent with a 'no opinion' interpretation of the parenthetical. For example, (25a) could not be used felicitously if the subject of the parenthetical had no expectations or was undecided. On that reading, the NEG of the parenthetical would modify the verb of the secondary and hence would violate condition (19), explaining the absence of the 'no opinion' interpretation.

Chapter 19

1. Another counterexample to the view that Classical NR functions systematically across clause types was noted by Seuren (1974a:192). He claimed that Classical NR is impossible in imperatives, citing these examples:

(i)   a. *Don't think he has found it yet.
       b. *Don't think he'll find it until tomorrow.

2. Aspect also influences whether or not Classical NR is possible, a fact for which we can offer no account:

(i)   a.   I don't think that Sally knows jackshit$_A$ about physics.
       b. *I am not thinking that Sally knows jackshit$_A$ about physics.

Chapter 20

1. We would like to stress a factual and methodological point distinct from an actual linguistic result. As our work on this monograph progressed, it became increasingly clear to us that any argument potentially relevant to Classical NR involving a scope-taking strict NPI in a complement clause C was fraught with difficulties. This followed because given our syntactic, multiple-occurrence view of scope representation, scope higher than C offers the possibility that a main clause NEG could achieve its surface position without raising out of C (but rather by raising from the NPI in high-scope position). In any case where that is a real possibility, no argument for Classical NR can be solid until the high-scope alternative is isolated and excluded. This is typically quite difficult. The reader will recall that we raised this issue on multiple occasions in chapters 9, 14, and 16.

A consequence of this methodological point is that particular discussions and data citations in the literature may show considerably less than what they might seem to because the possibility alluded to above appears to never have been taken into account. We believe the cases from Lindholm 1969 cited in Horn 1978 (see note 9 of chapter 14) provide an example.

Another example is provided by Horn's (1978:146) citation of (i):

(i)   Joe isn't going to have to be able to pay a red cent.

Here *a red cent* is a strict NPI, but one separated from the NEG permitting it by three non-CNRPs: *able*, necessitative *have to*, and future *going*. At first glance, this is a disastrous case for any claim that *a red cent* requires a local NEG. But if this is a case of a high-scope occurrence of [NEG a red cent] as in (ii), (i) actually would not bear on the locality claim for the NPI:

(ii)   Joe isn't (= NEG$_1$) [<[NEG$_1$ a red cent]$_3$> [going to have to be able to pay DP$_3$]]

Whether it is correct or not that (ii) provides the right meaning for (i), something like 'No amount of money x is such that Joe is going to have to be able to pay x' (and it seems plausible to us that it is correct), the mere possibility of such an analysis supports the present remarks to the effect that argumentation about Classical NR cannot ignore such possibilities.

2. Although we have covered a great deal of ground in this monograph, there are certain key facts we have not addressed. For example, Gajewski (2007:313) and Romoli (2012) explain the failure of Classical NR in certain cases originally discussed by Horn (1971:120–121), where one CNRP is embedded under another:

(i) a. I don't believe John wanted Harry to die until tomorrow.
  b. *I don't want John to believe Harry died until yesterday.

Gajewski (2007) gives an ingenious account of this contrast in terms of the way that *want* and *believe* project the presuppositions of their complements. Furthermore, these properties of *want* and *believe* are independently needed.

We agree with the judgments of (ia,b), but also we believe that a much more extensive investigation of so-called cyclicity phenomena is needed. Not only must the facts be examined for every pairwise combination of CNRPs, they must be examined for a much wider array of strict NPIs as well.

At this point, we are skeptical of the claim that Classical NR can be cyclic. In particular, it is unclear to us what the scope of *until tomorrow* is in (ia). Furthermore, we believe that strict NPIs can more easily take high scope out of nonfinite clauses than out of finite ones. Such a difference may be enough to explain the contrast between (ia,b) with no appeal to cyclic Classical NR. If so, it may be that Classical NR can never raise the same NEG more than once.

References

Adger, David, and Peter Svenonius. 2011. Features in Minimalist syntax. In *The Oxford handbook of linguistic Minimalism*, ed. by Cedric Boeckx, 27–51. Oxford: Oxford University Press.

Alexander, D., and W. J. Kunz. 1964. Some classes of verbs in English. Bloomington Indiana University Linguistics Research Project.

Anselm, Saint. The Lambeth fragments. In *Ein neues unvollendetes Werk des hl. Anselm von Canterbury*. Münster i. W.: Aschendorff (1936).

Atlas, Jay David. 1996. 'Only' noun phrases, pseudo-negative generalized quantifiers, negative polarity items, and monotonicity. *Journal of Semantics* 13:265–328.

Bartsch, Renate. 1973. 'Negative transportation' gibt es nicht. *Linguistische Berichte* 27:1–7.

Bolinger, Dwight. 1968. Postposed main phrases: An English rule for the Romance subjunctive. *Canadian Journal of Linguistics* 14:3–30.

Bosanquet, Bernard. 1888. *Logic*. Vol. I. Oxford: Clarendon Press.

Bošković, Željko. 1997. Pseudo-clefts. *Studia Linguistica* 51:235–277.

Bošković, Željko, and Jon Gajweski. 2008. Semantic correlates of the NP/DP parameter. In *NELS 39: Proceedings of the Thirty-Ninth Annual Meeting of the North East Linguistic Society*, ed. by Suzi Lima, Kevin Mullin, and Brian Smith, 1:121–134. Amherst: University of Massachusetts, Graduate Linguistic Student Association.

Bumford, Dylan. 2011. Not-raising. Ms., New York University.

Büring, Daniel. 2004. Negative inversion. Available at http://wurmbrand.uconn.edu/Germanic/C387611321/E459446832/index.html.

Carlson, Greg N. 1980. Any is existential. *Linguistic Inquiry* 11:799–804.

Carlson, Lauri. 1983. *Dialogue games*. Dordrecht: Reidel.

Cattell, Ray. 1973. Negative transportation and tag questions. *Language* 49:612–639.

Chierchia, Gennaro. 2004. Scalar implicatures, polarity phenomena, and the syntax/pragmatics interface. In *Structures and beyond*, ed. by Adriana Belletti, 39–103. Oxford: Oxford University Press.

Clinkenbeard, Joel. 1969. *Not*-transportation and related matters. Ms., MIT.

Collins, Chris. 1997. *Local economy*. Cambridge, MA: MIT Press.

Collins, Chris, and Paul M. Postal. 2012. *Imposters*. Cambridge, MA: MIT Press.

Collins, Chris, and Edward Stabler. 2012. A formalization of Minimalist syntax. Available at http://ling.auf.net/lingbuzz/001691.

Dayal, Veneeta. 1998. Any as inherently modal. *Linguistics and Philosophy* 21:433–476.

Déprez, Viviane. 1997. Two types of negative concord. *Probus* 9:103–143.

Deutscher, Max. 1965. A note on saying and believing. *Analysis* 105:53–57.

Dikken, Marcel den, and Anastasia Giannakidou. 2002. From *hell* to polarity: "Aggressively non-D-linked" *wh*-phrases as polarity items. *Linguistic Inquiry* 33:31–61.

Dowty, David. 2008. Resumptive negation as assertion revision. Available at http://www.ling.ohio-state.edu/~dowty/resumptive-negation.pdf.

Fauconnier, Gilles. 1971. Theoretical implications of some global phenomena. Doctoral dissertation, University of California at San Diego.

Fillmore, Charles J. 1963. The position of embedding transformations in a grammar. *Word* 19:208–231.

Fintel, Kai von. 1997. Bare plurals, bare conditionals, and *only*. *Journal of Semantics* 14:1–56.

Fintel, Kai von. 1999. NPI licensing, Strawson entailment and context dependency. *Journal of Semantics* 16:97–148.

Fodor, Janet Dean. 1970. The linguistic description of opaque contexts. Doctoral dissertation, MIT.

Gajewski, Jon. 2005. Neg-raising: Polarity and presupposition. Doctoral dissertation, MIT.

Gajewski, Jon. 2007. Neg-raising and polarity. *Linguistics and Philosophy* 30:289–328.

Gajewski, Jon. 2008. NPI *any* and connected exceptive phrases. *Natural Language Semantics* 16:69–110.

Gajewski, Jon. 2011. Licensing strong NPIs. *Natural Language Semantics* 19:109–148.

Geurts, Bart. 1996. On *no*. *Journal of Semantics* 13:67–86.

Geurts, Bart. 2009. Scalar implicature and local pragmatics. *Mind and Language* 24:51–79.

Giannakidou, Anastasia. 2000. Negative...concord? *Natural Language and Linguistic Theory* 18:457–523.

Giannakidou, Anastasia. 2011. Positive polarity items and negative polarity items: Variation, licensing, and compositionality. In *Semantics: An international handbook of natural language meaning*, ed. by Claudia Maienborn, Klaus von Heusinger, and Paul Portner, 1660–1712. Berlin: Mouton de Gruyter.

Haegeman, Liliane. 1995. *The syntax of negation*. Cambridge: Cambridge University Press.

Haegeman, Liliane. 2000. Negative preposing, negative inversion, and the split CP. In *Negation and polarity*, ed. by Laurence R. Horn and Yasuhiko Kato, 21–61. New York: Oxford University Press.

Haegeman, Liliane, and Raffaella Zanuttini. 1996. Negative concord in West Flemish. In *Parameters and functional heads*, ed. by Adriana Belletti and Luigi Rizzi, 117–179. Oxford: Oxford University Press.

Haspelmath, Martin. 1997. *Indefinite pronouns*. Oxford: Oxford University Press.

Heim, Irene. 1982. The semantics of definite and indefinite noun phrases. Doctoral dissertation, University of Massachusetts, Amherst.

Heim, Irene, and Angelika Kratzer. 1998. *Semantics in generative grammar*. Cambridge, MA: MIT Press.

Henry, Desmond. 1967. *The logic of Saint Anselm*. Oxford: Clarendon Press.

Hintikka, Jaakko. 1962. *Knowledge and belief*. Ithaca, NY: Cornell University Press.

Hoeksema, Jack. 2000. Negative polarity items: Triggering, scope, and c-command. In *Negation and polarity*, ed. by Laurence R. Horn and Yasuhiko Kato, 115–146. Oxford: Oxford University Press.

Hoeksema, Jack, and Henny Klein. 1995. Negative predicates and their arguments. *Linguistic Analysis* 25:146–180.

Hoffmann, Maria. 1987. *Negatio contrarii: A study of Latin litotes*. Assen: Van Gorcum.

Homer, Vincent. 2010. Neg-raising and positive polarity: The view from modals. Available at http://semanticsarchive.net/cgi-bin/browse.pl?search=homer.

Honcoop, Martin. 1998. *Dynamic excursions on weak islands*. The Hague: Holland Academic Graphics.

Hopkins, Jasper. 1972. *A companion to the study of St. Anselm*. Minneapolis: University of Minnesota Press.

Horn, Laurence R. 1971. Negative transportation: Unsafe at any speed? In *Papers from the Seventh Regional Meeting of the Chicago Linguistic Society*, 120–133. Chicago: University of Chicago, Chicago Linguistic Society.

Horn, Laurence R. 1972. On the semantic properties of logical operators in English. Doctoral dissertation, University of California at Los Angeles.

Horn, Laurence R. 1975. Neg-raising predicates: Toward an explanation. In *Papers from the Eleventh Regional Meeting of the Chicago Linguistic Society*, ed. by Robin E. Grossman, L. James San, and Timothy J. Vance, 280–294. Chicago: University of Chicago, Chicago Linguistic Society.

Horn, Laurence R. 1978. Remarks on neg-raising. In *Pragmatics*, ed. by Peter Cole, 129–220. New York: Academic Press.

Horn, Laurence R. 1989 [2001]. *A natural history of negation*. Chicago: University of Chicago Press.

Horn, Laurence R. 1991. *Duplex negatio affirmat . . .*: The economy of double negation. In *Papers from the Twenty-Seventh Regional Meeting of the Chicago Linguistic Society*. Part Two, *The Parasession on Negation*, ed. by Lise M. Dobrin, Lynn Nichols, and Rosa M. Rodriguez, 78–106. Chicago: University of Chicago, Chicago Linguistic Society.

Horn, Laurence R. 2001. Flaubert triggers, squatitive negation, and other quirks of grammar. In *Perspectives on negation and polarity items*, ed. by Jack Hoeksema, Hotze Rullmann, Victor Sánchez-Valencia, and Ton van der Wouden, 173–200. Amsterdam: John Benjamins.

Horn, Laurence R., and Samuel Bayer. 1984. Short-circuited implicature: A negative contribution. *Language and Philosophy* 7:397–414.

Iatridou, Sabine, and Ivy Sichel. 2011. Negative DPs, A-movement, and scope diminishment. *Linguistic Inquiry* 42:595–629.

Israel, Michael. 2011. *The grammar of polarity: Pragmatics, sensitivity, and the logic of scales*. Cambridge: Cambridge University Press.

Jackendoff, Ray. 1971. On some questionable arguments about quantifiers and negation. *Language* 47:282–297.

Jackendoff, Ray. 1972. *Semantic interpretation in generative grammar*. Cambridge, MA: MIT Press.

Jackson, Eric. 1995. Weak and strong negative polarity items: Licensing and intervention. *Linguistic Analysis* 25:181–208.

Jacobs, Joachim. 1980. Lexical decomposition in Montague Grammar. *Theoretical Linguistics* 7:121–136.

Jespersen, Otto. 1917. Negation in English and other languages. Copenhagen: A. F. Høst.

Johnson, David E., and Paul M. Postal. 1980. *Arc Pair Grammar*. Princeton, NJ: Princeton University Press.

Kadmon, Nirit, and Fred Landman. 1993. *Any*. *Linguistics and Philosophy* 16:353–422.

Karttunen, Lauri. 1974. *Until*. In *Papers from the Tenth Regional Meeting of the Chicago Linguistic Society*, ed. by Michael W. La Galy, Robert A. Fox, and Anthony Bruck, 284–297. Chicago: University of Chicago, Chicago Linguistic Society.

Keenan, Edward L. 1987. Unreducible n-ary quantifiers in natural language. In *Generalized quantifiers*, ed. by Peter Gärdenfors, 109–150. Dordrecht: Reidel.

Keenan, Edward L. 1992. Beyond the Frege boundary. *Linguistics and Philosophy* 15:199–221.

Keenan, Edward L. 1996. Further beyond the Frege boundary. In *Quantifiers, logic, and language*, ed. by Jaap van der Does and Jan van Eijck, 179–201. Stanford, CA: CSLI Publications.

Keenan, Edward L., and Leonard M. Faltz. 1985. *Boolean semantics for natural language*. Dordrecht: Reidel.

Kempson, Ruth. 1985. More on *any*: Reply to Ladusaw. In *Proceedings of NELS 15*, ed. by Steve Berman, Jae-Woong Choe, and Joyce McDonough, 234–255. Amherst: University of Massachusetts, Graduate Linguistic Student Association.

Kiparsky, Carol, and Paul Kiparsky. 1971. Fact. In *Semantics: An interdisciplinary reader*, ed. by Danny D. Steinberg and Leon A. Jacobovits, 345–369. Cambridge: Cambridge University Press.

Klima, Edward. 1964. Negation in English. In *The structure of language*, ed. by Jerry A. Fodor and Jerrold J. Katz, 246–323. Englewood Cliffs, NJ: Prentice Hall.

Klooster, Wim. 2003. Negative raising revisited. In *Germania et alia: A linguistic Webschrift for Hans den Besten*, ed. by Jan Koster and Henk van Riemsdijk. Available at http://odur.let.rug.nl/koster/DenBesten/.

Klooster, Wim. To appear. Against negative raising. In *Festschrift for Kazimierz Sroka*.

Kratzer, Angelika. 1995. Stage-level and individual-level predicates. In *The generic book*, ed. by Gregory N. Carlson and Francis Jeffry Pelletier, 125–175. Chicago: University of Chicago Press.

Krifka, Manfred. 1995. The semantics and pragmatics of polarity items. *Linguistic Analysis* 25:209–257.

Labov, William. 1972. Negative attraction and negative concord in English grammar. *Language* 48:773–818.

Ladusaw, William A. 1979. Polarity sensitivity as inherent scope relations. Doctoral dissertation, University of Texas. Published, New York: Garland (1980).

Ladusaw, William A. 1992. Expressing negation. In *Proceedings of SALT 2*, ed. by Chris Barker and David Dowty, 237–259. Ohio State University Working Papers in Linguistics 40. Columbus: The Ohio State University, Department of Linguistics.

Ladusaw, William A. 1996a. Configurational expression of negation. In *Quantifiers, logic, and language*, ed. by Jaap van der Does and Jan van Eijck, 203–223. Stanford, CA: CSLI Publications.

Ladusaw, William A. 1996b. Negation and polarity items. In *The handbook of contemporary semantic theory*, ed. by *Shalom* Lappin, 321–341. Oxford: Blackwell.

Lakoff, George. 1970a. Adverbs and modal operators. Ms., University of Michigan Phonetics Lab.

Lakoff, George. 1970b. Pronominalization, negation, and the analysis of adverbs. In *Readings in transformational grammar*. ed. by Roderick A. Jacobs and Peter S. Rosenbaum, 145–165. Waltham, MA: Blaisdell.

Lakoff, George. 1971. On generative semantics. In *Semantics*, ed. by Danny D. Steinberg and Leon A. Jakobovits, 232–296. Cambridge: Cambridge University Press.

Lakoff, George. 1991. Cognitive versus generative linguistics: How commitments influence results. *Language and Communication* 2:53–62.

Lakoff, Robin. 1969a. Some reasons why there can't be a *some-any* rule. *Language* 45:608–615.

Lakoff, Robin. 1969b. A syntactic argument for negative transportation. In *Papers from the Fifth Regional Meeting of the Chicago Linguistic Society*, ed. by Robert Binnick, Alice Davison, Georgia M. Green, and Jerry L. Morgan, 140–147. Chicago: University of Chicago, Chicago Linguistic Society. Reprinted in *Semantic syntax*, ed. by Pieter A. M. Seuren,175–182. Oxford: Oxford University Press (1974).

Landman, Fred. 1991. *Structures for semantics*. Dordrecht: Kluwer.

Larrivée, Pierre. 2004. *L'association négative*. Geneva: Librairie Droz.

Lasnik, Howard. 1972. Analyses of negation in English. Doctoral dissertation, MIT. Reproduced by the Indiana University Linguistics Club, 1976.

Lasnik, Howard, and Juan Uriagereka. 1988. *A course in GB syntax: Lectures on binding and empty categories*. Cambridge, MA: MIT Press.

Lawler, John. 1971. *Any* questions. In *Papers from the Seventh Regional Meeting of the Chicago Linguistic Society*,163–173. Chicago: University of Chicago, Chicago Linguistic Society.

Lee, Felicia. 2003. Anaphoric R-expressions as bound variables. *Syntax* 6:84–114.

Lindholm, James M. 1969. Negative raising and sentence pronominalization. In *Papers from the Fifth Regional Meeting of the Chicago Linguistic Society*, ed. by Robert Binnick, Alice Davison, Georgia M. Green, and Jerry L. Morgan, 148–158. Chicago: University of Chicago, Chicago Linguistic Society.

Linebarger, Marcia. 1980. The grammar of negative polarity. Doctoral dissertation, MIT.

Linebarger, Marcia. 1987. Negative polarity and grammatical representation. *Linguistics and Philosophy* 10:325–387.

Liu, F.-H. 1990. Scope dependency in English and Chinese. Doctoral dissertation, University of California at Los Angeles.

Löbner, Sebastian. 1985. Definites. *Journal of Semantics* 4:279–325.

Martinon, Philippe. 1927. *Comment on parle en français*. Paris: Librairie Larousse.

May, Robert. 1985. *Logical Form: Its structure and derivation*. Cambridge, MA: MIT Press.

May, Robert. 1989. Interpreting logical form. *Linguistics and Philosophy* 12:387–435.

McCawley, James D. 1971. Where do noun phrases come from? In *Semantics*, ed. by Danny D. Steinberg and Leon A. Jakobovits 217–231. Cambridge: Cambridge University Press.

McCawley, James D. 1973. *Grammar and meaning*. Tokyo: Taishukan.

McCawley, James D. 1998. *The syntactic phenomena of English*. Chicago: University of Chicago Press.

Mittwoch, Anita, Rodney Huddleston, and Peter Collins. 2002. The clause: Adjuncts. In *The Cambridge grammar of the English language*, ed. by Rodney Huddleston and Geoffrey K. Pullum, 663–784. Cambridge: Cambridge University Press.

Moltmann, Friederike. 1995. Exception sentences and polyadic quantification. *Linguistics and Philosophy* 18:223–280.

Moltmann, Friederike. 1996. Resumptive quantifiers in exception sentences. In *Quantifiers, deduction, and context*, ed. by Makoto Kanazawa, Chris Piñon, and Henriëtte de Swart, 139–170. Stanford, CA: CSLI Publications.

Muller, Claude. 1991. *La négation en français*. Geneva: Librairie Droz.

Penka, Doris. 2007. Negative indefinites. Doctoral dissertation, Universität Tübingen.

Penka, Doris, and Arnim von Stechow. 2001. Negativen Indefinita unter Modalverben. In *Modalität und Modalverben im Deutschen*, ed. by Reimar Muller and Marga Reis. 263–286. *Linguistische Berichte, Sonderheft 9.*

Peters, Stanley, and Dag Westerståhl. 2006. *Quantifiers in language and logic.* Oxford: Oxford University Press.

Pollack, Jay Michael. 1974. A re-analysis of NEG-raising in English. Master's thesis, The Ohio State University.

Postal, Paul M. 2000. A remark on English double negatives. Ms., New York University.

Postal, Paul M. 2004a. A remark on English double negatives. In *Lexique, syntaxe et lexique-grammaire; syntax, lexis & lexicon-grammar: Papers in honour of Maurice Gross.* ed. by Christian Leclère, Éric Laporte, Mireille Piot, and Max Silberztein, 497–508. Amsterdam: John Benjamins.

Postal, Paul M. 2004b. *Skeptical linguistic essays.* Oxford: Oxford University Press.

Postal, Paul M. 2005. Suppose (if only for an hour) that negative polarity items are negation-containing phrases. Paper presented at Workshop on Polarity from Different Perspectives, New York University, March 2005.

Postal, Paul M. 2010. *Edge-based clausal syntax.* Cambridge, MA: MIT Press.

Potts, Chris. 2000. When even *no*'s neg is splitsville. Available at http://ling.ucsc.edu/Jorge/potts.html.

Poutsma, Hendrik. 1928. *A grammar of Late Modern English.* Groningen: P. Noordhoff.

Prince, Ellen. 1976. The syntax and semantics of NEG-raising, with evidence from French. *Language* 52:404–426.

Progovac, Ljiljana. 1994. *Negative and positive polarity.* Cambridge: Cambridge University Press.

Progovac, Ljiljana. 2000. Coordination, c-command, and 'logophoric' N-words. In *Negation and polarity*, ed. by Laurence R. Horn and Yasuhiko Kato, 88–114. New York: Oxford University Press.

Pullum, Geoffrey K. 2007. The evolution of model-theoretic frameworks in linguistics. In *Model-Theoretic Syntax at 10*, ed. by James Rogers and Stephan Kepser. 1–10. Dublin: Trinity College Dublin.

Pullum, Geoffrey K., and Rodney Huddleston. 2002. Negation. In *The Cambridge grammar of the English language*, ed. by Rodney Huddleston and Geoffrey K. Pullum, 785–849. Cambridge: Cambridge University Press.

Pullum, Geoffrey K., and Barbara C. Scholz. 2001. On the distinction between model-theoretic and generative-enumerative syntactic frameworks. In *Logical Aspects of Computational Linguistics: 4th International Conference, LACL 2001*, ed. by Philippe de Groote, Glyn Morrill, and Christian Retoré, 17–43. Berlin: Springer-Verlag.

Pullum, Geoffrey K., and Barbara C. Scholz. 2005. Contrasting applications of logic in natural language syntactic description. In *Logic, Methodology and Philosophy of Science: Proceedings of the Twelfth International Congress*, ed. by Petr Hájek,

Luis Valdés-Villanueva, and Dag Westerståhl, 475–496. London: King's College Publications.

Quine, Willard Van Orman. 1960. *Word and object*. Cambridge, MA: MIT Press.

Richter, Frank, and Manfred Sailer. 2006. Modeling typological markedness in semantics: The case of negative concord. In *Proceedings of the HPSG06 Conference*, ed. by Stefan Müller. 305–325. Stanford, CA: CSLI Publications.

Rizzi, Luigi. 1997. The fine structure of the left periphery. In *Elements of grammar*, ed. by Liliane Haegeman, 281–337. Dordrecht: Kluwer.

Romoli, Jacopo. 2012. Soft but strong neg-raising, soft triggers and exhaustification. Doctoral dissertation, Harvard University.

Romoli, Jacopo. 2013a. A scalar implicature-based approach to neg-raising. Ms., Macquarie University.

Romoli, Jacopo. 2013b. A scalar implicature-based approach to neg-raising. Talk given at New York University, May 6.

Ross, John Robert. 1967. Constraints on variables in syntax. Doctoral dissertation, MIT. Published as *Infinite syntax*, Norwood, NJ: Ablex (1986).

Ross, John Robert. 1973. Slifting. In *The formal analysis of natural languages*, ed. by Maurice Gross, Morris Halle, and Marcel-Paul Schützenberger, 133–169. The Hague: Mouton.

Sailer, Manfred. 2005. NEG-raising in an underspecified semantics framework. Paper presented at Colloque de Syntaxe et Sémantique, Paris. Available at http://www.cssp .cnrs.fr/cssp2005/index_en.html.

Sailer, Manfred. 2006. Don't believe in underspecified semantics: Neg raising in lexical resource semantics. In *Empirical Issues in Syntax and Semantics 6*, ed. by Olivier Bonami and Patricia Cabredo Hofherr, 375–403. Available at http://www.cssp.cnrs.fr/ eiss6.

Schmerling, Susan. 1971. A note on negative polarity. *Papers in Linguistics* 4:200–206.

Seuren, Pieter A. M. 1974a. Autonomous versus semantic syntax. In *Semantic syntax*, ed. by Pieter A. M. Seuren, 183–208. Oxford: Oxford University Press.

Seuren, Pieter A. M. 1974b. Negative's travels. In *Semantic syntax*, ed. by Pieter A. M. Seuren, 96–122. Oxford: Oxford University Press.

Seuren, Pieter A. M. 1985. *Discourse semantics*. Oxford: Blackwell.

Seuren, Pieter A. M. 1996. *Semantic syntax*. Oxford: Blackwell.

Seuren, Pieter A. M. 1998. *Western linguistics*. Oxford: Blackwell.

Smith, Steven Bradley. 1975. *Meaning and negation*. The Hague: Mouton.

Swart, Henriëtte de. 1998. *Introduction to natural language semantics*. Stanford, CA: CSLI Publications.

Swart, Henriëtte de. 1999. Negation and negative concord in a polyadic quantification framework. Available at http://www.illc.uva.nl/j50/contribs/deswart/.

Swart, Henriëtte de. 2000. Scope ambiguities with negative quantifiers. In *Reference and anaphoric relations*, ed. by Klaus von Heusinger and Urs Egli, 109–132. Dordrecht: Kluwer.

Swart, Henriëtte de, and Ivan A. Sag. 2002. Negation and negative concord in Romance. *Linguistics and Philosophy* 25:373–417.

Szabolcsi, Anna. 1992. Weak islands, individuals and scope. In *Proceedings of SALT 2*, ed. by Chris Barker and David Dowty, 407–437. Ohio State University Working Papers in Linguistics 40. Columbus: The Ohio State University, Department of Linguistics.

Szabolcsi, Anna. 2004. Positive polarity – Negative polarity. *Natural Language and Linguistic Theory* 22:409–452.

Szabolcsi, Anna. 2007. Strong vs. weak islands. In *The Blackwell companion to syntax*, ed. by Martin Everaert and Henk van Riemsdijk, 479–531. Wiley Online Library.

Szabolcsi, Anna, and Marcel den Dikken. 1999. Islands. *GLOT International* 4/6. Reprinted in *The second GLOT International state-of-the-article book*, ed. by Lisa Cheng and Rint Sybesma, 3–8. Berlin: Mouton de Gruyter, 2002.

Szabolcsi, Anna, and Frans Zwarts. 1990. Semantic properties of composed functions and the distribution of *wh*-phrases. In *Proceedings of the Seventh Amsterdam Colloquium*, ed. by. Martin Stokhof and Leen Torenvliet, 529–553. Amsterdam: University of Amsterdam.

Szabolcsi, Anna, and Frans Zwarts. 1993. Weak islands and an algebraic semantics for scope taking. *Natural Language Semantics* 1:235–284. Reprinted in *Ways of scope taking*, ed. by Anna Szabolcsi, 217–262. Dordrecht: Kluwer (1997).

Tobler, Adolf. 1882. Il ne faut pas que tu meures 'du darfst nicht sterben'. Reprinted in *Vermischte Beiträge zur französischen Grammatik I*, 3rd ed., 201–205. Leipzig: S. Hirzel.

Tovena, Lucia M. 2001. Neg-raising: Negation as failure. In *Perspectives on negation and polarity items*, ed. by Jack Hoeksema, Hotze Rullmann, Victor Sánchez-Valencia, and Ton van der Wouden, 331–356. Amsterdam: John Benjamins.

Uckelman, Sara. 2009. Anselm on agency and obligation. Chapter 3 of Modalities in medieval logic. Doctoral dissertation, University of Amsterdam. Available at http://dare.uva.nl/document/142270.

van der Auwera, Johan. 2011. On the diachrony of negation. In *The expression of negation*, ed. by Laurence R. Horn, 79–109. Berlin: Mouton de Gruyter.

van der Wouden, Ton. 1994. Polarity and 'illogical negation'. In *Dynamics, polarity, and quantification*, ed. by Makoto Kanazawa and Christopher J. Piñón, 17–45 Stanford, CA: CSLI Publications.

van der Wouden, Ton. 1997. *Negative contexts*. London: Routledge.

Vizitelly, Frank. 1910. *A desk-book of errors in English*. New York: Funk & Wagnalls.

Williams, C. J. F. 1964. Saint Anselm and his biographers. *Downside Review* 82:124–140. U.S. Department of Labor (2012).

Zeijlstra, Hedde. 2008. Negative concord is syntactic agreement. Available at http://ling.auf.net/lingbuzz.

Zeijlstra, Hedde, and Doris Penka. 2005. Negative indefinites in Dutch and German. Ms., Universität Tübingen.

Zwarts, Frans. 1998. Three types of polarity. In *Plurality and quantification*, ed. by Fritz Hamm and Erhard Hinrichs, 177–238. Dordrecht: Kluwer.

Name Index

Subject Index